CLIMBERS' CLUB GUIDES TO WALES
Edited by **Geoff Milburn**

8

North Wales

Limestone

by **Andy Pollitt**

Diagrams by **Greg Griffith**

Cover photographs by **Dave Summerfield**
    and **Andy Boorman**

Published by the CLIMBERS' CLUB

1976 Climbs on North Wales Limestone by Rowland Edwards.
Published by Cordee.

1981 North Wales Limestone by Andy Pollitt.
Published by Dark Peak.

1982 North Wales 1982 Supplement by Andy Pollitt.
Published by the Climbers' Club.

1983 Clwyd Limestone by Stuart Cathcart.
Published by Cicerone Press.

1983 North Wales Limestone Supplement by Andy Pollitt.
Published by the Climbers' Club.

© The Climbers' Club 1987

Pollitt, Andy
   North Wales Limestone. — (Climbers' Club guides)
   1. Rock climbing — North Wales
   I. Title   II. Climbers' Club
   III. Pollitt, Andy   IV. Series

   ISBN 0-901-601-40-3

front cover: Andy Pollitt on The Electric Cool-Aid Acid Test
               Photo: Dave Summerfield

back cover: Mick Lovatt on Charlton Chestwig (The Worlds
               Finest Climber) E5 6b
               Photo: Andy Boorman

Prepared for printing by: Microset, Royal Oak Barn,
Cartmel, Cumbria, LA11 6QB.
Printed by: Joseph Ward (Printers) Ltd, Dewsbury,
West Yorkshire, WF13 1HR.
Distributed by Cordee, 3a De Montfort Street,
Leicester, LE1 7HD.

CONTENTS

ACKNOWLEDGEMENTS

Since Rowland Edwards's 'Climbs on North Wales Limestone' was published in 1975 there have been one updated guide, three supplements and numerous articles containing further information on developments in this area. This guidebook is a collection of all the previously published works as well as all the recent information I could collect before the copy date.

Firstly I must thank again all those who supplied details and information for the last three guides.

Colin Goodey has been more than helpful in producing first ascent details, anecdotes and photographs of climbing in the fifties and sixties – a period only poorly covered in past works. Gary Gibson and Chris and Dave Lyon have helped in no small way on the more recent period. Dave especially as he solely produced the relevant details for the Crinkle Crags area, Craig Arwahan, Un-named Crag, Manor Crag and regularly contributed updated information on the area as a whole. Dave and Chris also supplied the photographs, which Bernard Newman printed up, for the basis for Greg Griffith's stunning crag drawings. Mark Hutchinson then of the British Mountaineering Council continuously helped in sorting out the many access problems – keeping bans and restrictions down to a minimum. The Great Orme Country Park Warden Mr. John Davies has over the past years been deeply involved in all access matters, helping on all our behalfs to keep the crags open. He is owed many thanks from us all.

Malcolm Campbell, Martin Crook, Dave Towse, Norman Clacher, Andy Boorman, Ken Wilson, Pat Littlejohn, Trevor Hodgson, Tom Jones, Steve Haston, Mike Owen, Chris Gore, Steve Lewis, Ben Moon, Martin Atkinson, Anthony Ingham, Keith Simpson, Frank Cannings, Rick Newcombe and Dave Peers have all given information on their routes and invaluable opinions on gradings in general.

Also thanks are due to the people who supplied action photos for the text.

Finally I must again thank: Greg Griffith for such excellent art work – all done at very short notice; Geoff Milburn for his unending support – along with Paul Williams – and for both their encouragement on the whole issue of getting this guidebook published.

A.P. March 1986

6

Introduction

Over the past few years the limestone crags of the North Wales coast have received an enormous amount of publicity through the climbing press. From continual access problems through to the blitz of 1983 when Pen Trwyn in particular saw a radical and frenzied transformation, the area has thrust itself to the very fore of British outcrop climbing in terms of abundance of easily accessible high-quality rock climbs.

Situated in the rain shadow area of the Welsh mountains the crags receive a great deal of fine weather – often better than the Tremadog and Gogarth areas. Contrary to popular belief the area is not just a 'hard man's playground' but also offers many excellent routes to climbers operating at all levels of difficulty. All the climbs are on carboniferous limestone of varying quality and texture; and protection, varies from crag to crag, e.g. the abundance of natural placements at Forwyn through to the mainly bolted Pen Trwyn routes.

The area covered in this book comprises three main crags. Firstly Craig y Forwyn, a typical inland outcrop – with Derbyshire qualities – seldom rising above 100 feet in height and within easy reach of the road.

The Great Orme – with Pen Trwyn in particular is undeniably Britain's most extensive roadside crag with never more than a five minute stroll to any particular buttress.

In complete contrast to the above two crags is The Little Orme. This enormous headland dominates the east end of the promenade, its vast complex front face stretching majestically out into the Irish Sea. It is the most serious of the three main crags due to the abseil approaches needed to reach many of the routes. Unfortunately, due to the lack of traffic and the annual nesting of many migrating sea birds a lot of the climbs often hold a fair amount of vegetation and nests. Nevertheless, the good routes on Little Orme are most worthwhile and generally offer extremely spectacular situations. The star system of quality probably means more here than on any of the other cliffs in the area.

Concerning the in-situ protection situation, the area has become well known for its abundance of in-situ gear. All of this – especially abseil slings, belays and fixed karabiners should be left in place as continual removal only causes problems for subsequent parties. One idiotic climber was heard to comment on his return from Pen Trwyn that: "No we didn't climb much but we nicked a load of tat and some steel 'biners". This attitude only enhances the need for safety for all our benefits.

WARNING: Many of the climbs on the Ormes have in-situ protection. It is advisable to take a cautious approach to the dangers of old bolts, pegs and pieces of tat. These will generally be replaced as time goes by. Perhaps by re-placing a few pieces of rope or tape when climbing there this re-gearing process may be helped.

The area as a whole has not been without its access problems and all visiting climbers are strongly urged to read and comply with the access notes – failure to do so can only lead to one end – a total ban on climbing there.

As far as camping is concerned, under no circumstances should climbers camp at Craig y Forwyn, unless given strict permission by the land owners at the farm beneath the cliff.

On the Great Orme climbers have used the roadside caves at the start of Pen Trwyn for a 'holiday home with a view' for several seasons but the land owners have not really taken kindly to this practice. The nearest camping site is opposite the Technical College at Llandrillo yn Rhos (old Llandudno – Colwyn Bay Road).
There are scores of cafes, pubs and nightclubs in Llandudno. Parisella's Ice Cream Parlour in the Happy Valley Gardens is a mere two minute walk from Pen Trwyn and is situated 200 yards from the Toll Gate. The popular pubs seem to be Tiffanys and the Cottage Loaf pubs which are next to and behind the cinema at the Upper Mostyn Street roundabout. The best breakfasting cafe is The Princes – again just at this roundabout. On the other side of the road is Lyons Sports where a new route book is available at all times. The shop also stocks climbing gear, chalk and guidebooks.

The area is also served well by public transport. The L1 Cymru Coastliner bus goes from Chester to Caernarfon and back at regular intervals throughout the year and stops at Llandudno and Llanddulas. British Rail has stations at Llandudno and Llandudno Junction. The A55 dual carriageway has seen much development over recent years and runs along the coast in this area.

A.P.

Access

The three main climbing areas covered by this guidebook each have some sort of access problem and it is in the interests of continued goodwill between visiting climbers and respective land owners and managers that we conform with the various requirements – without exception.

The symbol (R) alongside crag headings is by request of The Nature Conservancy Council to serve as a reminder of the ban on that particular crag.

CRAIG Y FORWYN

The land up to and above the crag is owned by several different people, the main owner being the farmer and caravan-site owner beneath the crag. Since the last guidebook was published this land has changed hands. The main problem is the use of this farmer's land when approaching the crag. In the past the gentleman concerned has been most tolerant but at the time of writing he is not taking kindly to hordes of climbers descending on him each weekend. It is suggested that until things calm down a little climbers wishing to climb at Craig y Forwyn pay him a courteous visit to ask for permission to enter his land. The B.M.C. and local Manpower Services Commission are at the time of writing negotiating an access agreement which includes the erecting of new fences, stiles and the clearing of a car-park. Consequently in the interest of all concerned it is advisable to keep a low profile, conform to the farmer's wishes and look out for further details issued from the B.M.C. in the climbing press.

THE GREAT ORME

Firstly it should be made clear that The Marine Drive is a one-way toll road. Under no circumstances should drivers turn around or attempt to reverse vehicles back out of the toll gate.

The access situation of The Great Orme is quite complicated so the problems are outlined in order of the crags – as they are approached via The Marine Drive.

On Pen Trwyn (except the initial cave routes) climbing above the road should be avoided during the daytime hours 9am – 5pm during the months July, August and the first week of September including other Bank Holidays and the Easter period.

The area is one of extreme interest to tourists and up to a hundred cars per hour can pass through the toll gate onto the

Marine Drive. Since the major developments of 1983 on Pen Trwyn the local council has expressed grave concern about the danger to the general public driving, cycling or walking on the Marine Drive, from climbing taking place close to or actually overhanging the road. They believe that in the event of an accident to a third party caused by climbing, the council and the owners could be held liable and have to pay compensation for any damage or injury.

Depending on the circumstances very large sums of money could be involved. Common sense dictates a very cautious approach to the problem of rock fall. Dislodged material should be cleaned up immediately and every effort taken to avoid causing any accident. An injury to a member of the public would undoubtedly have serious repercussions.

Apart from the obvious dangers of falling debris the area is also a special site of scientific interest. There are rare plants such as the Wild Cabbage, the Rock Sea Lavender and the unique Great Orme Berry growing in selected areas all over the Great Orme. In particular the area around the route Ozymandias should be avoided as specimens of the above flora are to be found there.

As for the remainder of the crags on The Great Orme the same restrictions as Pen Trwyn cover Middle Earth Buttress (Gandalf's Groove). Farther around the headland there is a voluntary bird ban on The Un-named Crag, Upper and Lower Craig Pen Gogarth (Astrodome, Hang Ten etc) Point Five Buttress and The Hornby Crags from 1st March to 31st July. Although much space has been given to the historical beginnings of Great Orme development, the crags where it took place — Creigiau Cochion and the Toll Gate Crags — should really be treated with great care due to their close proximity to the road. It has been suggested that no further developments take place in this area and that as with the other cliffs above the road they be covered by the voluntary ban during the busy periods — as for Pen Trwyn.

THE LITTLE ORME

There is a voluntary ban here to protect the group of sea birds known as Auks. This group includes Razorbills, Guillemots and Puffins and it is essential that they be protected due to great losses they suffer at sea each year. So, in the following areas there is a ban: Auk's Buttress, The West Buttress of Detritus, The Allotment, Detritus Wall Area and the left-hand side of The Great Zawn from 1st March to 15th August and on The Diamond Buttress from 1st March to 31st July.

Finally, please do adhere to any restrictions outlined above, in the interests of us all.

For further information The Nature Conservancy Council's North Wales Regional office is at Ffordd Penrhos, Bangor, Gwynedd, LL57 2LQ (tel: 0248 355141).

The British Mountaineering Council's address is Crawford House, Precinct Centre, Booth Street East, Manchester, M13 9RZ (tel: 061 273 5835).

Historical

The following historical notes begin with a section of anecdotes, memories and factual information from Colin Goodey in November, 1985.

"To the very best of my knowledge myself and brother Brian were the first real pioneers of climbing on The Great Orme. Our interest in climbing and mountaineering began in 1947 when I was eleven years of age and my brother fifteen. We lived just below the crags of The Great Orme so it was really very convenient and in fact our only source of climbing in those days since it was too far to go to Snowdonia — having no transport, or money.

In actual fact there were very few people rock-climbing then compared to now and certainly there was no trace of any climbers having been on the Ormes.

Our first climbs apart from bouldering and top-roping on the small crags above the old convent at West Shore were on the West Tollgate Crags. These crags seemed similar to pictures we had seen in Milner's 'Rock for Climbing' which showed many spectacular pictures of Dolomite climbing. It was this book and Buhl's 'Nanga Parbat Pilgrimage' that became our inspiration.

Thus, the first climb on The Great Orme was *Pigeon's Chimney*, VD, which takes the very prominent chimney splitting the front face of The Toll Gate Crags above West Shore. I called this crag Pigeon Buttress (many pigeons lived and roosted in this chimney and it would appear that someone in the distant past encouraged this because there were remains of some loft structures high in the back of the chimney). So this first Orme route was climbed in the Summer of 1950 and it was followed by *The Kite*, D/VD on Tower Buttress (left of Pigeon Buttress). 1951 saw *Pinnacle Route*, VD, which followed the rake leading to the top of the detached pinnacle on Tower Buttress (C Goodey, D Williams). All these routes were climbed with a single 100-foot length of manilla rope and nailed boots.

Perhaps the best route of those early days was *Colin's Groove*, VS, which takes the obvious corner to the right of Pigeon's Chimney. This is a very good line and a quality route considering when it was put up – a single piton was used for protection and I climbed on to finish because I could not get back! (1st ascent C Goodey, D Williams, August 1952). On the same day we climbed a new route at the back of the great towering nose of Tower Buttress which we called *Dark Wall*, VD/S; this takes the left-hand wall of the gully which runs up behind the tower.

In June 1954 we discovered *Yellow Groove*, VS, on Creigiau Cochion overlooking the old gunsite on the south west side of the Orme. We used a peg for aid to surmount the overhang on the first pitch – again a good route for the period. An interesting point here is this climb's first and second ascents. I climbed it in the June of 1954 and made the second ascent 31 years later in the October of 1985! On this second ascent however the peg was only used for protection – hence the HVS grade.

By 1956 we had motor-cycles so we were able to get into Snowdonia and in consequence our interests were elsewhere – but in 1958 we renewed our acquaintance with the crags on The Orme. A small group of us including myself, Alan Davies, Mike Butler, Harry Groom, and Dave Birchley came back to practise our pegging for a trip to The Dolomites. We pegged many big faces all over The Orme, depegged them and made no record. By 1960 we were pegging across the huge ceiling of Elephant Caves and I was making repeated attempts on *'Penelope'* (a girl friend of mine in the late 50's). This climb eventually fell to Alan Davies and Harry Groom in June 1961. In the April of 1962 Barry Brewster and I made the Direct Start to this route. (Barry was killed on the Eiger North Face a few months later).

The Teal was climbed in June 1965 by Alan Davies, Dave Alcock and Dave Thomas (bach). Also, in December 1965 I made *Christmas Crawl*, HVS at Cochion with Dave Williams following.

In those early days of Orme exploration we also pegged many routes around Pen Trwyn but were of the opinion that they were too steep and too loose ever to be popular – how wrong we were proved to be.

Apart from a route done by Dave Yeats to the left of Penelope (possibly the line later climbed by R Edwards: Wall and Groove) in the late Sixties I can't remember anything else of significance until the arrival of Rowland Edwards and Andy Pollitt in the late Sixties and Seventies."

Goodey goes on to recall early days at Craig y Forwyn:

"The crag was 'discovered' by myself and Dave Thomas in September 1958 with ascents of both *Y-Chimneys*. Our first real attempt at a main line was during this month when we tried Scalar and the Great Flake or *The Shadow* as I eventually called it (this flake fell down in the late Seventies).

1959 saw the first major route on the crag with *Ivy Sepulchre*, climbed by Goodey and Thomas in May. The same pair pegged the big overhang of *Mojo* in the September and the very fine line of *The Shadow* finally succumbed to Goodey, Thomas and Alcock. Other pioneers started to arrive at that time: Frank Corner and Brian Thompson followed by Colwyn Bay climbers Dave Williams, Neil Sherry and Dave Patrick. Both Frank Corner and I (independently) pegged *Quick Step* during the very early Sixties. Also Barry Brewster did the climb using much less aid in the Spring of 1962.

Many climbers other than myself tried *Great Wall* during the period 1959 — 1967: Goodey/Thomas in 1959 and Goodey/Brewster in 1960/1961. On this 1961 occasion Barry succeeded in climbing free up to my highest peg which was almost mid-height! Attempts followed by Corner/Thompson and John Amatt (of Trolltind Wall fame) who took a very big fall when a peg came out at about mid-height. The wall finally succumbed to myself and Dr. Noel Dilly on October 14th 1967."

The other Forwyn pioneers Goodey mentions here were, over a period of seven to eight years responsible for such climbs as *Demolition, Twisting Chimney* and *Pterodactyl* by Frank Corner, but the main activists were Dave Patrick, Neil Sherry and Dave Williams who during this period kept themselves busy discovering and climbing *Scalar, Route 66, Stripper, Wacker, Fido's Redemption, Square Cut Chimney, Top Cat, Glade Arête* and more. Goodey, Corner and Williams climbed the mixed route *The Bat* and Goodey led *The Flue*.

From another letter in January 1986 Goodey recalls from this same early period:

"Castle Inn Quarry: We (Colin Goodey, Alan Davies, Dave Thomas, Harry Groom and Mike Butler) climbed here extensively from May 1959 till about 1962 when we focused all our attentions elsewhere. I certainly remember clearly making ascents of the main nose or buttress in 1959. One route, the most popular, straight up the middle and later on either side – all on top ropes. Only true ascent of middle route: C Goodey, A Davies in 1959 (after further inspection). Apart from this main buttress we recorded no other routes as such and used the area for 'bouldering' only."

April 1968 saw the first exploratory trips onto The Little Orme. Frank Cannings and Tim Lewis ascended *The Easy Way Off* – a HVS scramble involving three 'grass fields' en route. In the may of 1968 the pair climbed *Rhiwledyn*, a long and usually damp climb described as being 'A route of superb character, a sea cliff classic' by the first ascensionists. The route takes a line up the right-hand side of what was soon to be known as The Diamond Buttress. Shortly after this discovery Peter Biven and Mark Springett climbed *Thorfin Skullsplitter* a route over to the right of the above. Several points of aid were used to leave a small cave at half-height. For some unknown reason the route name got changed to *Shazam* the name by which we now know the climb.

Also in the May of 1968 Richard Isherwood and Ken Wilson added the next climb on Little Orme – *Sickle* – via the Right-Hand entry. Wilson recalls:

"This was a real epic. We knew very little about the cliff. We abseiled in on the right and pulled down our ropes. Then Dick Isherwood led that horribly loose chimney-crack pitch. Pitch 3 was more solid. Then we were in The Allotment. Not too difficult to escape from but then everything was overgrown. We took a horribly loose and poorly protected line well to the left (Loose Exit).

Thus, while the quality of the route was poor, the spirit of adventure and the commitment with which it was done was laudable; we had a real adventure."

Interestingly Ken Wilson and Tim Lewis both went on to edit the international climbing magazine Mountain.

Wilson adds:

> "The next adventure was with the Rev. Bob Shepton getting those photos. He pushed a pathetic sailing dinghy (without sails) into the choppy sea and rowed me (heavily laden with warm coats and cameras) across the foot of the cliffs. We kept rising up and down on the swell with me in the back taking pictures: No life-jackets: He was crazy – had God on his side."

During the early months of 1969 Rowland Edwards began to show great interest in this area. His first new route was *Gillies Groove*, climbed with Cliff Phillips. With Edwards leading, several other routes followed including the left-hand entry to The Sickle.

Edwards was to spearhead the attack over the coming five and a half years, adding almost all the routes to The Little Orme cliffs. Amongst the very many free-climbs Edwards was pioneering came *Detritus* and *The Wall of the Evening Light*, two of the longest and most committing artificial routes in the country.

At this same time the Rev. Bob Shepton was also busy whittling away at the many unclimbed lines on the Great Orme – The Hornby Crags to be exact. Due to their efforts there now existed over thirty routes on the cliffs and development started to accelerate with the discovery of new, hidden crags – on the Ormes especially. The first recorded climb in The Great Zawn was *Rabble Rouser*, a long exposed line which Edwards had spotted while on Detritus. After major gardening operations *The Big Flake* and *Genesis* were climbed by Edwards and Shepton in turn. The huge sweeping slab to the right of this trio of routes prompted exploration by Edwards and with Ken Toms partnering him he led the classic-to-be *Quietus* a route left unrepeated for quite some time.

Of these early Little Orme days Ken Wilson remembers:

> "Our final visit (to do *Rapunzel*) with Thexton and Roy Kligfield. It was hard. Somehow Shepton had got wind of the fact we were there and when we were engrossed in the route he suddenly came abseiling in on us out of the blue — Amazing bloke."

The period 1970-1971 was to produce a burst of activity at Forwyn by members and friends of the Bangor University Mountaineering Club – mainly Rick Newcombe, John Whittle, Dave Peers and Dave Archer who in a variety of combinations climbed *Knightsbridge*, *Thatcher Traverse*, *The Neurotic Woodpecker*, *The Groan* and *Jugular Start*. The line between Great Wall and Quick Step was pegged to give *Beeline* and similarly what we now know as *The Snake* was previously called Flake

Wall — courtesy of the the above team. They also climbed some very early — though unlikely the first — routes on the Left-hand Section of the cliff — namely *The Fox*, *Brer Rabbit*, and *Chatterley*.

In 1972 on The Great Orme Edwards discovered St. Tudno's Buttress and proceeded to climb each of the major lines in turn. *Ivy Wall* and *Oceanside*, the girdle, both needing some aid but were the finest discoveries here. On the big crag below, Edwards unearthed *The Red Sentinel*, known as 'Great Orme's Cenotaph Corner' (in fact it is bigger) and a long aid route *Hippodrome*.

Pen Trwyn received the sum total of seven new routes at this time — all from Edwards with the exception of one Jeff Connor route. *Mayfair* and *Oyster* both aid routes and the excellent free *Plumbline* were the best of these. The crag was then dismissed in favour of the less accessible crags beyond the headland. Though from these early Seventies days Edwards always maintained that the crag would eventually be fully developed.

In 1973-1974 a few more routes began to appear at Craig y Forwyn. Edwards was again the man to thank for such gems as *Sangfroid*, *Freedom* and *The Snake* with Les Holliwell.

The Latter route free-climbed the old aid route Flake Wall. Edwards then with P. Meads free-climbed The Bat, re-naming it *Sunset Strip*. It was also during this 1973-74 period that some very interesting new routes appeared on The Little Orme. Again it was Edwards, who with an ever-changing list of seconds, proceeded to climb *Hydro* — a classic from the outset, *Gemstone* — the longest route so far, *Moon Shadow*, *Midnight Blues* and *Peace Train*, *The Great Zawn Girdle* — beating even Gemstone for length, *Atlanta*, *Uranus* and the superb *Glass Wall*.

Without a shadow of a doubt the best discovery of this period was Castell y Gwynt, just beneath the lighthouse on the apex of The Great Orme. Edwards was later to write in an article on the cliff:

> "The first route was *Central Pillar* done in 1972 by me and Frank Harvey. During this ascent it had been noticed that there were possible free lines, particularly the girdles, but no amount of imagination could have foretold the lines which were to be done eventually."

During the following years Edwards produced many more fine routes on 'The Gwynt' including *The New Dimension* with Nigel Metcalfe (briefly) and Tim Jepson and *Appian Way* with Gerry Perry. (One of the very few rhyming climbers!). It is fair to say that *New Dimensions* as it got shortened to was the first major route to attract other climbers' attention to the Ormes. This route in particular caused quite a stir for reasons other than quality, for this was the time when chalk was starting to be used by certain climbers. Jim Moran who made the third ascent shortly after Frost and Lyon repeated the route used the 'magic white powder' and some thought his 'freer than Edwards' ascent invalid. As it has since been proved this is far from the case. It was Edwards, on the fourth ascent, who totally free-climbed the route.

Back at Craig y Forwyn Pete Livesey and Jill Lawrence were closely inspecting the then still artificial routes Great Wall and Quick Step. After a couple of yo-yo's Livesey reached the top of *Great Wall* and *Quick Step* was also quickly dispensed with by the same team. With these two free ascents accomplished a ripple went through the climbing world and heads began to turn as conversations about a great 'new' crag were overheard. Sometime around this period Livesey and Ron Fawcett girdled this area of rock to give *Great Whaler*. It was around this time that Edwards's interim supplement appeared – the first proper guide to climbing on these cliffs.

A little later, on 'The Gwynt', Edwards and Paul Williams forced the most difficult route up the very prow of the buttress to produce *Psychic Threshold*. Though some aid was used Dave Roberts, who made the second ascent, commented that he found it "equal to Right Wall on The Cromlech but with better protection".

During the late Seventies Edwards started developing the neighbouring Point Five Buttress and Upper Craig Pen Gogarth. His hardest route there was *Hang Ten* with Gerry Perry. Edwards was to round off his onslaught by climbing a last four routes – on the Upper Tier of St Tudno's Buttress. He seconded Paul Williams on the finest of these – *Gritstone Gorilla* – a similar route to New Dimensions in the sense that it sparked off new interest in the Ormes. By this time it seemed as if the area had perhaps given up its best lines and eventually Edwards left the area, only to take up a similar position on the granite sea cliffs of South West England.

The presumption that the area was 'worked out' was far from the truth however and several local climbers joined in the race for new lines making this the most concentrated period of development since Edwards first visited the cliffs.

The local Lyon brothers Chris and Dave added several routes to the Great Orme, early ones being *Astrodome*, a companion route to Edwards's Hippodrome, followed shortly by *Hoe Down*. They also added three fine routes to Central Hornby, which have since become popular.

During the first months of 1979 Andy Boorman – a teacher at Prestatyn High School and Andy Pollitt – a novice pupil, climbed extensively on the Left-hand Section of Craig y Forwyn. They climbed many routes from Difficult to Hard Very Severe. Some had definitely been climbed before while others were, in later years, to be claimed as new routes with different names to those the pair had made up. They made no record other than in personal diaries.

Later on in 1979 the young Pollitt met up with a similarly aged youth by the name of Tim Freeman and a new climbing partnership came to bloom. They turned their attention to the cliffs of The Great Orme and quickly reeled off free ascents of The Teal, Penelope and Wall and Groove. Their first new route together was *One Step Beyond* at Forwyn which was done only after their friend Nigel Radcliffe had hit the deck after stripping his gear.

Mike Owen, another local climber left his mark with such routes as the airy *Banana Moon* and the *Direct Finish to Mojo*.

Another young climber to cut his teeth on these crags was Jerry Moffatt – a resident pupil at the nearby St. David's College in Llandudno. It seemed obvious from the start that he should team up with the other two and firstly, pairing up with Pollitt sieged away the aid from Mayfair. This pair also added a fine Direct Finish to Sangfroid as well as making the long-awaited second ascent of Hedera Wall – an old Fawcett/Gibb creation at Forwyn.

By now the pace had quickened yet again and Ron Fawcett strung out a line up the rock left of Great Wall. Though very much an eliminate *Tears of a Clown* free-climbed the old aid route Beeline, and was a fine effort for the time – and certainly the hardest route on the crag so far.

Pollitt added several routes to Forwyn mainly with Pete Bailey including *High Steppa, Moonwind, Book of Dreams* and *High Plains Drifter*, as well as eliminating the aid points from Spike Driver and on Great Orme Edwards's Ivy Wall – the latter (and High Plains Drifter) with Chris Lyon.

John Redhead made an impressive contribution with his bold and brilliant *Plas Berw* as well as the equally exciting *Bittersweet Connection*, a free version of Central Pillar. He then went on to rid Fosse Way and Psychic Threshold of an aid point apiece – all climbed with Keith Robertson.

Visiting American Max Jones straightened out Alternative Three with Bill Wayman to give the harder *Rude Awakening*, while in

The Great Zawn the Lyon brothers put up *Father John* and *Mur yr Ogof*, the latter's rest point being dispensed with by Mike Owen and Dave Cowans on the second ascent.

With all the recent developments Edwards's excellent interim guide was fast becoming dated and Pollitt started compiling a new manuscript.

Kim Carrigan and Dougie Hall visited the area and amongst other things repeated Tears of a Clown and Moonwind. They also put up a fine variation to Mayfair's first pitch. Their best achievement however was their on-sight free ascent of Psychic Threshold.

Mel Griffiths, taking time off from his activities in the Moelwyns paired up with Leigh McGinley and added *Axle Attack* a superb route to the left of Mayfair. The line was an incomplete aid route by Chris Lyon and Paddy Elliot. It was this route more than any before it, on Trwyn, that gave a realistic impression of the wealth of new climbing waiting to be done.

A 'new' buttress was discovered in the trees right of Forwyn's Main Cliff where Chris Lyon's *Making Movies* and Pollitt's *Skateaway* have both become popular.

The Lyon brothers returned once more to The Great Zawn to climb possibly the finest route there – *Old Sam*. Also on the Little Orme, Shazam received a free ascent from Pollitt and Bailey who had previously reduced the aid on the nearby Midnight Blues from five points to one.

With the guidebook near completion a final few routes were squeezed in. The steep finger-crack in the arête right of Gritstone Gorilla fell to Pollitt and Griffiths to give *Goliath*. Steve Haston and Ian Johnson climbed the enormous roof of *Dumbell Flyer* which was to spark off great interest in that part of Pen Trwyn. Pollitt and Norman Clacher added the similarly spectacular *Crazy Horses* through the roof right of Mojo.

Geoff Roberts and companions also concluded their beavering on Pen Trwyn adding a host of middle-grade routes and showing others the true potential of the Pen Trwyn crags.

In a final effort to check routes for the manuscript Pollitt and Norman Clacher spent two days on the Little Orme. On the Monday the pair abseiled in to climb the magnificent *Gemstone*. At about 100 feet Pollitt was stopped by a vicious fulmar and was forced to retreat. By this time Clacher was knee-deep in the fast approaching tide and the pair being totally cut off were forced to scramble farther and farther out along the boulders beneath this gigantic crag. They soloed up the deathly-loose Rubble Buttress, 150 feet onto its manky plateau, where they proceeded to fail on two routes there, due to appalling rock. Descent by abseil back to a huge boulder above the high-tide mark was not so simple. The rope snagged this forcing a re-solo up then back down this horrible buttress. After a several hour wait the pair waded back to the abseil point to find the rope wind-blown and caught high on the face. Escape was eventually made by climbing Shazam with more aid than it had originally been climbed! As if that was not enough the following day, whilst on the sixth pitch of the Great Zawn Girdle, the sky turned black and the two were caught in a torrential rainfall. They tried in vain to climb out, in socks, barefoot, and using any gear they could get in but it was not enough. The idea of lowering Clacher 160 feet straight into the sea to swim to Llandudno and get help from the Lyons was shelved. So Pollitt tied the two ropes together and abseiled from an atrocious belay peg (now re-placed!) and made several 40-foot swings to reach the amphitheatre. From there a gripping solo up vertical soaking wet grass led to the top, where he could lower a rope down to his waiting partner. "If I'd have known he'd unclipped from the creaking peg when I abseiled off, I'd have bloody left him there a good couple of days."

Only three days later Pollitt and Bailey were in The Great Zawn in fading light when the inshore lifeboat zoomed into the Zawn. Insisting they needed a rescue they let them know a team was preparing to drop a rope from above. The climbers stuck to their guns and the boat left to rescue a boy who had fallen 50 feet into the Allotment while looking for birds' eggs!

So, in 1981, the guidebook appeared and climbers in their scores headed for the area.

Two major additions were just too late for inclusion in the book: Chris Lyon and Ant Moore's *Tunnel of Love*, a very committing route up the most exposed part of The Great Zawn and Pollitt and Bailey's Direct version of Moonwind, the latter instantly received many repeat ascents and a claimed 'classic' status. It was shortly after this that Pollitt soloed Great Wall and Quick Step.

Over the winter months Forwyn yielded a mass of new routes. Pollitt, mostly with Clacher, climbed *Jungle Love, Wackeroo Direct Finish, The Texas Shuffle, Street Stroller* and *The Maiden*, and with Pete Bailey freed the Orme's Goliath Crack and Hoe Down. John Redhead bouldered out a collection of roofs left of Dumbell Flyer and Tim Freeman later soloed it (The Burning Sphincter).

Clacher and friends blitzed the left-hand section of Forwyn producing many lines the best of which were *Larks a Bumbly* and *The Last Grasp*.

The bulging wall left of Cutter was climbed using some aid by a youthful Trevor Hodgson (later to join the merry band of Llanberis 'slateheads'). During an attempt to eliminate the aid Pollitt fell and grounded out from the crux. Ron Fawcett and Bill Wayman then stepped in to climb the route *Imminent Crisis*.

Over on the Little Orme Pollitt and Bailey were too slow in trying a line they had cleaned and prepared and Kevin Howitt and Dave Towse top-roped the crux then led the pitch. Pollitt joined them four days later and the team added a more independent finish. *Doenitz* was later to become a seldom-climbed gem.

The roof and ramp-line right of Gritstone Gorilla had apparently been climbed using aid on the roof and Pollitt and Bailey over two evenings freed the roof to give *Puerto Rican Harlem* the area's first claimed 6c.

Hodgson returned and climbed the first route on the Upper Tier of Two Tier Buttress at Forwyn with his tricky *Physical Diagnostic*. *The Breck Road* was Tom Jones's roof-climbing contribution left of Dumbell Flyer. While Freeman bagged the delightful *Big Licks* Clacher and Keith Simpson traversed the Lower Tier to produce the exciting *Water Margin*. The Gibson Brothers, Gary and Phil, beat other contenders to the immaculate *Space Mountain* and shortly afterwards John Codling partially solved a 'last great problem' by climbing the big wall left of Sangfroid.

Attention suddenly switched to Pen Trwyn again and it was to become really clear as to what was possible on the blanker sections of rock that abound in the area.

Between Redhead and Pollitt the lines of *The Bloods*, Oyster (almost free), and Connor's Folly (free) fell whilst the most important route so far was *The Disillusioned Screw Machine*. Unfortunately an aid bolt was used on 'The Screw Machine' but that was eliminated by Tom Jones although he did not complete the pitch.

Up at the Castle Inn Quarry Pollitt and Hodgson added four excellent new routes while on the Little Orme The Bender lost its aid point to Mark Lynden and Dave Towse.

Fawcett once more grabbed a plum with the elimination of the aid bolt on The Bittersweet Connection – a big sustained lead (and very Raven Tor-ish). Bill Wayman then pushed the boat out by climbing a slanting line up the wall left of Plumbline to give *Gold Rush*. Nearby at the Elephant Caves, Redhead and Martin Crook were attacking the huge horizontal flake and after a concerted effort succeeded in climbing *Separate Elephant* possibly Britain's largest free roof.

Pollitt teamed up once more with Freeman and they powered their way up the leaning wall right of the old pillbox to give the sustained *Chain Gang*.

All these routes were included in the North Wales New Climbs supplement which was published in 1982 and contained over seventy new routes in this area and since its publication an astonishing number of new routes have appeared.

Mel Griffiths put the limestone section of the supplement out of date virtually straight away with his ascent of *The Visitor*. About the same time Dave Towse, Martin Crook and Kevin Howitt discovered *Flakeaway, Firefly* and *Scary Canary* three superb routes.

Bill Wayman with Nigel Shepherd then climbed *After the Gold Rush* which was to be the beginning of his blitz. *Klondike, Solid Gold* and *Price of Gold* followed shortly afterwards with Fred Crook. Dave and Chris Lyon squeezed in *Yellow Belly* and *Pershing II* while Towse and various partners bagged *The Jehad, Masada, Primrose Walk* and *Melkor*, the latter being the first route on Yellow Wall.

Pollitt and Clacher then grabbed Forwyn's most dramatic route with *Space Case*. Meanwhile back on Pen Trwyn Fred Crook and Wayman alternated leads on *Precious Metal, Lucky Strike, Gold Star, Krugerrand* and *Pure Gold*. Dave Lyon and Clacher climbed *Alchemist's Dream* and *Pale Shelter* whilst Pollitt and Paul Williams did *Quicksilver*. It was about this time that Ron and Gill Fawcett appeared on the scene. It was obvious from that point onwards that routes would fall thick and fast.

Fawcett and Williams climbed *Sheik Yer Money* while Wayman and Crook got *En Gedi* to its right. Gary and Phil Gibson paid a fleeting visit, adding *The Violator* – one of the longer and more exposed Trwyn routes. The Wayman/Crook team also produced *Love over Gold* the same day.

One of the biggest plums of the time was a completely free ascent of The Screw Machine which Pollitt and Williams achieved two days later. That evening *Gorgo* fell to the same team.
They were also responsible for the twin classics *The Bearded Clam* and *Anchovy Madonna*.

Jerry Moffatt teamed up with Elfyn Jones for *Rapture* between the above routes which turned out to be another gem. Towse partnered Mike Raine on *String of Pearls* whilst to their left Pollitt, Williams and the Fawcetts climbed *The Pirates of Pen Trwyn*.

Moffatt after much effort climbed the excellent headwall left of Gold Rush to give *Wings of Perception* – the area's most technical route to date. Griffiths renewed his acquaintance in the Axle Attack/Visitor area producing the brilliant *King Krank* in between. The right arête of Monster Buttress went to Fawcett, Williams and Pollitt to give the humorously named *Charlton Chestwig (The World's Finest Climber)*. That evening the same team put up *Pen Trwyn Patrol*. Pollitt and Williams then broke out of Charlton Chestwig to give 'him' his *Continuing Adventures*. Dave Lyon came out with *Private Investigation, Too Low For Zero, Power Failure* and *The Magical Ring*, then Pollitt and Williams retorted with *Carrigan's Groove Direct Start, Pocket City, Mr. Chips, Captain Fingers, The Golden Goose* and *Gold Digger*.

Over the ensuing fortnight Fawcett snatched *Body Torque, The Electric Cool-Aid Acid Test* – perhaps the most technically intricate route so far, *Sourdough, Fall Back, Ward 10* and *Mr. Olympia* – an impressive list though probably his best effort was freeing the aid pitch of Central Pillar on Castell y Gwynt – an outrageous piece of climbing.

Gary Gibson returned to Pen Trwyn and mostly with Adam Hudson and Andy Popp climbed *Menincursion* and *The Peppermint Pig*, the Black Wall's first routes. He also found *Paradise* and *The Bounty Hunters* nearby. *The Wall of Blutes* went to Paul Williams and a cast of thousands while Pollitt and Clacher went direct on The Violator to produce *Birdbrain* an even more exposed route than its neighbour.

The Lyons beat other contenders to *Twisting by the Pool* a much eyed line on the Lower Tier. This route had many quick repeats but amazingly the crag lay virtually untouched for another year.

Up above, Pollitt, Andy Grondowski and Williams found a superb top pitch to The Bloods and following that the very neat *Visionary*. Williams then took the lead on *The Arc of Eternity* another fine line. Gibson and friends continued to whittle away at the spaces on Black Wall coming up with *Willowbrook's, Let's Lynch the Landlord, Salty Dog, Pure Mania, Spine Chill, Second Sense, Storm Warning* and *Drip Drip Drip*. That same week Towse climbed *Pen Trwyn Pilots* and *Liquid Lust*.

Paul Williams on the Hole of Creation.

Julian Taylor—Williams collection

Chris Gore on Oyster.

Martin Atkinson

Hot Space by the Lyons and the *Hole of Creation* by Williams and Julian Taylor became The Little Orme's first routes of the summer but despite the amount of potential there, activity remained firmly centred on Pen Trwyn.

The Lyons' *Jacuzzi Jive* was a worthy companion for Twisting by the Pool. Fred Crook and Chris Bundock climbed *Le Bingomaniaque* whilst Pollitt and Towse joined forces to attack the central overhang of Monster Buttress, *The Psychofant Roof* being their prize.

Hanging Rock – the quaint little buttress right of the Mayfair wall came in for some heavy treatment when Roland Foster, with Williams, Pollitt and Tim Freeman added *Slouching Towards Bethlehem*. Williams then fought his way up *De Torquemada* while Pollitt added *Jerusalem is Lost, Gripper Clipper, The Picnic* and *Babylon by Bus*. The horizontal break above the main crag gave Pollitt and Paul Clark *Spanish Train* but the nearby *Thunder Road* proved a bigger plum. Gibson's *The Thin Red Line* – a technical boulder problem – unfortunately required a rest point on the first ascent – dispensed with by courtesy of Pollitt and Wayman on the second. Gibson's *No Red Tape* however was not as difficult and saw many quick repeats.

About this time Moffatt eliminated Pen Trwyn's last aid point with his free ascent of *Oyster*, a desperate problem which has repelled many would-be ascensionists. He also climbed directly up the stunning headwall above Carrigan's Groove to give *Masterclass* – another phenomenal achievement.

After a brief lay-off from the Trwyn scene Wayman and Crook with Paul Clark put up *Prospectors* while on the same day Martin Crook and Andy Newton climbed *Silver Surfer*. Gibson popped back for *Once in a Blue Moon*.

With the activity tailing off somewhat, several parties took advantage of the quietude. Dave Towse, Martin Crook, Andy Newton and Kevin Howitt between them put up *Karma* and *Back to the Egg* on the Little Orme and *Tips, Silent Voices, Gandalf's Groove* and *Big Kazoo* on The Great Orme.

Wayman and Crook discovered *Beaverbrook, White Seam* and *Too Pooped to Whoop*. Paul Williams returned for a final fling, adding *The Cynical Pinnacle* and *Tokoloshe Man* with Ian Sayers.

Visiting climbers Ian Carr and Chris Hardy found *The Gold Coast* while Wayman and Crook added *Uaeba* and *Pen Trwyn Pillar* to their seemingly inexhaustible list of new routes. The Lyons put up *Goodbye Mickey Mouse* and this was followed by Wayman and Crook's *Gold 'n Delicious, Gold Wall Girdle Part II* and *Meanstreak* which were added in a race against time as the Pen Trwyn 1983 supplement went to press.

1984 saw yet another onslaught instigated by Gary Gibson. Over the initial months of that year with a variety of seconds he cleaned and climbed several routes right of Hodgson's Physical Diagnostic. *The Black Hole, Livingstone I Presume, Bush Doctor* and more were followed by a trio of Lyons' routes on the left-hand side of the same buttress – *Notta Bleck, Good Friday Groove* and *Into the Gap*.

Back on Trwyn Gibson found yet another instant classic with *Homo Sapien* as well as equipping the wall to its right but not managing to complete the pitch.

In the May period Dave Lyon and Norman Clacher visited an area spotted by the Lyons some years previously. They wandered under the Crinkle Crags and Dave abseiled down the Wonderwall. Over the ensuing months the pair put up most of the routes on the walls then Clacher with Chris Lyon started to work out Surprise Zawn. Chris put up this particular area's hardest routes with *The Flim Flam Man* and *Tel Shady* and Dave the best with *The Reflex*. Clacher was to add a few more routes and Pete Leavers and some pupils from St. David's College later worked out some easier climbs.

Back down on Lower Pen Trwyn Dave Lyon and Clacher climbed *New Moon on Monday* which was the turning point for development on this wall. Steve Lewis's *Krankenstien* and Pollitt's *Ape's Hit* both plugged obvious gaps up above.

The scene was then set for some tremendous new routing back down by the sea. Over a few weeks in June Pollitt climbed *Libertango* and *La Bohème* and Lewis *Face Race* and *Mean Mother*. Pollitt made a brief excursion back to the main crag to bag *Readers' Wives*.

At this time Ben Moon was busy bolting a remarkable line through the steepest part of the Lower Tier. He spent about eight days trying to link a series of very technical moves until finally he succeeded in climbing *Statement of Youth* a route destined to be amongst the top few in Britain.

Dave Lyon and Clacher continued to fill gaps in the Wonderwall area and Pollitt with Martin Atkinson completed Gibson's unclimbed line right of Homo Sapien to give *White Hopes*.

On Monster Buttress the wall right of Charlton Chestwig went to Pollitt – *Dive, Dive, Dive* and the short crack right again to Lewis – *Crunchy Toad IX*.

Farther round the headland Dave Lyon and Dave Summerfield were busy climbing some nice routes on the clean walls of Unnamed Crag. Up above, Pollitt spent two days alone on a rope cleaning and equipping three very obvious problems on Castell y Gwynt. The next day he returned with Atkinson and climbed the first of the three, *Blast Peru*. Atkinson repeated the route and while doing so his attention was drawn to the slender pillar to its left. He cleaned and equipped it the following day. That day Pollitt spent the afternoon attempting the huge bulging wall left of Psychic Threshold but after numerous scary falls was forced to retreat. Atkinson proceeded to deal with his route taking a mammoth flyer in the process – *Sidekick* being his chosen name. Back the next day Pollitt managed to climb *Teenage Kicks* then the pair abseiled in to the stance on New Dimensions where a line of bolts lead directly up the soaring groove above. Pollitt led *Good Taste!* to complete development there so far. Later that same day with Atkinson out in front the pair climbed the groove-line up the left-hand side of Lower Trwyn to give *Under the Boardwalk*.

Lewis had been attempting a line right of 'Statement' and finally succeeded in producing the excellent *Rompsville*. Pollitt climbed a line just right again, *Night Glue*.

Gibson filled the gap between The Bloods and Mayfair with *Contusion* and climbed the fine *Skin Deep* on the right-hand side of the Lower Tier. The groove above The Bloods/Contusion was an obvious gap and gave Pollitt *The Senile Penile Extension*.

Martin Crook and Andy Newton found *Alien Forces* a good route round on the Hornby Crags and Dominic Staniforth climbed *The Pink Pinkie Snuffs It* on the Lower Tier. Just to its left Pollitt, Williams and Atkinson did *Voodoo Child*, then Pollitt went on to add *Wall of Voodoo* just left again.

The later months were to see a decline in activity though Dave Lyon continued to plug gaps with his *Methylated Laughter, SS20, Nuclear Winter, Eliminator* and the very good *Welcome to the Pleasure Dome*.

Christmas day was not spent in front of the telly by Gibson. He was at Forwyn adding *The Fun House* up the stepped wall left of *Purple Haze*.

The first of January 1985 saw Towse, Crook and Redhead on the Hornby Crags putting up *Hom Day Wall* whilst down on Trwyn Gibson did *The Complicated Muse* and *The Star Spangled Banner*. Over the ensuing weeks Gibson and friends put up many routes including *Norman's Wisdom, No Arc No Bark, Barking up the Wrong Tree, Beauty is Only* and *Burslem Boys*. Meanwhile the Lyons discovered *Testament, Talisman* and *Touchstone*. Gibson's biggest and best addition however was *Foolish Ghoulish* a powerful line up the much-eyed wall left of Mr. Olympia.

Clacher put up *Hagar the Horrible* and *Chock a Block* at the right-hand side of the crag while Paul Williams unearthed *Jungle Jive* and *Wu-shu Boys*.

The Middle Tier of Craig y Don on the Little Orme saw its first ever routes courtesy of Gibson and Clacher when they gardened and climbed *Crab Slab, Just Along for the Ride* and *The Get Along Gang*. The same day Gibson added *Capturing the Coelacanth* over on Trwyn.

Towse returned to the Meadow Walls for *Slime Crime* the hardest route there.

The Upper Tier of Craig y Don came in for similar treatment when Mike Hammill mainly with Chris Lyon climbed *Hydraulic Transmission, New Wave* and *The Cruel Sea*. Over on the Great Orme Dave Lyon was busy cleaning more routes in the Craig Arwahan area. *Bodyworks, Self Abuse* and *Mystic East* were his routes.

Back on the Little Orme the fun continued. Hammill and friends bagged *Nimitz, Frozen Moment, Exocet* and *ECM* while Towse and George Smith stepped in to climb *Dough Nutz* – the last of a string of fine additions.

On the Hornby Crags Mike Ryan and Dominic Staniforth got *Opus Pistorum* and Dave Lyon and Summerfield discovered *Big Mac, French Fries, Squall, The Brotherhood, Vaquero, Watcher in the Woods* and *When the Lion Feeds*.

Ryan found a further two routes at the extreme right-hand end of Pen Trwyn *Reading Henry by the Road* and *Treat Me Like a Rag Doll* climbed with Staniforth then Dave Leadbetter and Rona Owens respectively.

The Lyon/Summerfield team continued to find new climbs this time coming up with *Wind and Worrying* and *Life's a Joke*.

Clacher discovered *Cockleshell Bay* in another new area and also climbed the exciting *Adam's Roof*. The big plum here however was Dave Lyon's *Future Days* (*Here's to*) over to the right of Adam's Roof.

Pat Littlejohn showed interest in the area and with Sarah Bishop and Steve Briggs eliminated the tension traverse on Midnight Blues. He also climbed a new line *The Lizard of Oz* over on Trwyn. His most important achievement by far was when, teamed up with John de Montjoye he reduced the aid on Detritus to only 4 points. A magnificent piece of free-climbing will be the prize for the first person with enough stamina to cross the great initial traverse without falling off. However, it was not all roses for Littlejohn during his Orme exploration. In a letter dated February 1986 he explained:

> "My best epic on the Orme happened this October when I tried to swim around Little Orme to get a good view of all the crags. It was a dull cold day and a couple of people walking the beach must have thought I was committing suicide as I left my clothes in a pile and strode out in my T-shirt and undies. Anyway I soon had major problems as there are lots of submerged rocks in that first bay with incredibly sharp barnacles on them. I got several minor cuts, then just as I was about to land on the first beach (beneath Evening Light) I got a really nasty gash on my knee which bled copiously into the water. I soon went off the idea of swimming round the headland and decided to turn back. There was a fair swell and I kept getting dumped onto the rocks, so by the time I made the beach I was in a hell of a state, blood all over my legs and arms. Luckily there was no-one on the beach to observe me."

Littlejohn continues with another bad luck tale of visiting the Little Orme.

> "I decided to go bouldering on one of the little outcrops above the crags. On the first problem I tried I was pulling round an overhang when the whole thing came away. I hit the ground then the roof landed on my head. I was knocked out for a short time and my hair was matted with blood from head cuts. I just sat there feeling very sick and woozy for about an hour then as no-one seemed likely to pass that way to give me a hand, I wobbled off down to the car. Luckily I am not superstitious or I would have thought Little Orme was jinxed for me. The funny thing about both these incidents was that I had to pick up my girlfriend from

college at the end of each day, and I was always in
such a state that her friends thought I was some sort
of desperado!"

A little later on Colin Goodey with his daughter Katherine
returned to old haunts and produced a further four routes on
Creigiau Cochion, the area where he originally began his Orme
explorations in the 1950s.

To round off activity for 1985 Dave Lyon and Dave Summerfield
produced a number of worthwhile pitches the best of which
were *The Fourth Protocol* and *Edge of Darkness*.

1986 began with another promise of many new lines on the Pen
Trwyn cliffs. Between Clacher and Lyon routes such as
Alexandra Sagnenko and *Nostradamus* were discovered. Mike
Raine and George Smith continued development on Hamburger
Buttress coming up with four routes of which the hardest was
Heightmare – a five-foot roof. Another difficult roof problem was
Tom Jones's Direct Start to Doenitz. Clacher was first to breach
the previously ignored second cave system at the start of the
crag with his route *Mumbo Jumbo*. Dave Lyon steamed in
immediately afterwards to add a further seven routes to the
same buttress of which all have had several repeats with
favourable comments coming from the repeat ascensionists.
Clacher and Keith Simpson discovered a few more routes but
the hardest routes to appear for some time were Tim Freeman's
Up to the Hilt which takes the central roof of Monster Buttress
at its widest point, a fine effort, and Craig Smith's *Sèverine* right
of White Hopes.

In addition Anthony Ingham with Pete Bailey girdled the Yellow
Wall to give *Trivial Pursuits*.
The Lyon brothers were also bringing to fruition a 'new' area
called The Manor Crag where between them several short steep
routes were discovered.

George Smith and Perry Hawkins found an impressive line called
Primeval up the back of Surprise Zawn shortly after.
The Lyon/Summerfield partnership continued to find new
routes, their best discoveries being *Speed Livin'* and *Red
October* on St. Tudno's Buttress followed by *Telegraph Road*
and *Opal Moon* – two excellent Gwynt additions.

Against All Odds was next to fall to Dave Lyon and Clacher – a
major sweeping girdle of The Detritus Wall. Mick Lovatt and
team solved the previously equipped but unclimbed nose at the
far end of Pen Trwyn – calling their route *Physical Abuse*.

As the guidebook manuscript neared conpletion a few final routes were received barely in time for inclusion. Smith's *Crinkle Crack* and *Crinkle Crank* take fine lines in the Crinkle Crag area.

Once again it is Dave Lyon who has been responsible for major developments on The Ormes. His tally of new routes rising slowly but surely above any other Orme pioneers. The strong 'Beris team of Hodgson and Paul Pritchard left such routes as the excellent *Aerial Multigym, Confuse the Aardvark, Space Delivery* and *Rupture* – the latter done on-sight. "Breck" Mike Collins free-climbed the old aid route right of Llanddulas Cave to produce the desperate *Wirral Whip* while Dave Lyon found *Moon Madness, Top Gun* and *Planned Obsolescence* amongst others.

Johnny Dawes bouldered out *Snakes and Ladders* between White Hopes and Sèverine and other teams continued to search the crags for worthwhile gaps.

So, after many delays and months of waiting, the manuscript for this latest North Wales Limestone Guide goes off to the printers, and, as the sun slowly sets over the Great Orme, all is still but for a few gulls calling overhead and the distant drone of Dave Lyon's new battery powered bolt drill.

So, what of the future for the North Wales Limestone area? Rowland Edwards is rumoured to have once said he thought there was more limestone on The Ormes than there is in the whole of Derbyshire. Though this seems a rather far-fetched statement, with each passing season the amount of new routes climbed in the area grows and thus adds strength to the general point Edwards was making.

With Edwards's futuristic attitude in mind a final quote from the man himself seems rather appropriate. It also proves the point that he knew exactly what he was talking about regarding Orme development.

"I had always found it very difficult to get partners to show the same interest in the area as I had, and after having spent sixteen years climbing in Wales I was due for a change of scenery. As for not seeing the potential of Pen Trwyn this could not be further from the truth. I had actually thought of developing it quite early on but when I produced the first guide to the area I had been warned by the local council and the Mostyn Estates, that there was a very good possibility of them taking me to court if I produced a guide. It was only after some very nifty negotiations that I was able to proceed. If I had tried to climb extensively on the roadside crags there is no doubt that climbing would have been stopped on The Orme. As there was only myself involved there would have been no possibility of having any pressure group to back me up. Now it is different. There are hundreds of climbers who can present a united voice for access. I am certain that if I had proceeded with climbing above the road the position would have been a lot different to that of today. Anyway, there was so much other rock available at the time that to spoil it all for future climbers was not justified."

Craig y Forwyn

Craig y Forwyn is situated a mile or so up a pleasant valley running inland from the small village of Llanddulas. When approaching from the Colwyn Bay side take the A55 dual carriageway around the headland to a point about a mile beyond the large quarry workings on the right. An exit left (signposted) from the dual carriageway leads into the village itself. Drive straight through and immediately on leaving the village turn right at the old school. Follow the lane for about a mile to the Plas Newydd Farm and caravan site. The crag is situated directly above this in the trees.

If approaching from the Rhyl side take the road straight through Abergele until after two miles the road drops down into Llanddulas. Take the first turning left at the old school and follow the lane, as above, to the crag.

From the road a path leads up through the trees to the Staircase Gully area. The gully itself (90 feet Moderate) is the simplest and most convenient means of descent for this part of the crag. The Main Crag leads rightwards from this point while to the left of Staircase Gully the crag extends a long way, though it is seldom more than 50 feet high. The routes are approached by traversing leftwards along the narrow rock ledge from the foot of the gully and are described from right to left as one traverses this ledge.

Please avoid crossing fences above the crag and leaving any litter.

LEFT-HAND SECTION
The short corner crack near the base of Staircase Gully has been climbed at Very Severe, 4c. Also the arête to its left **Squatter's Rights** at a slightly higher grade. Neither is particularly worthwhile.

Un-named Route1   50 Feet   Hard Very Severe
Start just left of the arête.
1   50 feet. 5a. Climb the wall to the roof. Surmount this via the wide crack to finish.

Scum Bag   45 feet   Hard Very Severe   (30.6.82)
Start just left of the last route.
1   45 feet. 5a. Climb the shallow groove and wall above to gain the roof. Pull over this on good holds to finish.

Hooter   45 feet   Hard Severe   (5.71)
Start below a shallow corner just left of Scum Bag.
1   45 feet. 4b. Ascend the corner and go over the little roof onto
a ledge. Move up left then back up the crack on the right to finish.

23 Skidoo   50 feet   E2   (5.71/18.6.82)
Rather loose and not particularly worthwhile.
1   50 feet. 5c. Climb the overhanging groove, then the wall
above finishing over a small roof 5 feet right of The Fox.

The Fox   45 feet   Hard Very Severe   (1969)
Start just left again beneath an obvious overhanging black
corner crack. (Previously known as Un-named Route 2.)
1   45 feet. 5a. Climb the corner crack and pull over the roof onto
a small ledge. Go straight up to finish over another roof.

Fading Colours   50 feet   E2   (2.1.83)
A line up the wall left of The Fox starting beneath a short
blankish groove. Bold but fairly good climbing.
1   50 feet. 5b. Go up the groove to its top and exit left onto the
wall. Climb this at its centre over a few bulges and left of easy
ground to the right.

Moonwalk   50 feet   Very Severe
Start at the far end of the terrace below a large roof.
1   50 feet. 4c. Go leftwards up to the roof (peg) cross the wall
leftwards by the undercut crack and finish up easier rock above.

A descent from the terrace to follow the path for 50 feet leads
to the next buttress.

Coulombe   65 feet   Very Severe   (4.3.79)
Start as for Chatterley beneath the obvious overhanging crack.
A good route.
1   65 feet. 4c. Go up rightwards over several bulges to a tree
root. Finish direct.

Chatterley   45 feet   Hard Very Severe   (1969)
1   45 feet. 5a. Climb up into the wide crack and follow it steeply
to the top. Polished. (Previously known as Clem.)

Think Void   40 feet   E2   (16.7.82)
Start as for Chatterley.
1   40 feet. 5c. Climb the steep wall left of the crack to the roof.
Pull through this at its weakest point and finish up a short wall.

Extinction Crack   40 feet   Very Severe
Start just left of Chatterley beneath another crack.
1   40 feet. 4c. Climb the crack, go over a small bulge and finish
up the wall on the right.

★ **The Crunge**   50 feet   E1   (14.3.79)
Takes the arête of this buttress. Start below an obvious undercut
flake.
1   50 feet. 5c. Move up to the flake and follow it rightwards until
a long reach leads to good holds above. Go up left into a scoop
and exit rightwards to finish up the short slab above.

The Cringe   45 feet   E2   (13.3.82)
1   45 feet. 5c. Climb the wall just left of the arête of The Crunge.

Vole   50 feet   Very Difficult
Takes the obvious corner, through ivy, immediately left of the
last route.

Whitewash   50 feet   Very Severe   (9.4.82)
1   50 feet. 4c. Takes the obvious corner 20 feet left of Vole.

The right arête of Whitewash has been climbed: **Gear Freak**,
Very Severe, 4c.

Immediately left again is a broad, blank wall this has been
climbed on its right-hand side at 5c and up the centre (**Sunny
City**, E2, 5c, (9.5.81).

Just left again a large flake crack trends up to the right. This is
the start of the next route.

★ **Arian**   60 feet   Hard Severe   (12.6.71)
1   60 feet. 4b. Climb the flake to its top then traverse left above
the roof to an in-cut corner. Finish up this.

Variations
Arian Direct Finish   60 feet   Very Severe   (1981)
1   60 feet. 4c. From the top of the flake step right and climb the
crack direct to the top, or, the wall just to its left, (E1, 5b, (1984).

Arian Direct Start   50 feet   Very Severe
1   50 feet. 5a. Enter the corner on the left and move up to the
roof. Step right and pull over to join Arian at the in-cut corner.
Finish up this.

Dave's Wall   40 feet   E2   (9.1.83)
1   40 feet. 5c. The bulging wall just left of Arian Direct Start –
not particularly good.

Ivy Line   40 feet   Hard Severe
Start just left of Dave's Wall.
1   40 feet. 4a. Climb the vague crack over several bulges.

Paul's Wall   50 feet   E1   (9.4.82)
A worthwhile route. Start just left of Ivy Line.
1   50 feet. 5b. Go up rightwards and over a small roof. Step back
left and climb the wall direct, with a tricky finishing move.

Plas Newydd Groove   40 feet   Very Severe   (21.2.82)
1   40 feet. 4c. Climb the cleaned groove left of Paul's Wall.

The next routes are to be found a further 50 yards along the path
below a clean wall with a long capping roof.

Hairline   40 feet   Hard Very Severe   (18.2.79)
Start below the thin crack on the right-hand side of the wall.
1   40 feet. 5a. Go up the crack finishing right of the roof at the
top.

Spike Driver   50 feet   E2   (20.1.80)
Start just left of Hairline.
1   50 feet. 5c. Climb direct to a small flake under the roof. Pull
over on huge holds and trend leftwards to a difficult finish.
'Friends' useful.

Kiwi   60 feet   Severe
Start as for Spike Driver.
1   60 feet. 4a. Climb diagonally leftwards across the wall and
make a hard move round below the left-hand side of the roof.
Go up right to an easier finish.

Variation
Kiwi Direct Start   50 feet   E1   (12.5.82)
1   50 feet. 5b. Go straight up the bulging crack to join Kiwi at
the end of its traverse.

★ **The Last Grasp**   50 feet   E2   (16.4.82)
A good route with a strenuous crux. Start left of Kiwi at the foot
of the corner capped by a 4-foot roof.
1   50 feet. 5b. Take the right wall of the corner then the roof
direct on good holds.

★ **Larks a Bumbly**   50 feet   Severe   (10.4.82)
A little gem.
1   50 feet. 4a. The overhanging corner has huge holds. Finish
on the left arête. The left arête climbed direct is Hard Very
Severe, 5a.

Farther along the path are two obvious grooves.

Un-named Route 4   40 feet   Very Difficult
1   40 feet. 3b. Climb the right-hand groove passing a tree stump
just below the top.

Heart Attack   40 feet   Hard Severe
1   40 feet. 4b. Climb the left-hand groove.

Un-named Route 3   40 feet   Hard Very Severe
Start on a ledge just left of Heart Attack.
1   40 feet. 5a. Enter the slot out left and pull up into the crack up left again. Finish steeply up this.

Dyslexic's Delite   50 feet   Very Severe   (13.5.81)
1   50 feet. 4c. From 10 feet left of Un-named Route 3 climb into a vague groove starting at a short arête.

Hugh's Groove   50 feet   E3   (7.82)
1   50 feet. 5c. Climb the obvious slim groove up the next buttress, finishing leftwards at the top.

Legal Separation   40 feet   E2   (9.4.83)
1   40 feet. 5c. The short, steep wall left of Hugh's Groove. Thread runner.

Farther along a path leads rightwards to an obvious chimney.

Ann   30 feet   Severe
1   30 feet. 4a. Go straight up the wall right of the chimney to a tricky final move.

Golden Gate   30 feet   Difficult
1   30 feet. Climb the outside of the chimney finishing up a small corner on the left.

Claustrophobia   30 feet   Very Difficult
1   30 feet. Climb the inside of the chimney, passing under two large chockstones to finish on a large ledge at the top.

Temptation   30 feet   Very Difficult
1   30 feet. Start left of the chimney at a small roof. Pull over the roof and go straight up finishing via a roof crack.

Krag Rat   45 feet   Very Severe
1   45 feet. 4c. From the top roof on Temptation traverse right around the arête and finish up a short steep wall.

To the left again is a vegetated gully.

Otto   30 feet   Very Difficult
1   30 feet. Climb the left wall of the gully.

Beeline   30 feet   Hard Severe   (1969)
Start as for Otto.
1   30 feet. 4a. Go left for about 15 feet then ascend to the roof. Traverse back right to finish up a little corner.

Beeline Direct   30 feet   Hard Severe
Start 10 feet left of Beeline.
1   30 feet. 4a. Pull over the roof to join Beeline at the end of its initial traverse.

Naughty Bits   30 feet   Severe
Start just left of Beeline Direct.
1   30 feet. 3c. Climb the short groove, finishing up the arête on the left.

Cling   30 feet   Hard Severe
Start left again beneath a crack.
1   30 feet. 4a. Climb the crack leftwards to the top.

A couple of little routes exist over the fence from here. **Kite**, Difficult and **Cervix**, Severe, take obvious little features.

CRAIG Y BOTEL
This obvious pillar in the adjoining field has been climbed on its outside face.

THE MAIN CLIFF
To the right of Staircase Gully is The Main Cliff, which provides the best climbing on the crag. The routes are described from left to right, ending just before the foot of a second descent gully, at the far end of the crag.

Human Menagerie   60 feet   E1   (7.7.77)
A strenuous route up the wall just right of Staircase Gully.
1   60 feet. 5b. Climb the wall to a hollow flake. Follow the thin crack above, moving right then back left to finish. (The left arête of this route has been climbed.)

Swinger   100 feet   Hard Very Severe   (28.5.80)
A traverse of the left-hand end of the crag. Start as for Human Menagerie.
1   50 feet. 5a. Pull up to a small roof then traverse right crossing Pterodactyl and The Flue to belay on a ledge on the arête.
2   50 feet. 5a. Traverse right into the corner and go around the arête into the chimney. Cross to the right and pull up into the scoop at the top of Yam. Finish direct as for Yam.

Knightsbridge   60 feet   Very Severe   (5.70)
Start at an obvious sentry box 30 feet right of Staircase Gully.
1   60 feet. 4c. Leave the sentry box with difficulty to finish up the wide crack above.

Variation   60 feet   E2   (1979)
1   60 feet. 5c. From the sentry box break out left and take the short groove and wall above to the top.

Banana Moon 60 feet   E3   (2.10.79)
Start just right of Knightsbridge.
1 60 feet. 5c. Go up leftwards to a point just right of the roof
of Knightsbridge. Pull over the bulge here and make a thin move
up onto the wall above. Finish up the overhanging flake on the
left at the top.

★ **Pterodactyl** 60 feet   Hard Very Severe   (9.68)
Takes the wall and groove directly below a tree at the top of the
crag.
1 60 feet. 5a. Climb up to the groove and layback this to the
top of the crag.

★ **The Flue** 60 feet   Very Severe   (6.67)
An excellent crack route. Start 10 feet right of Pterodactyl
beneath the steep flue-like crack.
1 60 feet. 4c. Enter the crack with difficulty and climb it over a
bulge at half-height to reach good finishing holds.

One Step Beyond 60 feet   E2   (9.2.80)
A good climb up the wall right of The Flue.
1 60 feet. 5c. Pull rightwards over the roof at the base of The
Flue and ascend direct to a wide scoop. Cross to the left for a
few feet then go straight up via a short crack to a ledge. Move
back right to finish.

Snotty Arête 60 feet   E3   (1980)
A serious pitch up the shattered arête right of One Step Beyond.
1 60 feet. 5c. Traverse right beneath the roof and move up onto
the arête. Go straight up this avoiding easier ground on the right.

Zig Zag 70 feet   Very Difficult   (1967)
Start round to the right from The Flue at a large open corner.
1 50 feet. 3c. Climb up to a huge perched block then traverse
the break leftwards, passing a small bush to belay at an in-cut
corner.
2 20 feet. Finish up the corner exiting left at the top.

Little Neb 70 feet   Hard Very Severe   (11.76)
Takes the roof crack left of the corner.
1 70 feet. 5b. Follow Zig Zag for 30 feet then climb the obvious
crack up to the roof. Go straight out over this to a strenuous
finish.

The roof just right of Little Neb has been climbed at E2, 5c
L'Indienne, (27.1.82).

★ **Softly Softly** 70 feet   Severe   (19.11.67)
A fine route taking the huge corner.
1 70 feet. 4a. Climb straight up the corner to a roof at 50 feet.

Craig y Forwyn — Main Crag Left-Hand

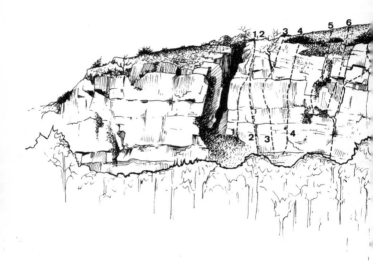

1	Human Menagerie	E1
2	Knightsbridge	VS
3	Pterodactyl	HVS
4	The Flue	VS
5	Zigzag	VD
6	Little Neb	HVS

7	Softly Softly	S
8	Imminent Crisis	E5
9	Cutter	S
10	The Arête	VS
11	Fido's Redemption	HVS
12	Freedom (+ Var. Fin)	E2

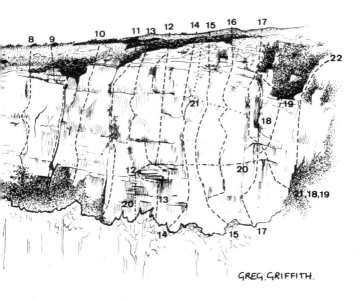

GREG. GRIFFITH.

13 Mojo	E1	18 Demolition	VS
14 Quick Step	E4	19 The Texas Shuffle	E2
15 Space Case	E6	20 High Steppa	E5
16 Great Wall	E4	21 High Plains Drifter	E3
17 Book of Dreams/		22 Twisting Chimney	VS
Magnum Opus	E4/E5		

Traverse right a few feet and move up left into a short corner to finish.

The right arête of the corner is taken by a poor route: **Grotty Arête** Very Severe, 4c, (22.4.65). Right again are two obvious chimneys. The left wall of which has been climbed. (**Gary**, 65 feet, E4, 6b, (6.9.85).)

THE Y CHIMNEYS

★ **Left-hand Branch**   70 feet   Very Difficult   (9.58)
1   70 feet. 3b. Climb the wall leftwards to a jammed chockstone. Ascend the outside of the chimney past a second chockstone and finish up the short gully.

★ **Right-hand Branch**   70 feet   Hard Very Difficult   (9.58)
1   70 feet. 4a. Go up the back of the chimney then make a long stride right onto the wall. Surmount the roof and move back left above it into the continuation chimney which leads to the top.

Yam   70 feet   Hard Very Severe
This route follows the obvious jutting arête which forms the right wall of the chimneys.
1   70 feet. 5a. Climb the wall just left of the arête to a scoop near the top. Pull up into the scoop and finish direct, OR, from the scoop swing out right to finish. Tree belay.

Jungle Love   60 feet   E3   (27.10.81)
A good route with an exposed finish. Start just right of Yam at a short corner.
1   60 feet. 5c. Climb the corner, then go diagonally leftwards across the wall to the arête, peg. Climb the arête and top roof direct to finish.

Just around the corner from Jungle Love is an area of cleaned rock in a vegetated bay.

★ **Imminent Crisis**   60 feet   E5   (5.5.82)
A very steep and strenuous route with the crux right at the top. Start 10 feet left of Cutter.
1   60 feet. 6b. Climb the wall keeping left of a peg at 20 feet to a horizontal break and an excellent thread. Cross the bulge rightwards then pull up left to a poor resting position 10 feet from the top. Step right to a pocket, then with an enormous reach gain a jug and then the top.

Cutter   60 feet   Severe
Start on the rock ledge on the left-hand side of the bay.
1   60 feet. 4a. Climb the corner crack exiting left at the top.

The wall immediately right of Cutter has been climbed at Very Severe, 4b.

The Arête   70 feet   Very Severe, 4c   (4.65)
Start on the right-hand side of the obvious arête in the centre of the bay. A pleasant route.
1   70 feet. 4c. Go up leftwards onto the arête. Move up left then back right into a shallow groove in the arête. Go up this finishing up an in-cut corner.

The vegetated gully is **Fido's Folly**, Very Difficult, (14.5.65).

The next buttress along, The Great Wall Area, provides some of the finest routes on the crag.

Clap Trap   80 feet   E3   (31.3.84)
An interesting pitch up the right wall of the vegetated gully. Start on the path directly below the arête.
1   80 feet 5c. Climb the left wall of the arête past an obvious flake hold to the last of three threads. Move left and go up the wall to a rest position then back right to finish up the last 10 feet of the arête.

⋆ **Fido's Redemption**   100 feet   Hard Very Severe
                                                    (17.7.65/ 1.7.83)
A superb route with an airy top pitch. Start beneath the arête.
1   50 feet. 5a. Move up right for a few feet then go straight up the wall passing a thread and peg to belay at the yew tree.
2   50 feet. 4c. Step onto the wall and move up left onto the arête. Go up this for a few feet then pull onto a ledge on the right. Step right and finish direct.

Variation
Jugular Start   50 feet   E1   (1.71)
Start 10 feet right of the normal start at a steep black corner.**1**   50 feet. 5b. Climb the corner to a small roof. Pull over this then move out left onto the arête. Go straight up through a small overhang moving left to the yew tree. Belay.

⋆ **High Steppa**   200 feet   E5   (10.1.81)
A bold and technical traverse crossing Great Wall at half-height. Begin as for Jugular Start.
1   90 feet. 5c. Climb the corner to the top roof, swing right to the pegs on Freedom. Pull over here and traverse right along the lip, passing the peg belay and the bottomless corner of Crazy Horses to a hanging stance at the ring peg on Quick Step.
2   90 feet. 6b. Move right to good holds, then boldly cross the wall to join Great Wall. Carry on then go straight up and over the bulge (Demolition) to a tree belay.
3   20 feet. 4b. Climb the easy groove behind the trees exiting left at the top.

Great Whaler   170 feet   E2   (1976)
A lower girdle of this area. Sustained on pitch two. Start as for
High Steppa.
1   60 feet. 5b. Go up the corner for 15 feet to an obvious traverse
line leading rightwards. Cross this and swing round the arête
into Mojo. Follow this up to the roof (wooden wedge runner).
Move right and pull up to the next roof, peg. Traverse delicately
right to a peg belay on the arête.
2   90 feet. 5c. Step down and move right, peg, then continue
traversing into Great Wall, peg. Move up to a thread then do the
traverse of Great Wall into the middle of the wall. Pull up to the
next thread then go out right onto the wall and traverse right
again until moves straight up lead over the bulge to tree belays
as for High Steppa.
3   20 feet. 4b. Climb the easy, groove behind the trees exiting
left at the top. (As for High Steppa). For those with strength to
spare, to continue along High Plains Drifter gives an excellent
pumpy finale.

Freedom Direct Start   50 feet   E3   (19.8.82)
A strenuous alternative to a fine route. Start just right of Jugular
Start.
1   50 feet. 5c. Boulder out the problem start to reach the break
then long reaches between better holds lead to the top roof. Step
right and pull over as for Freedom, traversing right to the peg
belay. 'Friends' useful.

✱✱ Freedom   100 feet   E2   (1.74)
An excellent route with two exciting and differing pitches. Start
below the obvious corner in the middle of the wall.
1   50 feet. 5c. Climb the wall just right of the corner to a small
roof. Step into the corner and go up to the next roof, wooden
wedge runner. Traverse left to the arête, pegs, and pull over to
a short crack. Traverse right to a niche and peg belays.
2   50 feet. 5c. Traverse right and step up to the thin crack in the
steep slab above. Climb this into a short corner then either go
straight up or traverse left under a little roof to an easy finishing
groove.

✱✱✱ Mojo   100 feet   E1   (6.59/12.5.75)
A magnificent first pitch through the huge roofs.
1   50 feet. 5b. Follow Freedom to the large roof, wedge runner,
then move right and go up into a bottomless corner, peg.
Traverse left to the lip passing several pegs and pull over on
huge holds to a niche and peg belay.
2   50 feet. 4a. Traverse left and move up into a groove. Climb
this passing a tree to finish.

Variation
★ **The Direct Finish**   50 feet   E3   (19.7.79)
2a 50 feet. 5c. Climb the wall via a series of thin moves, directly above the stance.

The first pitch of Mojo, if combined with the top arête of Fido's Redemption gives a fine route.

★ **Crazy Horses**   90 feet   E3   (15.9.81)
Although very much an eliminate the climbing is superb.
1 90 feet. 6a. Pull over the roof just to the right of the start of Freedom/Mojo and move up rightwards to a second roof. Go over this and straight up to the huge overhang. Step left and follow Mojo, pegs, almost to its lip, then make a hard move back right and pull into a bottomless corner, peg. Go up this to the roof and exit left onto a ledge below the top crack of Freedom. Follow this to another roof on the right. Go over this rightwards finishing easily up the top wall of Quick Step.

★ **Quick Step**   90 feet   E4   (1960/5.75)
A brilliant route up the stepped arête between Mojo and Great Wall. Strenuous and sustained. Start as for Crazy Horses.
1 90 feet. 6a. Pull over the first roof and traverse right to the arête. Climb this to a peg at the right-hand side of the large roof. Move round the arête on the right, then climb leftwards with difficulty to a ring peg in a little hole. Follow the thin crack above, thread and step left onto the arête. Climb the flake crack to the next roof and pull over this finishing up the short wall above.

Variation
★ **Direct Finish**   90 feet   E4   (1969/1979))
1 90 feet. 6b. From the thread, gain the continuation crack above with great difficulty and follow it direct to the top.

★ **Space Case**   90 feet   E6   (2.6.83)
A stunning pitch taking the vague groove between Quick Step and Great Wall. Start as for Great Wall.
1 90 feet. 6b. Follow Great Wall to the first peg then step left and make hard moves straight up over the bulge. Trend up leftwards to a point just right of Quick Step's ring peg then climb directly up into the shallow depression which curves up rightwards. Follow this boldly to a bolt then make hard moves straight above it to gain the break. Move left to climb a thin crack at the top.

★ **Great Wall**   90 feet   E4   (14.10.67/5.75)
Without doubt one of the finest pitches in the area. The climb offers steep, sustained climbing on perfect rock. Start directly below some large pockets in the middle of the wall.

1   90 feet. 5c. Ascend leftwards to a peg then traverse right, beneath a high thread, to gain the main line. Go straight up on long pockets passing another thread to a niche and a good resting place, threads. Step left and climb the obvious white pillar, then go up rightwards to a small flake crack. Cross left to a broken flake, then go straight up, bolt, to the top.

★ **Book of Dreams**   110 feet   E4   (6.3.81)
A wandering line but good climbing. Start just right of Great Wall.
1   110 feet. 6a. Go straight up the black streak to a small roof then up left with difficulty to meet Great Wall at the end of its traverse. Pull up to the thread then traverse right for 20 feet then straight up over a small bulge to a tree. Move left and climb a second black streak/groove to the break and traverse left into Great Wall to finish.

Variation
★★ **Magnum Opus**   90 feet   E5   (17.4.84)
A much more direct version with a difficult start. Start a few feet right of the normal start.
1   90 feet. 6a. Go straight up to a small horizontal slot, small 'hex' and Tri-cam, then pockets above lead to better holds and a thread on the right. Go up to and over the bulge to the tree. Step left and climb the black groove to the break finishing up rightwards.

The next routes start from the obvious curving chimney right of Great Wall. A traverse line leads out left onto the wall from here.

★★ **High Plains Drifter**   140 feet   E3   (29.3.81)
A strenuous girdle across the top of Great Wall in a very exposed position with good protection.
1   140 feet. 6a. Traverse left out of the chimney, just above a small bush, then go up left and over the bulge to a tree. Step left and climb the black groove (Book of Dreams) to the break. Traverse left into Great Wall then continue traversing with increasing difficulty to a hard finish at the crack of Quick Step Direct.

Demolition   80 feet   Very Severe   (6.60)
Start as for High Plains Drifter.
1   50 feet. 4c. Traverse out left and climb leftwards to the bulge. Surmount this to the tree and belay.
2   30 feet. 4b. Climb the easy groove behind the trees, exiting left at the top.

The Texas Shuffle   80 feet   E2   (17.1.82)
Good climbing up the bulging wall right of Demolition
1   60 feet. 5c. Follow Demolition to the first small bush, then

climb up to the bulge above. Go over this then straight up on small flakes to a ledge and belays.
2 20 feet. 4b. Move left and exit as for Demolition.

Variation
The Direct Start E3, 6a   (1982)
A boulder-problem start joining the parent route at the small bush at 20 feet.

Washington Waltz 80 feet E2   (4.3.84)
Start as for Demolition
1 60 feet. 5b. From the start of Demolition go straight up the wall to the base of a slim groove/crack. Follow this, small wires, to the ledge.
2 20 feet. 4b. Exit left as for Demolition.

Twisting Chimney 80 feet Very Severe   (6.60)
Start inside the chimney at a large cavern.
1 80 feet. 4c. Bridge up and climb the left wall to the outside of the chimney, then go straight up the outside edge past a jammed block to the top.

The Norman Conquest 70 feet Hard Very Severe   (2.4.81)
A good jamming crack when clean. Start as for Twisting Chimney.
1 70 feet. 5a. Move out right and up to a short groove. Climb this and step left to a fine crack. Follow this over the bulge then go rightwards over easier rock to finish.

The broken wall and obvious open groove to the right of Twisting Chimney gives a poor and vegetated route **Ivy Union**, Very Difficult, (25.4.65).

★ **The Neurotic Woodpecker** 110 feet Very Severe (6.2.71)
To the right of Ivy Union is a clean-cut orange groove behind some bushes. A popular route.
1 110 feet. 4c. Ascend the groove to a small roof, then climb the crack on the left to a ledge. Go straight up the wall to a little roof. Either go straight up over the roof or climb the left-trending flake moving back right above the roof (better) then straight up to finish. (A harder finish has also been done moving left at the top of the flake.)

Ivy League, (1965) a poor Severe takes a parallel line a little to the left of the next route though it is not really very worthwhile.

Street Stroller 110 feet E1   (27.1.82)
Basically just an easier approach to Scalar Arête. Start around the corner from the last route in a corner. Often vegetated.

1 50 feet. 5b. Climb up to the roof, then take the wide crack on the left up and into a niche. Pull up right to a small ledge and belay.
2 60 feet. 5a. Go up the slab to a break. Traverse this rightwards and pull up onto a loose ledge. Finish up the arête in a fine position.

Scalar Arête   115 feet   E4   (5.11.76)
A strenuous line up the wall and arête containing two obvious large peg runners, just right of the last route. Start in the corner.
1 115 feet. 6a. Climb the right arête of the corner to the roof then go up right to a small roof, peg on right. Go up left to two large pegs, step left then back up right to the roof. Traverse left to a resting place on the arête. Climb the left arête of the groove above, stepping into the groove at its top. Pull up onto a loose ledge, then climb just left of the arête to a good ledge at the top and tree belay.

★★ **Scalar**   120 feet   Very Severe   (1962/1963)
An excellent route crossing the big wall. Start as for Scalar Arête.
1 60 feet. 4c. Climb the corner to the roof, then make a rising traverse rightwards, peg, into a corner/crack. Ascend this to a good ledge and belay.
2 60 feet. 4c. Follow the corner to the roof, peg, and surmount this to gain a wide crack. Climb the crack to finish.

Variation
The Direct Start   60 feet   Hard Very Severe
Start at a short corner and ledge 15 feet right of the normal start.
1 130 feet, 5b. Go straight up then over the roof to join Scalar at the corner/crack. No gear until the original route is joined.

★★★ **Moonwind**   (Direct)   130 feet   E5   (9.4.81)
Superb climbing up the big wall right of Scalar Arête with a tremendous finale on the steep white headwall above the roofs. Start below the short steep wall just right of Scalar Arête.
1 130 feet. 6b. Go straight up the wall to a small roof and peg. Move up left then back up right to another peg under the first of two central roofs. Pull up to gain a horizontal crack. Traverse this wildly left and pull over on a prominent sloping hold. A hard move to reach a jug above the next roof then a step right leads to a good finger flake and pocket. Pull straight over then move up right to a small flake and resting place. Climb straight up the middle of the wall finishing up a short crack.

The Maiden   100 feet   E3   (28.1.82)
Start as for Hedera Wall.
1 50 feet. 5b. Climb leftwards to the arête and follow it to the stance on Scalar. Loose in places.

2 50 feet. 6a. Re-gain the arête and climb up right to the peg on Hedera Wall. Move left to the arête and an in situ thread, then steeply climb the arête until a step left into Scalar leads to the top.

Hedera Wall   110 feet   E3
This route follows the steep wall between Scalar and the obvious deep crack of Ivy Sepulchre. Start directly beneath the wall.
1 110 feet. 6a. Go straight up for 15 feet. Move up right then back left. Go up for a few feet then good holds lead to a peg just below a scoop. Pull into the scoop with difficulty and exit rightwards on rather dubious holds. Climb straight up the wall exiting left at the top on to a good ledge and belays.

★ **Ivy Sepulchre**   110 feet   Very Severe   (16.5.59)
A good climb up the deep crack.
1 60 feet. 4c. Go straight up the crack to a bulge. Surmount this, then go up the crack again. Move up right to a good ledge and belay.
2 50 feet. 4c. Move back left to the crack and follow it to the top of the crag.

★ **Titus**   110 feet   Hard Very Severe   (1963)
Start just right of Ivy Sepulchre.
1 60 feet. 5a. Climb the short corner to the roof then step right to reach the crack. Ascend this over a bulge at its top to a good ledge and belay.
2 50 feet. 4b. Climb the thin crack in the wall directly behind the belay to the top.

Wackeroo   160 feet   E2   (1964/1975)
Start just around the arête from Titus.
1 60 feet. 5b. Climb up to a peg then enter the groove on the left. Follow this over a bulge into a scoop and pull out leftwards onto the arête to belay as for Titus.
2 100 feet. 5c. Step back onto the arête and climb this to gain a traverse line crossing the steep slab on the right. Follow this, peg, to its end and make a hard move up into a groove. Climb up leftwards and pull onto a small ledge. Traverse left to the arête (loose) and finish up this.

Variation
Direct Finish   50 feet   E1   (1982)
A worthwhile pitch.
2a 50 feet. 5b. Follow the arête on its left-hand side to a small bulge and thread. Step right then go straight up to reach jugs and the top.

Craig y Forwyn — Main Crag Right-Hand

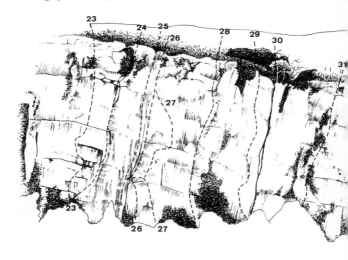

23	Moonwind (Direct)	E5
24	Scalar	VS
25	Ivy Sepulchre	VS
26	Titus	HVS
27	Wackeroo	E2
28	Rocker	HVS

29	Space Mountain	E5
30	Ash Groove	VS
31	Glade Arête	VS
32	Thatch	S
33	Stretch	VS

GREG GRIFFITH

34	Burgess Wall	E2		39	Sunset Strip	HVS
35	Panorama	E3		40	Route 66	VS
36	The Groan	E3		41	Sangfroid	HVS
37	Square Cut Chimney	HS		42	Sangfroid Direct	E2
38	Duchess	HVS		43	The Snake	E2

The Hurting   110 feet   E3   (6.6.83)
Quite serious and with a tricky start. Start 15 feet right of
Wackeroo.
1   110 feet. 6a. Climb the bulging wall rightwards to a thread
runner on the arête then climb up left to join Wackeroo at the
end of its traverse. Pull up into the groove (as for Wackeroo)
(possible belay) and climb to its top. Go rightwards into a
shallow scoop, climb this, then finish direct.

Mad World   130 feet   E4   (25.4.84)
Takes a line between The Hurting and Rocker, starting as for
Rocker.
1   130 feet. 6a. Climb Rocker until it is possible to swing left to
a wider crack and thread. Step left to a ledge then climb the wall
above to a peg. Surmount the bulge to reach two threads and
easier ground above which leads leftwards to finish as for The
Hurting.

The slanting groove to the right of Wackeroo is taken by **Rocker**,
Hard Very Severe, 5a (1964) a poor route with much vegetation.

*** Space Mountain   90 feet   E5   (26.7.82)
An excellent pitch, continuously steep with only sufficient
protection. It follows a line of shallow scoops up the white wall
left of Ash Groove. Start just left of Ash Groove.
1   90 feet. 6a. Step left from the tree stump and climb up into
the first scoop. Balance up rightwards to good holds in the break,
peg on the right, then fingery moves lead up left into another
scoop. Ascend rightwards past a thread to jugs, then move back
left into a slim groove. Follow this to jugs below the final bulge.
Step left and surmount the bulge finishing direct past another
thread.

Ash Groove   90 feet   Very Severe
Start at the back of the bay at the foot of an obvious chimney.
1   90 feet. 4c. Move left into the crack/groove and follow it over
a bulge at 70 feet to belay on the large ash tree at the top.

* Sinister Chimney   90 feet   Severe   (1962/1963)
Start at a cavern at the base of the obvious chimney.
1   90 feet. 4b. Bridge up the chimney to the roof, then move on
to the left wall, peg. Re-enter the chimney above and follow it
in the same line, moving out right for the final moves.

Savage the Cabbage   80 feet   E1   (17.4.85)
Start as for Sinister Chimney.
1   80 feet. 5b. Climb the right arête of the chimney via a
shattered groove and move onto the tower on the right at
half-height. Ascend this, thread, to finish.

Eight-Footed Exercise   110 feet   Hard Very Severe   (2.1.82)
A scrappy approach to a good finishing crack. Start below an
open groove right of Sinister Chimney.
1   110 feet. 5a. Climb the easy groove, over a bulge, and the
steep finishing crack.

The Electric Butterfly   130 feet   Very Severe   (19.4.81)
Start midway between Sinister Chimney and Glade Arête
beneath an obvious flake crack.
1   130 feet. 4b. Ascend the wall to the flake and climb this to its
top. Step left then go straight up to a tree. Take the slab on the
left, trending right to finish.

Glade Arête   130 feet   Very Severe   (9.65)
The obvious arête, usually containing a fair amount of
vegetation, gives an interesting climb. Start below the left-hand
side of the arête.
1   130 feet. 4c. Ascend rightwards to the arête then go back up
left to a ledge (possible belay). Go right onto the arête again,
peg, and follow it to a ledge beneath the final steep slab. Either
go straight up the arête on small holds (best) OR traverse left
and climb a short, easy groove.

∗ The Fun House   130 feet   E4   (25.12.84)
A strenuous line up the wall just round to the right from Glade
Arête. Start 10 feet left of the stile.
1   60 feet. 6a. Climb steeply up to a flake with two old pegs at
its top. Swing up left to a hole, thread, then climb the
overhanging wall past a peg into a very faint groove. Climb this
to easy ground then traverse left to belay just around the arête.
2   70 feet. 5c. Step back around the arête and climb the wall just
to its right avoiding easier alternatives to the left, past two
threads.

∗ Purple Haze   130 feet   E3   (1977)
Start at the stile just right of the last route.
1   60 feet. 6a. Step off the stile and climb up to a ledge with a
perched block, peg. Traverse right and make a hard move into
the corner. Ascend this to the roof, then pull out onto the right
arête. Go leftwards, then straight up the wall above to a
triangular ledge.
2   70 feet. 5c. Move left to a friable hold. Climb straight up then
slightly right and climb the wall direct.

Variation
The obvious corner just right of the stile has been climbed at 5c
joining Purple Haze at 25 feet.

Gone with the Gonads 50 feet   E1   (26.8.84)
Start just right of the corner, right of the stile.
1 50 feet. 5c. Climb the wall trending rightwards to a bolt on
Thatcher Traverse. Abseil off or traverse right to a belay in
Thatch.

Just right again is an obvious deep chimney crack which gives
the next climb.

★ **Thatch** 120 feet   Severe   (15.4.64)
1 50 feet. 3a. Scramble up over easy rock to a good belay in a
shallow groove.
2 70 feet. 4a. Move up to the roof then step onto the arête on
the right. Climb the arête and re-enter the chimney above.
Follow this finishing through the thatch at the top.

Variation
Thatcher Traverse 150 feet   Hard Very Severe   (1970)
2a 60 feet. 5a. Traverse left from the cave to belay on Glade
Arête. One bolt runner.
3a 90 foot. 4c. As for Glade Arête.

Stretch 110 feet   Very Severe   (1962/1963)
Start just right of Thatch.
1 70 feet. 4c. Climb the short wall to a groove. Follow this and
the crack above, then go rightwards over some blocks to a good
ledge.
2 40 feet. 3c. Climb the wall behind the stance for 10 feet then
traverse left around the arête into Thatch up which it finishes.

To the right of Stretch the wall steepens and several good routes
are to be found.

The Space Race 120 feet   E4   (27.4.84)
Start just right of Stretch.
1 80 feet. 5c. Climb up to a small roof. Surmount this, thread,
and climb the slim groove above, peg, to an in-cut corner.
Ascend this to a ledge. Belay on the right.
2 40 feet. 6a. Gain the thin crack in the wall above with difficulty
and climb this, peg, to finish.

★ **Burgess Wall** 120 feet   E2   (4.76)
A strenuous route with adequate protection. Start 10 feet right
of The Space Race below a peg at 20 feet.
1 80 feet. 5c. Climb leftwards at first then go back up right to
the peg. Enter the slim groove on the left and climb it to a little
overhang. Surmount this then go up the in-cut corner above to
belay on the ledge as for Stretch.
2 40 feet. 3c. Finish as for Stretch.

★ **Burgess Wall Right-Hand**   120 feet   E4   (16.6.82)
A strenuous first pitch leads to an exciting finish over the top
bulge. Start as for Burgess Wall.
1 80 feet. 6a. Ascend steeply to a ledge at 20 feet then go up
rightwards, crux, to the horizontal break. Traverse 5 feet left then
move up to a slim right-trending groove above. Follow this and
the short, slabby wall to the ledge and belay as for Stretch.
2 40 feet. 5c. Climb the wall behind the stance for 10 feet then
traverse left onto the arête (as for Stretch). Move up, then gain
the bulge on the right via a good flake. From the peg in the break
above, move left and finish with a long reach.

★ **Man Alive Direct Start**   80 feet   E3   (3.7.82)
Start 15 feet right of Burgess Wall.
1a 80 feet. 6a. A line of obvious flakes leads directly up the
bulging wall to a small thread in the break at 25 feet. Go up
rightwards to join Man Alive in the incut corner. Climb this but
instead of moving left, continue in the same line until a higher
traverse left gains the stance.

★ **Panorama Direct Start**   80 feet   E3   (10.8.85)
1a 80 feet. 6b. Go straight up the wall between Man Alive Direct
Start and the ordinary start of Panorama past two threads. More
in keeping with the upper pitch.

★ **Panorama**   120 feet   E3   (3.8.82)
Good climbing up the pocketed wall left of The Groan. Start just
right of Man Alive Direct Start.
1 80 feet. 6b. Boulder out the initial wall, thread, to reach the
break then climb up leftwards into the incut corner. Step out
right and climb straight up on good pockets until a traverse right
leads to the stance on The Groan. Poor belays.
2 40 feet. 6a. Climb the overhanging groove/crack above the
belay, past a bomber thread placement at half-height, moving
slightly rightwards at the top.

Man Alive   120 feet   E1   (1971)
Start at the base of the chimney right of Panorama. An obvious
line leads left across the wall.
1 80 feet. 5b. Move up a few feet then traverse left across the
steep wall and pull up onto a ledge below an incut corner. Climb
the corner for a few feet then swing out left on to a good hold.
Cross over to the ledge on the left and belay as for Stretch.
2 40 feet. 3c. As for Stretch.

★ **The Groan**   110 feet   E3   (13.6.71)
Takes the groove and bulging wall left of the chimney. Start as
for Man Alive.
1 70 feet. 5c. Climb up to the foot of the groove and follow it
to a ledge and poor belay.

2 40 feet. 6a. Traverse out right a few feet then go straight up the bulging wall, peg, to the top.

Square Cut Chimney 130 feet Hard Severe   (30.7.65)
This route climbs the obvious chimney right of The Groan.
1 50 feet. Climb up a short easy slab and gain a crack. This leads to a ledge and belay at the foot of the open chimney above.
2 80 feet. 4c. Climb the chimney for 30 feet then swing out right on to the arête. Ascend rightwards to the foot of a left-trending groove. Climb this to finish.

Variation
★ **The Direct Finish** 70 feet Hard Very Severe
2a 70 feet. 5a. Climb the chimney to where it closes completely, then pull over the bulge, good nut placement, and finish direct.

★★ **Duchess** 140 feet Hard Very Severe   (29.8.79)
Square Cut Chimney is bounded on the right by a long slabby wall. Start midway between the chimney and the arête.
1 140 feet. 5a. Climb up to a thin crack in the slab then follow this to a small grassy ledge. Move right for 5 feet then ascend leftwards on excellent pockets to a broken crackline which provides the finish.

Variation
★ **Variation Start** 60 feet Hard Very Severe   (3.3.82)
1a 60 feet. 5a. The slab 15 feet right of the thin starting crack provides an interesting alternative joining Duchess at the grassy ledge at half-height.

★ **Sunset Strip** 160 feet Hard Very Severe   (1968/4.74)
Another fine route up the slab. Start down right from Duchess in a corner.
1 40 feet. 4c. Climb the corner to the roof, then traverse leftwards to the arête and belay on small ledges.
2 120 feet. 5a. Enter the groove behind the stance and move right into a thin crack. Follow the crack until a move left onto the slab is made, then climb up to a flake which leads to a ledge. Step right and climb the short, steep wall to finish.

Variation
The Direct Start 30 feet Hard Very Severe   (3.82)
1 30 feet. 4c. A poor variation, taking a line of dubious flakes directly to the stance.

Autobahn 140 feet E3   (22.5.82)
Start as for Sunset Strip.
1 140 feet. 5c. Climb the right arête of the corner then cross left and pull leftwards between two small roofs to reach a ledge on the arête. Climb the arête to another ledge. The wall above, peg,

is the crux and leads to better holds rising left onto the arête up which the route finishes. A hold has since disappeared – the route may now be a little harder.

⋆**Route 66**   140 feet   Very Severe   (1962/1963)
A fine, popular route. Start below the corner as for Sunset Strip.
1   90 feet. 4c. Climb the corner for 20 feet then traverse right to the arête. Ascend the arête to a steep wall and climb this exiting left or right on to a good ledge and belay.
2   50 feet. 4b. Follow the obvious corner behind the stance to finish.

⋆**Manhattan**   140 feet   E5   (13.8.82)
Excellent climbing up the lower part of the huge wall right of Route 66. Start below the middle of the wall.
1   140 feet. 6a. Ascend to a peg at 20 feet then go straight up again, difficult. Trend leftwards to a second peg in a horizontal break. Shuffle left past the peg then go straight up to an undercut flake. Move left to another flake then a long reach gains holds above leading left into Route 66 up which it finishes.

⋆**Variation**   140 feet   E4   (3.8.85)
1a   140 feet. 6a. Alternatively climb directly up the wall just left of the normal start, thread, over a small roof to a junction with the original route.

⋆**Sangfroid**   160 feet   Hard Very Severe   (21.11.73)
An excellent route. The best of its grade on the crag giving steep climbing in airy positions. Start right of Manhattan below an obvious flake high on the wall.
1   30 feet. 4a. Climb easy ground to a small bush. Belay.
2   130 feet. 5a. Climb up past several small ledges to gain the base of the flake. Follow this to its top then make an exposed traverse left across the wall stepping down onto the arête at the end. Move left and finish up the corner.

Variation
⋆**Sangfroid Direct**   120 feet   E2   (30.1.81)
A superb pitch taking a very direct line.
2a   120 feet. 5c. Follow Sangfroid to the top of the flake. Pull out right to another flake on the steep headwall and climb this to a small ledge. Follow the shallow corner above to reach a ledge and finish either direct or by a short traverse onto the left arête.

The wall and wide crack leading up to and through the roof 10 feet right of Sangfroid has been climbed at E1, 5b.

** **The Snake**   130 feet   E2   (2.5.71/1.74)
A very good route taking the twin flakes high on the arête right
of Sangfroid. Start in a shallow corner directly beneath the
jutting roof.
1   80 feet. 5c. Climb the corner to the roof then step right onto
the arête. Pull over the small bulge to a crack. Climb this to its
top then transfer to another steep crack on the right. Ascend this
to a rubble-covered ledge.
2   50 feet. 5c. Climb leftwards to a small ledge at 20 feet. Go up
the shallow corner above and either finish direct or by a short
traverse onto the arête on the left.

Variations   (1981)
2a   60 feet, E3, 5c. Climb the wall behind the stance leftwards
at first then back right to finish. Bold.
2b   50 feet, E2, 5b. A better way to climb the pitch. Go straight
up into the niche, pull up, then exit rightwards to finish through
the fence at the top.

** **The People Mover**   140 feet   E5   (31.3.84)
A superb, hard route taking the fine white wall right of The
Snake. Start 20 feet right of The Snake.
1   80 feet. 6b. A shallow groove leads past two threads to twin
bolts below the headwall. Go straight up for 10 feet then transfer
right and move up to a thread with difficulty. Continue direct to
the big ledge.
2   60 feet. 5c. Move out left as for The Snake pitch 2 then attack
the wall above direct via a black streak and a final huge jug.

Stripper   100 feet   Severe   (1963)
The deep chimney crack right of The People Mover.
1   70 feet. 3c. Climb the crack to a small ledge and go over this
to enter the chimney above. Follow this to an awkward exit
under a large chockstone to finish on a huge grassy ledge with
tree belays.
2   30 feet. 3b. From the tree go 10 feet left and climb a short
groove to finish.

Sour Grapes   110 feet   E2   (31.1.81/1984)
Takes the arête right of Stripper. Start at the foot of the arête on
its right-hand side.
1   80 feet. 5c. Climb the arête for 15 feet then move up leftwards
to a small roof, peg on the right. Pull over by a prominent jug
on its lip and move rightwards to a short flake. Go up leftwards
to the large grassy ledge. Tree belay.
2   30 feet. 5a. Climb the cleaned wall directly behind the large
tree.

Di's Delight   70 feet   E2   (18.8.83)
1 70 feet. 5b. A filler-in up the slabby wall between Sour Grapes and Top Cat finishing any way from the grassy ledge.

Zonesthesia   220 feet   E1   (11.80)
An interesting girdle of the right-hand side of the cliff. Start as for Top Cat.
1 40 feet. 5a. Climb Top Cat for 30 feet then traverse left around the arête to a belay in Stripper.
2 50 feet. 5a. Drop down a few feet then make a rising traverse across the steep white wall to the arête. Move round and go up to a belay on Sangfroid. A bold pitch.
3 70 feet. 5a. As for Sangfroid to a belay in Route 66.
4 60 feet. 5a. Traverse left onto the arête of Sunset Strip then go leftwards to a ledge. Take the easier ramp over on the left to finish.

Top Cat   120 feet   Very Severe   (1965)
To the right of Stripper a crackline in the wall provides a mildly pleasant route.
1 90 feet. 4c. Climb up to a small ledge, step left and climb the crack to reach the huge grassy ledge. Tree belay.
2 30 feet. 3a. Over to the right of the ledge is a vegetated groove. Climb this to the top.

TWO TIER BUTTRESS

The most recently developed part of the crag. The Upper Tier is clearly visible from the road while The Lower Tier is hidden by trees below and to the right.

To approach, walk 500 yards down the road from the main crag approach path, and ascend a scree slope, through trees, until The Lower Tier is reached. This is clearly recognizable by its bulging central wall. The wall here being about 60 feet in height.

For The Upper Tier, walk leftwards under the Lower Tier and climb over the wall. Go through bushes and scramble up left to a ledge running back right to the foot of the steep striped slab.

LOWER TIER

Limestone Cowboy   30 feet   Severe   (1.6.82)
1 30 feet. 3a. The corner round the arête right of Making Memories.

Making Memories   60 feet   E2   (26.2.85)
1   60 feet. 5c. Climb the groove right of Making Movies, moving left at its top and up to a bolt. Trend up right to a flake and finish on the left.
N.B. Has been led without the bolt runner.

★ **Making Movies**   60 feet   E3   (3.6.81)
A fine sustained little route on excellent rock. Start just right of the middle of the wall.
1   60 feet. 6a. Climb to a thread at 10 feet then go up again to a peg. From the peg move up right to the start of a shallow left-trending groove. Ascend this past two small threads then step left on to a small ledge. Straight up the wall above to the top. Peg belays.

★ **Skateaway**   60 feet   E3   (12.6.81)
A nice companion route to Making Movies. Start just to its left.**1**   60 feet. 6a. Go straight up the bulging wall to a thread at 20 feet. From the thread move up left to the foot of a slim groove. Climb this, over a small roof and finish up the easier wall above. Peg belays.

Eastbound Train   60 feet   Hard Very Severe   (6.6.81)
Start below the arête left of Skateaway.
1   60 feet. 5a. Climb the arête until it is possible to move on to the wall on the right. Ascend this into the slim groove of Skateaway. Cross this and move up onto a ledge. Finish straight up.

Rock On, Severe, 3a, (6.6.82) and **Face Value**, Very Severe, 4c, (6.6.82) take parallel lines up the wall left of Eastbound Train. Rock On is the crackline on the left while Face Value more or less follows the right-hand arête.

Jackdaw Chimney   70 feet   Very Difficult   (30.5.81)
Start at a deep chimney left of Eastbound Train.
1   70 feet. Climb the chimney, go over a large jammed boulder, and move up left to finish up a wide crack and easy wall.

Romeo   70 feet   Very Severe   (30.5.81)
Start left of the chimney at an obvious corner/crack.
1   70 feet. 4c. Climb the right wall of the corner then move up rightwards into a chimney. Hand-traverse out left to a wide flake crack and ascend this to finish.

Juliet   65 feet   E1   (5.7.81)
Strenuous jamming up the initial crack leads to an unpleasant battle through vegetation to finish. Start just left of Romeo below a steep crack.
1   65 feet. 5b. Enter the crack and follow it over a bulge at the top onto a ledge. Finish either left or right.

Amateur Dramatics   40 feet   E2   (3.8.83)
1   40 feet. 5c. Climb the loose crack and groove just left of Juliet.

UPPER TIER

Into The Gap   50 feet   E3   (20.4.84)
Start 30 feet right of the deterioration of the crag at the foot of
an obvious tower.
1   50 feet. 5c. Climb the wall steeply (wide crack on the right)
to the break. Move up and right to a crack in the headwall and
finish up this. Large 'Friends' useful. There is a peg belay in the
platform 20 feet back.

Good Friday Groove   50 feet   E1   (20.4.84)
Start 15 feet right of Into The Gap.
1   50 feet. 5b. The crack/groove is climbed in its entirety to
finish over an unsound block. Belay as for Into The Gap.

Notta Bleck   50 feet   Hard Very Severe   (20.4.84)
Start 5 feet right of Good Friday Groove.
1   50 feet. 5a. Climb the scoop to the remains of a slender flake
and pull onto the ledge above. Ascend the groove moving left
at the top with some loose rock to finish. Belay as for Into The
Gap.

Physical Diagnostic   60 feet   E3   (17.6.82)
Good climbing up the shallow groove right of Notta Bleck.
1   60 feet. 6a. Boldly gain the groove and follow it to a flared
slot at its top. Swing out onto the left arête and climb this, peg,
to the top.

Napalm Sunday   70 feet   E4   (14.4.84)
A very bold route crossing The Black Hole from left to right. Start
between Physical Diagnostic and The Black Hole.
1   70 feet. 6b. Climb the slab then step right onto a ledge just
above the thread on The Black Hole. Go straight up to the peg
on The Black Hole then move up right to reach a thin break. Make
a hard move up and right on an undercut for a good hold, thread,
then lunge for the top.

★ **The Black Hole**   65 feet   E4   (7.4.84)
A superb bold pitch up the centre of the slab right of Physical
Diagnostic starting 15 feet right of that route.
1   65 feet. 5c. Go straight up the grey wall to a scoop at 20 feet,
thread on its left side. Pull directly out of the scoop and go
straight up the wall on the right into a second scoop and peg.
Move up to the thin break above then swing left to finish up a
slight groove.

★ Livingstone, I Presume?   65 feet   E4   (7.4.84)
An immaculate pitch, bold to start but with a well-protected crux.
Start 15 feet right of The Black Hole, near a tree.
1   65 feet. 6a. Climb up into a very slim groove and follow it
boldly to a peg. Pass this directly via a slight groove to a good
hold and continue direct up the flake crack above to the top,
thread.

Bush Doctor   65 feet   E2   (7.4.84)
The next slim groove to the right gives a neat pitch. Start just
right of the tree.
1   65 feet. 5b. Climb grey rock direct into a scoop, thread. Step
up left then ascend into the obvious groove/crack, thread. Climb
this directly to the top.

Bush Rush   60 feet   Very Severe   (15.4.84)
The partly cleaned slab right of Bush Doctor gives an awful
route.
1   60 feet. 4b. Climb a dirty crack to a ledge, trend rightwards
then go up back left to finish. Yeuch!

Electric Avenue   60 feet   E1   (7.4.84)
1   60 feet. 5b. The long black slab at the right-hand side of the
wall is climbed passing a thread and peg.

Castle Inn Quarry

About a mile and a half up the road from Craig y Forwyn, near
the village of Llysfaen is a buttress in the car park of The Castle
Inn.

Follow the road for about a mile to an off-set cross roads. Go
straight across (actually diagonally left) then up a hill bearing
left as it dictates. The pub is on the right after a further 200 yards.

Solid 6   50 feet   E3   (1.83)
1   50 feet. 6a. Takes a direct line up the wall 5 feet right of
Driving The Dumper, past a peg at 10 feet.

Driving The Dumper   50 feet   E3   (31.8.82)
Short but worthwhile.
1   50 feet. 6a. Start 10 feet right of Route 1. Climb the wall to a
steep slab, then step up right to a peg under a small roof. Fingery
moves lead straight up to a ledge and easy finish.

★ Route 1   60 feet   Hard Very Severe   (1959/1962)
Start on a ledge just right of the arête. Bold but reasonable
climbing.

1 60 feet. 4c. Climb the wall for 15 feet then step onto the arête. Follow this, passing the stalactites, (threadable) to the top.

Vienna 100 feet E4   (31.8.82)
A superb bold pitch taking a sweeping line across the face. Start as for Route 1.
1 100 feet. 6a. Climb up to a ledge on the arête then a delicate traverse leads left crossing Route 2 to a point just above the peg on Route 3. Go straight up for 10 feet then traverse left under the roof to finish up the short side wall.

Route 2 60 feet E2   (1959)
A bold lead up the front face of the buttress. Start 5 feet left of the arête.
1 60 feet. 5b. Climb up to a peg at 10 feet then go straight up on small holds to finish up the easy groove on the left.

Route 3 (Direct) 70 feet E3   (1959-62/1982)
The best route on this wall offering bold, fingery climbing. Start 10 feet left of Route 2.
1 70 feet. 6a. Go straight up to a peg at 20 feet. Pass it direct then boldly climb the steep slab above to finish up a small corner on the right.
N.B. The original version moved right into Route 2 at 20 feet.

The Cake Walk 80 feet E3   (31.8.82)
Good climbing up the wall left of Route 3.
1 80 feet. 6a. Follow Route 3 to the peg, then traverse left along a thin break to a small ledge. Go straight up the wall to the roof, then traverse right until it is possible to pull up to good holds. Finish easily up a shallow corner.

Variation E3   (20.5.84)
Gain the small ledge direct from the ground. Go straight up as for the original to the roof. Finish direct.

School Mam 80 feet E3   (20.5.84)
1 80 feet. 5c. From the ledge on The Cake Walk Direct, step left and climb the vague thin crack and continue to a break below a small nose. Finish leftwards over this.

Several easy routes have been climbed on the walls over to the left of this buttress but do not warrant inclusion in the guide.

LLANDDULAS CAVE
The cave is situated at the very mouth of the valley and is directly above the road into Llanddulas (from the Abergele side). A very obvious feature is a broad white wall with a huge cave on its right-hand side. A path leads up through trees to the cave.

Early Bird   110 feet   E3   (1.7.84)
Start at the mouth of the cave on the left-hand side.
1   110 feet. 5c. Ascend the vague groove just left of the cave,
passing two threads to a ledge (care needed with loose rock).
Climb the wide crack to finish. Belays on the right.

Main Overhang   100 feet   A2/Very Severe
A mixed route taking the obvious line of pockets and cracks
crossing the cave roof to a belay over the lip. Free climbing
above leads to the top.

Guano on Sight   60 feet   E2   (29.6.84)
1   60 feet. 5c. Climb the centre of the inside wall of the cave
past two large threads.

The wall immediately right of the cave provides the next route:

The Wirral Whip   50 feet   E6   (11.86)
1   50 feet. 6c. Climb the wall with great difficulty to a bolt belay.
Lower off.

** **Pearl from the Shell**   60 feet   E4   (27.6.84)
Start 10 feet right of The Wirral Whip.
1   60 feet. 6a. Climb the wall past two bolts, and a peg on their
left, to finish rightwards. Belay on a huge thread on the
right-hand side of the upper wall.

* **Searching**   60 feet   E4   (27.6.84)
Start 8 feet right of the last route.
1   60 feet. 6a. Go straight up the wall past two bolts and a
thread.

P.C. Wimpout   50 feet   E2   (27.6.84)
1   50 feet. 5c. Climb the obvious groove right of Searching past
a thread.

* **After Glow**   50 feet   E2   (27.6.84)
Start as for P.C. Wimpout.
1   50 feet. 5c. Traverse right for 10 feet then climb the wall
trending leftwards to finish.

The Great Orme

The Great Orme's head is situated at the west end of Llandudno's north shore promenade. The headland contains many crags of varying heights, rock structures and aspects. The one main factor common to all the crags is the total ease of access. The most popular of the crags here is Craig Pen Trwyn which is the first cliff one travels beneath when circling the Orme via the Marine Drive. This road is a toll road and is extremely popular with tourists both in cars and on foot – hence the access requirements. Farther around the Orme the majority of the crags are situated below road level so the problem with tourists does not exist; however certain cliffs are covered by the annual bird ban. See access notes.

CRAIG DINAS
From the toll gate a path leads up through the Happy Valley Gardens to an old quarried cliff. This is Craig Dinas and it is easily recognizable as it is undermined by some huge caves (The Elephant Caves). The first routes start to the right of the cave's entrance. For the routes starting from the half-height terrace scramble up behind the caves to reach the terrace.

Penelope Direct 140 feet E4   (1982)
A serious and committing lead in an exposed position. Start at the right-hand arête of the huge cave entrance.
1 140 feet. 5c. Go up the arête to poor runners, then go diagonally rightwards to the end of Penelope's traverse. Climb the corner, then pass the pegs on the right onto a ledge. Climb the short wall behind to another ledge, then make a hard exit left onto a narrow ledge. From the left-hand end of this climb the faint groove in a very airy position to a serious finish.

Separate Elephant 35 feet E5   (21.11.82)
Considered the ultimate challenge of its day, this potentially dangerous route has now been reassessed. Start at the back, open end of The Elephant Cave at a horizontal flake, 10 feet above the slope.
1 35 feet. 6c. Swing courageously right along the detached flake for about 20 feet. Make a 90-degree turn and pull over the lip via a good undercut hold. Traverse right to a peg and lower off to avoid vegetation. Verdict: unjustifiable.

★ **Spitting Image** 50 feet E3   (8.8.86)
Start a few feet left of Wall and Groove below a V-groove at 20 feet.
1 50 feet. 6a. Climb the vague crack to a ledge below the groove. Climb the groove passing a bolt to the roof and move

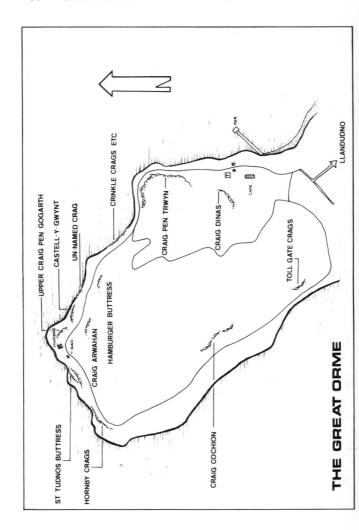

UPPER CRAIG PEN GOGARTH

CASTELL-Y-GWYNT

UN-NAMED CRAG

CRINKLE CRAGS ETC

ST TUDNOS BUTTRESS

HORNBY CRAGS

CRAIG ARWAHAN

HAMBURGER BUTTRESS

CRAIG PEN TRWYN

CRAIG DINAS

TOLL GATE CRAGS

CRAIG COCHION

PIER

CAFE

LLANDUDNO

THE GREAT ORME

out left onto ledges. Go straight up the wall to a bolt belay. Abseil off.

★ **Wall and Groove**   100 feet   E1   (4.70/23.10.79)
A good safe route with a strenuous first pitch and fine positions. Start on the terrace below a roof.
1   40 feet. 5b. Climb the wall to a peg in a niche. Traverse right across the steep wall, 3 pegs, to an airy stance on the arête. Peg belay.
2   60 feet. 5a. Go up the corner to the roof then swing onto the arête on the left and ascend the wall to finish, OR, from the roof step right and continue in the same line to the top of the crag.

Penelope   120 feet   Hard Very Severe   (1970/1979)
Takes the big face above and to the right of the huge caves by a rising traverse. Start right of Wall and Groove on the edge of the terrace.
1   70 feet. 5a. Step off the terrace and make a rising traverse right into a wide, open corner. Ascend the corner to a square-cut nose on the right (peg). Go up the right-hand side of the nose to a good ledge and belay.
2   50 feet. 4c. Ascend steep rock rightwards near the top then go back left to finish.

Craig Pen Trwyn   (R)

Pen Trwyn, the most extensive crag in this area starts about 100 yards along the Marine Drive at two sloping series of caves, both cave systems having been quite well worked out. Just beyond here is the showpiece of Pen Trwyn – the main Mayfair Wall Area. Immediately right again is Hanging Rock a small compact buttress containing several miniature routes. The next main feature is approximately 200 yards beyond and is a large arched overhang, above the grassy slope leading down to the road. Farther right is a long series of walls averaging 50 feet high. These walls continue right round the headland, past the coastguard lookout and an old disused pill box to terminate in a convenient descent gully (containing some telegraph poles). Immediately right again is Monster Buttress – recognizable by a huge central roof and an obvious right-trending rampline.

A slender white pillar to the right again separates Monster Buttress from the aptly named Yellow Wall, in turn becoming Black Wall. Beyond these the crag eventually terminates in the form of a final rounded buttress. The rock in general on Pen Trwyn is sound but nevertheless any rocks falling down onto the Marine Drive should be removed immediately. The final and some would say the finest section of Pen Trwyn is The Lower Tier. This is the obvious long buttress and wall at sea level beneath the aforementioned arched overhang. Access is only restricted by the tide and this part of the crag is **not covered by any ban.**

Please note that climbing **above** the Marine Drive is covered by the access ban.

Starting from the first roadside cave the routes are described as one scrambles up leftwards below the cave system.

Werry's Woof Woot   20 feet   E3   (5.83)
1   20 feet. 6b. A bolt-protected roof problem starting just left of the cave. Lower off from the second bolt or finish up poor rock.

Pumped in Pumps   60 feet   E3   (2.9.82)
A horrendous route, loose and unpleasant. Start outside the first pillar, up left from Werry's Woof Woot.
1   60 feet. 5c. Go straight up for 15 feet then swing right onto a ledge on the arête. Finish up leftwards.

★ **Aerial Multigym**   50 feet   E5   (24.10.86)
Start beneath the pillar just before Dumbell Flyer.
1   50 feet. 6b. Powerful climbing passing two bolts leads to an easier finish. Good.

Dumbell Flyer   70 feet   E4   (2.7.81)
A very strenuous roof leads to an easier but loose finish. Start about three-quarters of the way up the terrace in a cut-away under a large roof.
1   70 feet. 6a. Climb the short slab at the back of the cave to some large pockets. A long reach leads to an excellent jug which is used to gain a line of pockets and cracks crossing the roof. Follow these to a peg on the lip and move round onto the headwall. Climb this with sparse protection to finish on the upper terrace.

The Breck Road   50 feet   E4   (30.8.82)
A technical problem. Start 20 feet left of Dumbell Flyer.
1   50 feet. 6b. Pull over the roof on a sloping finger ledge and move up right to a bulge. Surmount this, bolt, to a good hold then go directly up the headwall to a loose finish.

The Burning Sphincter   50 feet   E4   (4.3.82)
More serious and sustained though not technically as difficult as The Breck Road. Start just left of the latter.
1   50 feet. 6b. Pull over to a peg, then move left to clip a hanging sling. Step back right and make long reaches to a good hold

below the upper roof. Pull through this on the left and climb a short wobbly flake to a final roof. Cross this rightwards to another loose finish.

Variation
The Direct Start   6c   (1982)
The aforementioned hanging sling can be reached direct from the ground by a desperate move over a 5-foot roof. From the sling pull straight over to jugs. A step right then leads to the break in the roof, and a junction with the normal route.

Apes Hit   60 feet   E4   (15.6.84)
Start about 20 feet left of the last route below a series of stepped roofs.
1   60 feet. 6b. Pull rightwards over the first roof into a crack in the slab, bolt. The next roof is slightly easier and leads past a peg to an easy finish.

A Touch Too Much   60 feet   E4   (9.1.83)
A very hard problem. Start 10 feet left of Apes Hit.
1   60 feet. 6c. Boulder out the first roof to reach a bolt on the slab. Climb straight over the next, larger, roof passing another bolt to finish up the short wall.

Stolen Corpse   50 feet   E4   (9.9.84)
1   50 feet. 5c. Climb the leaning corner, just left of the last route. Not particularly technical. Both rock and protection could be better.

The Graduate   35 feet   E3   (2.7.82)
1   35 feet. 5c. Take a direct line up the wall immediately left of Stolen Corpse. Unprotected.

Hom Rescue   35 feet   E2   (1982)
Start below a vague groove left of The Graduate.
1   35 feet. 5c. Climb the groove to a small niche (runner in a borehole on the right). Pull over the bulge and finish easily.

Apostle   40 feet   E3   (9.9.82)
1   40 feet. 6b. Strenuous climbing up the wall just left of Hom Rescue past a peg at 20 feet.

Green Flash   30 feet   Hard Very Severe   (1982)
1   30 feet. 5a. A poor route taking a rightward line through the overhangs just before the crag ends.

A little farther along the Marine Drive another cave system runs up leftwards. At the start of this system is an obvious roof and curving crack. This gives a poor route: **Polit Bureau**, E1, 5b (1983).

Farther up the terrace are to be found the following routes. The first route starts at a niche just as the ground flattens out at the top of the approach slope, and below a pink blob at 30 feet.

The Triad   70 feet   E4   (22.5.86)
An exposed and intimidating route traversing the roof from Pink and Black rightwards.
1   70 feet. 5c. Climb as for Pink and Black to over the small roof. Traverse down rightwards for 15 feet to a good hold in the break (as for Purple Tight Fright). Continue traversing rightwards then go up through the small roof above, bolt. Climb the wall above to a situ belay.

Purple Tight Fright   70 feet   E4.   (11.5.86)
A harder finish to Pink and Black.
1 70 feet. 6a. As for Pink and Black to good holds over the small roof. Traverse down rightwards to the good break in the large roof after 15 feet. Bolt on the lip. Layback past this to gain a standing position above then go left to the belay bolt on Pink and Black.

Pink and Black   60 feet   E4   (8.5.86)
1   60 feet. 6a. Climb up to a shot hole on the left then go horizontally rightwards for 10 feet to a good slot. Pull directly over the roof to gain the large break beneath the roof above. Bolt on the lip. Layback past this then go up to an in-situ belay.

All Fall Down   50 feet   E2   (4.12.86)
Start as for Pink and Black.
1   50 feet. 5b. Go up leftwards then follow the obvious right-leading line to join and finish up Fears for Tears.

Top Gun   160 feet   E2   (7.12.86)
1   90 feet. 5b. Follow the last route until a swing down into Fears for Tears above its second bolt. Carry on in the same line to belay under The Irishman Must Go.
2   70 feet. 5b. Go left as for Brothers in Arms and follow the break to finish up the easy groove of Parting Shot.

★ **Fears for Tears**   50 feet   E3   (4.5.86)
A direct on Tears as Souvenirs.
Start about 40 feet left of the last route, just left of a small arête and bolt over the roof.
1 50 feet. 6a. Climb up and over the roof to good holds. Climb the wall above moving left to join Tears as Souvenirs at the layback. Finish up this.

★ Tears as Souvenirs 50 feet E2   (4.5.86)
Start 10 feet left of the last route beneath a bolt at 15 feet.
1 50 feet. 5c. Climb up and past the bolt to a good break leading
rightwards. Move right for 10 feet to beneath another bolt.
Ascend past this then go diagonally rightwards to a break in the
roof at the arête. Layback into the groove above and finish easily.
Bolt belay.

★ Mumbo Jumbo 60 feet E2   (12.4.86)
Start 10 feet left of the last route and below another bolt at 15
feet.
1 60 feet. 5c. Go up past the bolt to a ledge. Move rightwards to
a small roof, bolt, and climb straight up to a thread below the
bigger roof. Pull over this leftwards and go up to an in-situ belay.

The Irishman Must Go 60 feet E3   (27.5.86)
Start as for Mumbo Jumbo.
1 60 feet. 6a. Instead of going right at the first roof pull over
direct via an obvious crack. Move left and finish up Brothers in
Arms.

★★ Brothers in Arms 70 feet E3   (27.4.86)
Takes a line through the roof left of Mumbo Jumbo via the
obvious brown corner. Start just left of Mumbo Jumbo.
1 70 feet. 6a. Climb directly to a bolt at 20 feet. Pass this then
ascend leftwards to beneath the first roof. Move left and go up
into the brown corner, bolt. Hand traverse right and layback
round the roof to a good shot hole. Climb the left side of the
depression above to finish.

★★ Parting Shot 60 feet E4   (29.5.86)
The open corner/groove left of the last route, gained by the roof
below. Start from beneath a niche at 10 feet left of Brothers in
Arms.
1 60 feet. 6b. Climb bubbly rock to the niche. Traverse left on
the good break to a bolt over the lip. Pull over the roof and move
up right to a jug. Ascend the groove to an in-situ belay. 'Friends'
needed.

Planned Obsolescence 60 feet E2   (14.12.86)
Climbs the vague corner at the left-hand end of the crag.
1 60 feet. 5c. Ascend the rib just left of the large roofs until it
is possible to swing right around a nose of rock into the corner.
Climb this to finish.

Farther along the Marine Drive is the Main Wall of Pen Trwyn,
a 150-foot crag easily recognizable by its many large scoops and
grooves. Descent from these routes is either by in-situ abseil
slings or by walking down a narrow sloping terrace above the
crag.

High on the left-hand side of this Main Wall is a 40-foot thin crack – the top pitch of Birdbrain. For simplicity's sake the routes are described first leftwards then rightwards from below this crack.

★★ **The Lizard of Oz**   120 feet   E4   (10.10.85)
An interesting and well-protected route. Start 15 feet left of Birdbrain, just left of a black groove.
1   90 feet. 6b. Climb the clean wall to the break. Strenuous moves through the bulge above, peg, gain the groove. Climb this, move right a few feet then go up into another shallow groove. Ascend this bearing rightwards to a large hold and pull up right to join Birdbrain at its belay.
2   30 feet. 5a. Climb the corners left of the top crack of Birdbrain.

★★ **Edge of Darkness**   100 feet   E4   (12.85)
A fine route taking a line into the bottomless corner left of The Lizard of Oz via an overhanging pillar. Start beneath the groove, at a green cross painted on the rock.
1 100 feet. 6b. Gain the slab on the right and follow it for 30 feet to the break. Move left along this to a small cave, bolt. Climb the pillar on the right and with difficulty gain the bottomless corner passing two bolts. Climb the corner to a ring bolt and lower off.

★★ **Nostradamus**   100 feet   E5   (1986)
Another good climb. Start as for Edge of Darkness at the green cross.
1 50 feet. 6a. Climb up to a bolt at the start of a groove. Pull into this and gain its right arête. Go up left to a left-trending ramp and follow this with increasing difficulty until holds lead past a peg to a thread belay in the break.
2 50 feet. 6a. Climb the wall above the belay, thread on the right, to gain a good ledge. Climb the open corner above moving left at its top to a bolt belay. Lower off.

★ **Alexandra Sagnenko**   70 feet   E2   (11.1.86)
Start 40 feet left of Edge of Darkness below a small roof at 20 feet.
1 70 feet. 5c. Climb towards the roof, bolt, and move right to a big flake. Ascend straight up to a thread then move left into a chimney. Go up this exiting right at its top to a crack in the wall. This leads to a bolt and thread belay. Abseil off.

The next two routes finish on the narrow terrace which runs down rightwards to reach the road just beyond Hanging Rock.

★★ **Birdbrain**   130 feet   E3   (3.7.83)
A poor start leads to fine exposed climbing above. Start directly below the obvious crack in the wall high on the crag.

1 30 feet. 5b. Climb a short corner to a small roof, peg. Go rightwards over this to the cave. Peg and bolt belays. (Optional).
2 60 feet. 6a. Exit left from the cave past a peg to reach a large flake; peg on the right. Go straight up the wall passing two ring pegs onto a slab. Climb this, thread, to a ledge with thread and bolt belays.
3 40 feet. 5c. The thin crack in the headwall gives a fine finale. Two threads.

The Violator   100 feet   E3   (12.6.83)
An exposed route. Start just right of Birdbrain.
1 30 feet. 5b. Climb a shallow corner and loose wall to the cave. Peg and bolt belay (optional).
2 70 feet. 6a. Exit left as for Birdbrain, peg, and move right, peg, into a shallow right-trending groove. Follow this to a bulge after 60 feet. Surmount this, thread, to reach a grassy bay and belays.

The Visitor   70 feet   E2   (3.83)
Start 20 feet left of Axle Attack below a roof at 15 feet.
1 70 feet. 6a. A difficult first wall, bolt, leads to the vague depression on the right, peg, follow thin cracks and flakes and make a hard move to enter the groove above. Follow this until a pull out left leads to a ledge and bolt belay. Abseil off.

Bonking the Donkey   230 feet   E3   (12.9.86)
A girdle taking the break from The Visitor leftwards. Start as for The Visitor.
1 50 feet. 6a. Climb The Visitor, bolt and into the cave from the left to belay as for The Fourth Protocol.
2 110 feet. 5c. Traverse left along the break to a bolt. Step down and hand traverse across to Edge of Darkness. Step down again then make some hard moves to the thread on Nostradamus. Belay a few feet further on – good threads.
3 70 feet. 5c. Continue the traverse to reach Alexandra Sagnenko at the thread. Follow this to the top and abseil off.

The Fourth Protocol   100 feet   E4   (13.11.85)
Start as for The Visitor.
1 40 feet. 6a. A hard move past the bolt gains the initial groove of The Visitor which is followed for 20 feet then move left, thread, to a cave and belay.
2 60 feet. 6a. Climb rightwards from the cave via a large flake, bolt, then climb the slim groove and ramp to a niche. Exit rightwards from this to a thread then go up left into another slim groove which leads to the belay at the top of The Violator.

Craig Pen Trwyn – Mayfair Wall

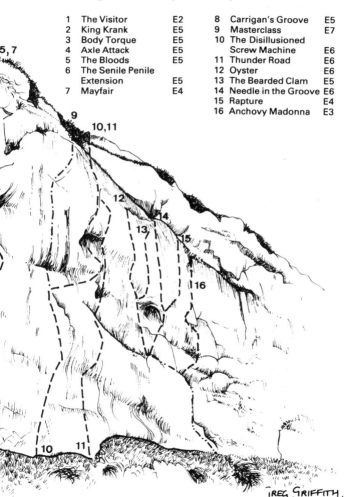

GREG GRIFFITH.

★ **King Krank**   70 feet   E5   (25.6.83)
Immaculate, fingery climbing up the fine scooped wall left of
Axle Attack. Not hard for its grade.
1   70 feet. 6b. Pull rightwards over a small roof, peg, then go
easily up to the first scoop. Pull directly out of this, bolt, to better
holds leading to the next, larger scoop. Move out to a thread
and peg on the wall on the right and pass these via a thin move
to reach the stance of Axle Attack. Abseil off.

★ **Body Torque**   70 feet   E5   (1983)
Although an eliminate line the climbing is good – and very hard.
Start as for Axle Attack.
1   70 feet. 6c. From the second peg on Axle Attack move up left
onto the wall and climb this to a scoop right of King Krank. Move
up right, bolt, and go up to a peg. Difficult moves then lead up
rightwards to join Axle Attack at the top of its groove. Follow
this to the stance. Bolt belay. Abseil off.

★★★ **Axle Attack**   70 feet   E5   (6.81)
A superb, sustained pitch taking the obvious bolt ladder up the
middle of the wall. Represents the lower end of the grade. Start
at two embedded boulders beneath a bottomless black corner.
1   70 feet. 6b. Make a hard move into the corner, peg, then
move up rightwards, thread, onto the wall. Go straight up this,
bolt and peg, to a semi-resting place beneath a shallow groove.
Enter the groove and climb it with difficulty, bolts, to a good
flake hold at its top. Move up to a peg then go diagonally
leftwards to a ledge and bolt belays. Abseil off.

★★ **The Bloods**   150 feet   E5   (7.8.82/5.7.83)
An excellent route with two fine pitches. Start a few feet right of
Axle Attack.
1   90 feet. 6b. Go straight up the wall to a wide niche. Move left
then pull over the bulge, bolt. Go strenuously up right to a
second bolt then go straight up the wall above to a bolt stance.
2   60 feet. 6a. Traverse right along the break for 10 feet until it
is possible to pull up onto the wall above. Go straight up this to
another break and thread. Step left and climb the steep bulge
passing another thread and so to the top. Thread belays on the
left.

Variation
★ **The Senile Penile Extension**   40 feet   E5   (1984)
2a   40 feet. 6b. From the belay climb the steep groove above,
peg, to the bulge. Step left to a bolt and then go straight up to
finish. Thread belays. A good pitch.

Contusion   70 feet   E4   (22.9.84)
Takes the wall between The Bloods and Mayfair with a serious
start. Start at a small ramp just right of The Bloods.
1   70 feet. 6b. Ascend the ramp, step left then continue to the
bulge. Move right and pull over, bolt, to good holds leading up
to a hole, peg on the left. Pull up out of the hole past two threads
and belay as for The Bloods. Abseil off or take either finish to
The Bloods.

★ **Mayfair**   150 feet   E4   (11.72/16.3.80)
The old aid route now provides a sustained free route with
in-situ protection. Start at the lowest point of this face where a
line of bolts leads over a bulge into a cave.
1   55 feet. 6b. Go up the wall, bolt, to the bulge. Surmount this
onto the steep slab above and climb this till a step right into the
cave, peg belay.
2   95 feet. 6b. Climb the wall behind the stance, leftwards to a
thread in the break. Ascend rightwards, bolts, to the foot of an
easy groove (its original finish – 5a). Move out left and climb the
headwall passing two threads (as for The Bloods pitch 2) to a
thread belay on the terrace.

★ **Carrigan's Groove**   (Direct)   40 feet   E5   (5.81/27.6.83)
A fine pitch. Start 10 feet right of Mayfair.
1   40 feet. 6b. Climb straight up the wall to a tiny spike at the
foot of the groove. Enter the groove with difficulty and climb it
trending right to a bolt belay. Abseil off.
N.B. Can be used as a variation 1st pitch to several routes.

★ **Masterclass**   110 feet   E7   (8.83)
A phenomenal route taking the stunning headwall above
Carrigan's Groove.
1   40 feet. 6b. As for Carrigan's Groove.
2   70 feet. 6c. Climb up to large pockets in the bulge and use
these to clip the first bolt. Go straight up on tiny holds to a
second bolt then up and right to the third bolt. Pass this and
climb the faint groove above finishing diagonally rightwards at
the top.

★ **The Disillusioned Screw Machine**   120 feet   E6   (27.7.82/
14.6.83)
One of the finest routes in the area with continuously steep and
exciting climbing. Start 20 feet right of Mayfair.
1   50 feet. 6a. Climb up to a large hole and a good spike. Pass
the bolt above with difficulty and pull up leftwards over the
bulge onto a steep slab. Climb this, keeping left of the flake to
reach the stance. Bolt belays.
2   70 feet. 6b. Traverse right to twin bolts and with great
difficulty enter the large scoop above. Exit left, bolt, to a huge

Craig Pen Trwyn – Mayfair Wall

GREG. GRIFFITH.

pocket then boldly continue to a good resting place in the middle of the headwall. Go straight up again to a horizontal break then step left and finish direct past a peg just below the top. Peg belays on the terrace.

★★ **Thunder Road** 120 feet E6   (30.7.83)
Basically a direct version of the last route, though not quite so fine. Start just right of The Disillusioned Screw Machine.
1 50 feet. 6a. Climb the wall, thread, to the bulge. Cross this rightwards, bolt, to jugs leading to a ledge and peg/thread belays.
2 70 feet. 6b. Climb straight up, bolts, into The Screw Machine cave. Exit directly out of this and gain the groove above with difficulty. Climb this to its top moving left to finish up the last 20 feet of The Screw Machine.

★★ **Oyster** 100 feet E6   (11.72/8.83)
A horrendously difficult route with wild positions. Start 20 feet right of Thunder Road at a large left-facing flake.
1 40 feet. 4a. Climb the flake then cross left to a ledge and thread belay.
2 60 feet. 6c. Pull over the bulge to horizontal slots and climb up left, thread and bolts, to a shake-out below the huge bulge. Cross this, pegs, in extremis and pull round into a groove above the lip. Follow this with less difficulty to a ledge and bolt belay. Abseil off.

★★★ **The Bearded Clam** 110 feet E5   (16.6.83)
A sensational route, one of the best on the crag.
1 40 feet. 4a. As for Oyster pitch 1.
2 70 feet. 6b. Follow Oyster, bolts, to the roof then make wild moves, bolt, to gain and enter the bottomless groove on the right. Climb this to a peg at its top then step out right onto the arête. Climb this to a break above, move right a few feet and follow a second groove to a bolt belay. Abseil off.

Variation
★ **Readers' Wives** 70 feet E5   (27.6.84)
A short, bold alternative finish.
2a 70 feet. 6b. From the peg in the groove move out onto the left wall and climb up the middle of this moving left to the stance on Oyster. Abseil off.

★★ **Needle in the Groove** 110 feet E6   (1983)
An excellent and very strenuous route.
1 40 feet. 4a. As for Oyster pitch 1.
2 70 feet. 6b. Climb up right into a scoop, bolt. Go up to a second bolt then long reaches between good layaways lead through the bulge above and into a groove. Climb this direct to the top. Bolt belay. Abseil off.

** **Rapture**   110 feet   E4   (17.6.83)
Another superb groove line in a fine position.
1   40 feet. 4a. As for Oyster pitch 1.
2   70 feet. 6b. Go up right into a scoop. Step right, peg, and
boulder out the short wall, bolt, to gain the groove above, peg.
Climb this to a step right at its top, peg. Go straight up the flake
above to a bolt stance. Abseil off.

** **Rupture**   110 feet   E5   (8.11.86)
Start as for Rapture.
1   40 feet. 4a. As for Oyster pitch 1.
2   70 feet. 6c. Exit right from the scoop of Rapture, peg and bolt,
but pull out left to a peg at the base of a groove in the arête.
Step left and either climb the arête or finish up the groove of
Needle in the Groove.

** **Anchovy Madonna**   110 feet   E2   (17.6.83)
A cracking route taking the fourth of the dominant groove lines.
Start on a ledge on the right of the top of Oyster's initial big flake.
1   40 feet. 4a. As for Oyster pitch 1.
2   70 feet. 5c. Move up to the bulge and surmount it directly,
three threads, to reach a groove on the left. Climb this to the
next bulge then step out right onto a small ledge. Go back up
left on deep 'goutes' to the foot of a short rib which leads to a
stance. Bolt belay. Either abseil off or do:

Spanish Train   160 feet   E2   (27.7.83)
A fine exposed pitch with good views down the hard routes to
the left.
1   40 feet. 4a. As for Oyster pitch 1.
2   70 feet. 5c. As for Anchovy Madonna.
3   50 feet. 5c. From the top stance of Anchovy Madonna reverse
the rib for 10 feet to the break. Traverse left along this, peg and
thread, all the way to the stance at the top of Oyster. Bolt belays.
Abseil off.

Bored Daughter meets the Power Bulge Boys   30 feet   E5
                                                                 (17.9.86)
Just before The Wall of Blutes is a minute buttress with a tiny
groove in the middle.
1   30 feet. 6b. Go up to the buttress and enter and climb the
groove passing two bolts and a thread to a fixed belay. Lower
off.

The next routes start to the right again beneath an obvious
disjointed groove just before the crag reaches the road. This
groove is Connor's Folly.

★ **The Wall of Blutes**   70 feet   E3   (3.7.83)
A good route taking the slim groove in the left arête of Connor's
Folly. Start below this.
1   70 feet. 6a. Boldly enter the groove to a peg and climb it using
a good flake on the left arête to reach huge 'goutes' on the slab
above. Go straight up this finishing on the terrace above. Peg
belay inside and to the left of a small chimney.

Connor's Folly   70 feet   E1   (11.72/6.8.82)
A reasonably good route. Start directly beneath the groove.
1   70 feet. 5b. Enter the groove and follow it trending slightly
rightwards to the terrace. Peg belays on the left (inside and to
the left of a small chimney).

Le Bingomaniaque   65 feet   E2   (21.7.83)
Start 10 feet right of Connor's Folly.
1   65 feet. 5c. Boldly layback up into a long flake groove and
climb it up to and over a small bulge, peg. The short wall above
leads to the terrace.

Burslem Boys   35 feet   E4   (24.2.85)
Start 15 feet right of Le Bingomaniaque below a roof.
1   35 feet. 6a. Climb through the roof, bolt, by a large span, and
climb the wall above, bolt, to a peg and nut belay. Lower off.

HANGING ROCK
This is the small compact buttress at road level just right of the
last route. Unfortunately much of the in-situ protection has been
stolen and needs replacing.

The Wall of Goutes   40 feet   E2   (25.7.83)
Start on a grassy ledge at the left-hand side of the crag.
1   40 feet. 5c. Pull up to a horizontal break then step up onto
this. Good holds above lead up and right to a thread belay.
Lower off. Since its first ascent this route has now grassed over.

Gripper Clipper   40 feet   E4   (26.7.83)
Start just right of the last route.
1   40 feet. 6b. Go straight up to the break and a thread. Go
rightwards passing a second thread to reach good holds leading
straight up to the thread belay on Wall of Goutes. Lower off.

★ **Slouching Towards Bethlehem**   40 feet   E4   (23.7.83)
Start 10 feet right of Gripper Clipper.
1   40 feet. 6b. Step up to an undercut and use this to reach an
obvious pocket. Go straight up from this onto holds leading up
left to the thread belay on Wall of Goutes. Lower off.
This route was originally climbed with two in-situ wires for
protection. They may or may not be in place any more.

★ **De Torquemada** 40 feet   E5   (24.7.83/18.8.84)
Start 10 feet right of 'Slouching'.
1 40 feet. 6c. Climb up left and gain the central groove, bolt, with extreme difficulty. Follow it, thread, to its top. Bolt belay. Lower off.

★ **The Picnic** 30 feet   E5   (25.7.83)
As with the last route, a vicious little problem. Start 15 feet right of De Torquemada.
1 30 feet. 6b. Surmount the roof, bolt, to gain small pockets and thin cracks leading up to a thread belay. Lower off.

Jerusalem is Lost 30 feet   E3   (24.7.83)
Start just right of The Picnic.
1 30 feet. 6b. A boulder problem start leads to flakes which are followed, threads, to a thread belay. Lower off.

Perthy Thrower 20 feet   Hard Very Severe   (1983)
1 20 feet. 5a. The short flake system right of 'Jerusalem' is climbed to reach vegetation. V.S. descent to the right.

Babylon by Bus 50 feet   E3   (26.7.83)
A neat little girdle of the crag.
1 50 feet. 6a. Start up Perthy Thrower and step left into Jerusalem is Lost at its first thread. Move left into The Picnic then go left again, thread, into De Torquemada. Climb this for a few feet then go left once more to the thread belay on Wall of Goutes. Lower off.

Farther along the Marine Drive and up above the road is a massive arched overhang. This is bounded on its left-hand side by a long groove and scooped wall. Left again from here about 100 yards is an obvious cut-away at the foot of the big wall containing a corner crack in its top left-hand section. The next route begins at this cut-away at its right-hand end.

★ **Wu-Shu Boys** 120 feet   E3   (2.5.85)
1 120 feet. 6a. From a bolt under the cut-away, traverse the hanging slab to a peg. Follow the line on good holds to a grassy ledge. The top wall with a bolt and thread gives a fine finale. Scramble off rightwards.

The next routes start just left of the long groove, left of the arched overhang and below the scooped wall.

★★ **Testament** 50 feet   E4   (24.2.85)
Just left of centre is a black wall leading up to a niche.
1 50 feet. 6a. Climb the wall, peg and threads, to the niche and a bolt. Exit from this, thread to another bolt then go leftwards

past another bolt and go up to a fixed belay in a small niche. Abseil off.

★ **Talisman**   50 feet   E4   (1.85)
Just right of Testament is a steep groove.
1   50 feet. 6a. Follow the groove, two threads, to the small roof and a peg on the right. Pull over into the groove then go up the rib on the right into a scoop, bolt. Step left and climb the bulging wall above, bolt and thread, into the top scoop. Bolt belay. Abseil off.

★ **Touchstone**   60 feet   E4   (1.85)
At the left-hand end of the overhang, left of the big arch, an obvious line of holds crosses the roof.
1   30 feet. 6a. Climb across the roof passing various fixed runners and pull over to a small ledge. Ascend the groove above, thread, to a bolt belay at its top.
2   30 feet. 6a. Traverse the scoop rightwards and move up right, bolt, to a flake crack. Follow this, pegs, until it is possible to step left to the upper scoop. Bolt belay. Abseil off.

★★ **Jungle Jive**   150 feet   E2   (16.4.85)
The obvious long groove between Touchstone and Norman's Wisdom. The top pitch is very exposed and easier than it looks. Start 15 feet right of the base of the groove.
1   100 feet. 5c. Surmount the bulge and move up leftwards to an obvious hole, thread. Step down and make a descending traverse leftwards to reach the corner just above the lip of the overhang. Follow the groove passing a thread and peg to a hanging belay. (Bolts.)
2   50 feet. 5b. Climb carefully up left to clip a bolt above the second ledge. Step right and climb the groove system past a peg to the top. Scrambling leads to a peg and large nut belay after 30 feet.

Confuse the Aardvark For 3-5 year olds/Space Delivery
120 feet   E5   (26.10.86)
Start beneath the roof below and to the right of the long groove of Jungle Jive.
1   65 feet. 6b. Surmount the roof then climb the snappy wall above and clip the bolt belay with a long reach.
2   55 feet. 6b. Move left along the ledge then left again along the break, peg and bolt. Go up over the bulge above moving rightwards to finish. Peg belay well back.

Bored Games   65 feet   E4   (1986)
1   65 feet. 6b. Takes a line between Confuse the Aardvark and Norman's Wisdom. 1 bolt.

★ **Norman's Wisdom**   65 feet   E4   (19.1.85)
Start as for Jungle Jive.
1   65 feet. 6a. Pull over the roof and move left and up to the
hole, thread and bolt. Make technical moves up rightwards to a
good hold and bolt. Climb direct, thread, to a bolt belay. Abseil
off.

To the right of the arched overhang are twin leaning corners.

Gold Star   60 feet   Very Severe   (5.6.83)
1   60 feet. 4c. Climb the left-hand corner to a bulge which is
passed on the left, traversing back right to finish.

Lucky Strike   60 feet   E2   (5.6.83)
1   60 feet. 5c. Climb the lower leaning corner then the
secondary corner above. This is loose in places and leads once
more to the terrace above. Quite serious.

Uriah's Neck 50 feet, Very Severe, 4c takes the obvious wide
crack 20 feet to the right of Lucky Strike. Loose at the top.

Just right of Uriah's Neck are two shallow corners at 30 feet.

Gold Digger   60 feet   E2   (28.6.83)
Start beneath the left-hand corner, at a flake.
1   60 feet. 5c. Climb the flake and the wall above to reach the
corner. Climb this to a small ledge and a peg above. Move left
to finish.

The Golden Goose   60 feet   E2   (30.6.83)
Start 10 feet right of the last route.
1   60 feet. 5c. Go up leftwards to a small ledge and climb the
short groove right of Gold Digger and the wall above to finish.

About 20 feet right of The Golden Goose is an obvious grey
slabby wall. The next two routes start beneath the centre of this
wall.

★ **Platinum Blonde**   55 feet   E4   (17.2.85)
A good clean little climb up the white wall left of It.
1   55 feet. 6a. Trend easily leftwards to below the wall. Climb
the wall on small holds to a huge jug. Small wires protect on
the right. Swing right to a scrappy finish.

★ **It**   60 feet   E2   (21.10.82)
A very popular route.
1   60 feet. 5b. Climb twin cracks, then the slabby wall above,
direct to the path.

Precious Little   60 feet   E3   (6.1.85)
Quite a good little route direct through the line of Precious Metal.
Start just right of It below a short, brown groove at 10 feet.
1   60 feet. 5c. Use the groove to gain Precious Metal. Ascend a
large flake above then climb the bulge above, peg, and finish at
another peg. Either lower off this or traverse right to bolt belays
on Pyrites of Pen Trwyn.

★★ **Precious Metal**   65 feet   E2   (5.6.83)
Good climbing taking a left-trending line just right of It.
1   65 feet. 5b. Follow the crackline to join It 20 feet from the top.
Finish as for It.

★ **Pyrites of Pen Trwyn**   50 feet   E4   (12.1.85)
A good route. Start as for Precious Metal.
1   50 feet. 6b. Climb direct to the break and gain a thread in the
bulge above. Cross this rightwards, bolt, to an undercut flake,
then move right and finish up a short groove to a bolt belay.
Abseil off.

★ **The Bloxwich Blockhead**   45 feet   E4   (23.2.85)
A good problem through the bulge right of the last route. Start
just right of Pyrites of Pen Trwyn.
1   45 feet. 6b. Climb to a good ledge, threads above. Swing up
right through the bulges, bolt, to a bolt belay. Abseil off.

Midas Touch   65 feet   E4   (1983)
Start below a black leaning corner 35 yards right of the last route.
1   65 feet. 6a. Climb the corner via its left wall to a ledge on the
left. Step back right and climb the problematic little wall to the
bolts.

★ **Magical Ring**   65 feet   E4   (30.6.83)
Good moves on very sharp pockets. Start just right of Midas
Touch.
1   65 feet. 6b. Climb up to the bulge, peg, and surmount it, bolt
and thread, to gain a standing position in the niche above. Go
up to a ledge, bolt (possible belay) then step right to a thread.
Go straight up to finish. Bolt belay. Abseil off.

★ **Gold 'n Delicious**   75 feet   E5   (4.11.83)
The steep wall right of Magical Ring.
1   75 feet. 6b. Starting 10 feet right of Magical Ring climb
straight up the wall and go over the bulge by a bolt. Continue
up a shallow open groove, then move up and right to a peg over
a bulge. Make hard moves up to gain a line of undercut flakes
and follow these left (bold) to the belay of Magical Ring. Abseil
off.

★ **Pure Gold**   65 feet   E4   (8.6.83)
Start round to the right of Gold 'n Delicious at an embedded block.
1   65 feet. 6b. Move up to the bulge and go over it into a short groove. Go diagonally leftwards to a bolt (possible belay). Climb the flakes above this, peg and thread to finish.

Capturing the Coelacanth   60 feet   E5   (20.4.85)
The fine upper wall right of Pure Gold gives very sustained climbing for 15 feet.
1   60 feet. 6b. From the top of the groove on Pure Gold climb direct up the wall past two bolts to a hole. Pull up and move left to the bolt belay.

★ **Love over Gold**   60 feet   E4   (12.6.83)
To the right of Pure Gold is a long, shallow groove.
1   60 feet. 6a. Climb the groove to a scooped ledge then take the bulge above direct passing a peg to a peg and thread belay. Abseil off.

Flash in the Pan   60 feet   E3   (26.6.83)
Start 15 yards right of Love over Gold, below a short left-facing corner at 30 feet.
1   60 feet. 5c. Climb up into the left-facing corner and move up to a peg in the right wall. Traverse left below a roof to the foot of another corner. Finish up this.

★ **Miner Forty-Niner**   60 feet   E4   (12.1.85)
A good route. Start below the centre of the white wall right of Flash in the Pan.
1   60 feet. 6b. Start up a thin crack which leads onto the wall and climb this by a hard move (side runners) to good holds. Swing up left to a sloping ledge. Climb the scoop above mainly by its right arête to a groove. Use the bolts of Power Failure on the right for descent.

★ **Power Failure**   55 feet   E4   (27.6.83)
Better than it looks. Start just right of the last route.
1   55 feet. 6a. Climb the wall to the second recess then hard moves lead straight up into a flake system which leads to a bolt stance. Lower off.

★ **After Thought**   60 feet   Hard Very Severe   (17.2.85)
Start below a large flake, left of Zig.
1   60 feet. 5a. Climb the flake and swing out left and up to a ledge, thread. Go straight up to finish up the final groove of Zig.

Zig 60 feet E1   (14.1.72)
A poor route. Start at a flat-topped boulder beneath a slanting
groove above half-height.
1 60 feet. 5b. Go up into the first groove then step right and
climb a second groove to the roof. Traverse left to a small ledge
then climb straight up the wall and left trending groove above
to the top.

** **Wings of Perception** 70 feet E5   (6.83)
An excellent and very difficult pitch. Start as for Zig.
1 70 feet. 6c. Climb the right arête of Zig's first groove to a good
ledge and peg. A very sustained 30 feet then leads straight up,
moving rightwards above a bolt to better finishing holds.

Gold Rush 70 feet E5   (28.10.82)
A very bold pitch up the wall right of Wings of Perception. Start
below a groove at 15 feet.
1 70 feet. 6b. Boulder up into the groove, go up the right wall
of this, then round the roof on its right-hand side to a good rest
on the ledge on the left. Boldly cross the wall rightwards to a
small corner then pull up through the roof to finish up a short
wall.

*** **Plumbline** 65 feet E3   (1973)
A superb and sustained route. Start just right of Gold Rush at
the foot of an obvious groove – crowds permitting!
1 65 feet. 5c. Gain the crack and follow it over a bulge into a
groove. Climb this exiting left at the top.

** **Scary Canary** 70 feet E5   (4.83)
Start just right of Plumbline.
1 70 feet. 6a. Climb the flake to where it ends then bold, thin
climbing leads to a bolt. Move up left to a short flake and follow
this and pockets above to finish. Peg and bolt belays. A runner
in Flakeaway reduces the grade to E4.

** **Flakeaway** 70 feet E5   (3.83)
Start 10 feet right of Scary Canary.
1 70 feet. 6b. Go up the easy flake to reach a line of small
pockets rising directly to a bulge. Cross this rightwards to a large
flake hold then pull back up left to an easier finish. Peg and bolt
belays.

Zag 70 feet Hard Very Severe   (14.1.72)
Start below the left-facing corner just right of Flakeaway.
1 70 feet. 5a. Climb the corner, difficult in the middle to its top.
Step right then go up to the top. Peg Belays.

★ **Welcome to the Pleasure Dome**   60 feet   E4   (2.11.84)
1   60 feet. 6a. Climb the overhanging arête right of Zag passing two threads to a peg on the right. Climb the bulge above to finish.

The vegetated ramp and short corner right again is **The Stairs of Cirith Ungol** Hard Severe, 4a.

Into A Game Hard Severe, 4b is the crack, moving into the last route for the last few moves, starting just around the arête again.

★ **Hot Club**   60 feet   E4   (21.2.85)
The fine white wall left of Vagal Inhibition.
1   60 feet. 6a. Climb the thin crack to a good ledge. Arrange protection up and left then climb direct up the wall to a peg. Go up left from this to a bolt and thread in the bulge. Make an interesting move to a bolt belay. Abseil off.

Vagal Inhibition   70 feet   E2   (13.5.83)
To the right of Into a Game is an obvious left-facing groove. Start below its left wall.
1   70 feet. 5c. Climb the wall to reach a small roof at the top of the groove. Pull rightwards over this and finish up a short wall.

Gold Wall Girdle – Part II   230 feet   E3   (5.11.83)
1   100 feet. 5c. Start as for Vagal Inhibition until over the bulge. Traverse to the rest on Prospector then on to Price of Gold and up to the thread. Traverse right to the thread on Krugerrand. Step down and reverse the latter's traverse. Pull right round the arête into Quicksilver then traverse down rightwards to belay on the ramp of The Alchemist's Dream.
2   100 feet. 6a. Drop down and traverse right into Too Low for Zero. Follow this around the arête. Traverse into Klondike at its undercut and pull over the bulge on the right to a rest below the final crack of Pocket City. Reverse this to the right, to the flake on Sourdough. Go right across the wall into Solid Gold. Move down a couple of moves and belay.
3   30 feet. 6a. Make a hard move down right, across Captain Fingers then finish up Firefly.

Sussudio   60 feet   E4   (16.3.85)
Start just right of Vagal Inhibition at a vague groove.
1   60 feet. 6b. Climb the groove to the bulge, bolt. Move rightwards and pull back left to a good ledge. Climb the wall above moving rightwards past a thread to finish as for Prospectors. Bolt and thread belay.

Prospectors 65 feet E4   (21.9.83)
Start just right again.
1 65 feet. 6a. Go up to a thread at 15 feet then pull up right
over a bulge and move up right on small holds to the thread on
Price of Gold. Climb the left-facing flake to good finishing holds.
Bolt and thread belay.

** **Price of Gold** 65 feet E4   (12.5.83)
Start just right of Prospectors.
1 65 feet. 6b. Go straight up past a jammed nut (not always in
place) to a bolt at 20 feet. Traverse delicately left for 10 feet then
climb straight up to a thread above. Climb the thin crack right
of this to finish.

Variation
** **Price of Gold Direct** 60 feet E5   (22.8.84)
1 60 feet. 6b. From the bolt go straight up the blind flake above
to the thread on Krugerrand. Finish as for Krugerrand.

Krugerrand 65 feet E4   (5.6.83)
Start just right of Price of Gold.
1 65 feet. 6a. Climb the obvious groove to its top then traverse
left to a thread. Go back up right to finish.

* **Quicksilver** 65 feet E4   (10.6.83)
Start just right of Krugerrand.
1 65 feet. 6b. Go easily up right into a small corner. Move up
to a thread then go left to a second thread. Thin moves now lead
straight up passing a peg on the left.

*** **The Electric Cool-Aid Acid Test** 60 feet E5   (1983)
An absorbing problem. Start as for Quicksilver.
1 60 feet. 6c. From the small corner move up to a thread then
very technical moves lead straight up past a bolt to good holds
in the break. Step left then go up right to finish.

* **The Alchemist's Dream** 60 feet E3   (10.6.83)
Start 10 feet right of Quicksilver.
1 60 feet. 6a. Go straight up to a ramp below an open groove.
Climb the groove past a peg and thread directly to the top.

Slapstick 50 feet E4   (26.2.85)
Nice climbing but escapable. Start as for The Men in the Jungle.
1 50 feet. 6b. Go up to a block on the left at 10 feet then climb
the wall above on good holds moving left onto the ramp of The
Alchemist's Dream. Step right and climb the arête, bolt, to jugs
and a thread at the top.

The Men in the Jungle   60 feet   Hard Very Severe   (1979/1980)
A few yards right of The Alchemist's Dream is a crack/groove.
A poor route.
1   60 feet. 5a. Gain the ledge on the wall then follow the
corner/crack to the top of the crag.

Too Low For Zero   65 feet   E3   (25.6.83)
Start as for The Men in the Jungle.
1   65 feet. 5c. From the ledge traverse right, bolt, into Private
Investigation then go right again (or from 10 feet higher up the
groove) around the arête to holds leading rightwards across the
upper wall.

** **Private Investigation**   60 feet   E5   (27.6.83)
Start 10 feet right of Too Low for Zero.
1   60 feet. 6b. Pull over the bulge into the right-hand of two slim
grooves. Climb this and the bulging groove above passing a
thread to the top.

* **The Complicated Muse**   60 feet   E4   (1.1.85)
The roof start to Too Low For Zero. Start beneath a bolt on the
bulge.
1   60 feet. 6b. A problem move leads to an undercut above the
ledge. Move up left past the bolt to a good hold then go straight
up to ledges and a junction with Too Low For Zero. Finish up
that route.

** **Klondike**   60 feet   E4   (11.5.83)
Start just right of the last route below an open groove with a
prominent undercut at 30 feet.
1   60 feet. 6a. Go leftwards over the bulge into a niche then
climb leftwards to the undercut. Move up and slightly right then
go up a groove above to finish.

** **Pocket City**   60 feet   E4   (30.6.83)
Start as for Klondike.
1   60 feet. 6a. Pull straight up over a bulge and rock up onto a
small ramp. Move up right to a small niche and undercut
leftwards to the foot of a thin flake crack. Climb this direct.

** **Sourdough**   60 feet   E4   (1983/1984)
Start a few feet right of Pocket City and directly below a faint
groove in the upper wall.
1   60 feet. 6a. Climb straight up the bulging wall on holds which
are difficult to see from below to the base of the vague groove.
Climb this boldly to finish.

*** **Solid Gold**   60 feet   E3   (11.5.83)
Start below the obvious groove right of Sourdough.
1   60 feet. 6a. Steep moves up the wall lead to a narrow sloping
ledge. Layback up onto this then climb the flake/groove above.

** **Captain Fingers**   60 feet   E5   (30.6.83)
Just right of Solid Gold are two left-trending grooves.
1   60 feet. 6b. Follow the left-hand groove, thread, to a good
hold on the right. Hard moves lead straight up past a bolt to gain
a flake crack. Follow this stepping left at the very top.

*** **Firefly**   60 feet   E3   (3.83)
1   60 feet. 5c. Gain the right-hand groove direct past a bolt on
the first bulge and follow it direct past a thread.

** **Mr. Chips**   60 feet   E4   (1.7.83)
1   60 feet. 6b. From the thread on Firefly swing right to a second
thread then go straight up past a bolt to a thin flake crack. Climb
this finishing out left at the top.

* **After the Goldrush**   60 feet   E4   (4.83)
1   60 feet. 6a. Boldly enter the groove right of Mr. Chips and
follow it to the top. Side runners can be used to start.

Nailed up and Bleeding   60 feet   E1   (8.81)
1   60 feet. 5b. Climb the groove immediately right of After The
Goldrush. One peg.

Immediately right of this groove a smooth grey wall containing
a detached-looking flake runs into the vegetated gully on the
right.

* **The Star Spangled Banner**   60 feet   E4   (1.1.85)
Start directly below the flake.
1   60 feet. 6a. Climb the thin bulging crack to a good hold and
peg then gain the flake. Layback up this and exit via a short
groove.

* **Silver Surfer**   60 feet   E3   (21.9.83)
Start below the middle of the smooth slab.
1   60 feet. 6a. Climb leftwards past a peg at 10 feet then step
back right above it. Go up past two threads to a ledge. Step left
and finish over the bulge via a large pocket.

Variation
New Wave Finish   E3, 6a   (7.2.84)
From the ledge a hard move over the bulge on the right leads
to the top.

The vegetated gully right of the wall has been climbed – **Ozymandias** Severe, (1979/80). The obvious traverse line leading leftwards across the wall has also been done: **Jivin Around** Very Severe, 4c, (1979/1980). Both climbs however should be avoided due to their botanical importance.

★ **Span Ban**   50 feet   E4   (6.3.84)
1   50 feet. 6b. The right arête of Ozymandias is climbed direct with a hard move at half-height.

Ichneumon   60 feet   Very Severe   (20.6.81)
1   60 feet. 4c. Takes the obvious wide crack just right of Span Ban.

Just right of Ichneumon is a broad white wall. The climbing on this wall is superb throughout. Just above half-height is a pale white band crossing the wall.

★★ **Barking up the Wrong Tree**   60 feet   E5   (2.2.85)
An excellent, strenuous route. Start below a bolt at 15 feet, above a jumble of blocks.
1   60 feet. 6b. Hard moves past the bolt lead to a peg over a small roof. Strenuously now, bolt on the left, to a thread then move up and right across the wall to the hidden peg on No Arc, No Bark. Finish direct.

★★ **No Arc, No Bark**   65 feet   E5   (19.1.85)
Another fine route. Start 10 feet right of the last route and just below a short left-facing corner.
1   65 feet. 6b. From the corner pass a bolt with difficulty to reach a recess on the The Arc of Eternity. Step left then go straight up on good holds past another bolt. Continue to a good hold, peg, then direct to the top.

★★ **Call it Black**   70 feet   E3   (20.5.84)
A fine direct line. Start 20 feet left of the start of Excursion, and below and slightly left of the ramp on that route.
1   70 feet. 6a. Go straight up the problematic wall into The Arc of Eternity. Go direct through the bulge above to the foot of the ramp of Excursion. Step right to the deep slot then continue up to the bulge above, peg. Go over this into a shallow scoop on the left. Move back right to a niche in the roof and finish through its left side.

★★ **The Arc of Eternity**   70 feet   E4   (6.7.83)
Start as for Excursion.
1   70 feet. 6a. Go up and left on jugs for about 20 feet then make a long traverse left past an open recess to a bolt. Hard moves lead left then up to a second bolt. Traverse left to finish on a small ledge.

Craig Pen Trwyn – Excursion Wall

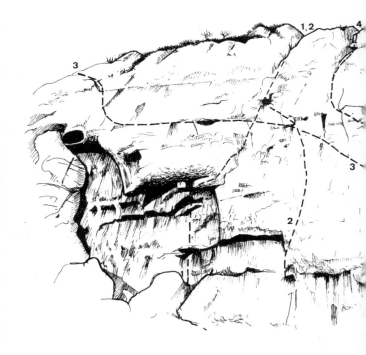

1	Barking up the Wrong		3	The Arc of Eternity	E4
	Tree	E5	4	Excursion	E2
2	No Arc, No Bark	E5			

GREG GRIFFITH.

5 The Visionary   E4   7 Beaverbrook   E4
6 Clear White Light E3

★★★ **Excursion**   70 feet   E2   (9.5.81)
A classic route. Start below the middle of the wall.
1   70 feet. 5b. Climb up then leftwards to an obvious vertical
slot. Move left onto a small ramp and gain jugs at its end. Climb
straight up, peg, to the top.

★★ **The Visionary**   70 feet   E4   (5.7.83)
Start just right of Excursion.
1   70 feet. 6a. Climb straight up and make the crux moves of
Clear White Light to reach the pale white band. Move left then
go up to a peg. Go rightwards from this to finish right of the roof
at the top.

★★ **Clear White Light**   70 feet   E3   (1.12.82)
Start 10 feet right of Excursion at a short flake crack above a
block.
1   70 feet. 6a. Go straight up to two black streaks then pull up
and move left to an obvious slot. Go straight up to the pale white
band, crux, then trend rightwards to a thread on the arête. Pull
up then step left to a flake crack which is followed to the top.

★ **Variation**   70 feet   E4, 6a   (20.5.84)
Where the original route goes left to the slot (protection),
continue straight up over the bulge to a spiky jug. Move
diagonally left to the pale white band and continue as for the
original route.

Beaverbrook   70 feet   E4   (8.10.83)
Start 10 feet right of Clear White Light.
1   70 feet. 6a. Follow the thin crack to a peg. Move left and
climb a shallow groove, go over a bulge, then continue in the
same line to finish.

The Exodus of Plastic Penguins   55 feet   Hard Severe
                                                          (1979/1980)
Starts at the large pinnacle at the next bend in the road.
1   55 feet. 4b. Ascend either side of the pinnacle then the wall
above moving rightwards.

Too Pooped to Whoop   60 feet   E5   (13.10.83)
The wall right of 'Exodus'.
1   60 feet. 6b. Climb a thin crack to a bulge where it peters out.
Traverse right to another thin crack, climb the bulge above, peg,
then finish up the thin groove above.

To the right again are two obvious black-stained grooves.

Nuclear Winter   50 feet   E3   (29.10.84)
Start beneath the left-hand groove.
1   50 feet. 6a. Climb the groove to the roof. Pull directly over this, bolt, finishing up the continuation groove above.

Gobachops   50 feet   E4   (26.2.85)
The arête between the two grooves.
1   50 feet. 6a. Climb easily up the arête to a peg and thread. Pull directly through the bulge to good holds, two threads, with easier climbing to finish.

Pershing II   60 feet   E2   (13.5.83)
1   60 feet. 5c. Climb the right-hand groove.

SS20   50 feet   E3   (29.10.84)
1   50 feet. 5c. Climb the crack to the vague scoop right of Pershing II. Pull rightwards round the roof and follow the rightward trending line past a dead bush to the top.

To the right of SS20 is a white wall with an overhang crossing it about 15 feet up. The next routes start here.

Cruise Missile   60 feet   E1   (1979/1980)
Start below the left-hand side of the overhang.
1   60 feet. 5c. A hard start leads to a ledge just below the overhang. Traverse right for about 20 feet then go straight up to finish.

★ **The Cold War**   60 feet   E3   (12.1.85)
Start between the two starts to Cruise Missile.
1   60 feet. 6a. Climb the short problem wall to good ledges. Pull through the overhang on the left, bolt, finishing direct.

Greenham Girls   55 feet   E2   (17.1.84)
Start as for The Cold War.
1   55 feet. 5c. Climb the wall to the ledges then move up to the overhang. Undercut rightwards around this then climb leftwards to finish.

Cruise Missile Direct Start, 5b, (1982). A short problem wall joining the original at the end of its traverse.

Insidious Practices   65 feet   E2   (28.10.82)
Start 15 feet right of Cruise Missile Direct Start.
1   65 feet. 5c. Climb the initial wall on slots and surmount the bulge to a ledge (crux). Climb the shallow corner above moving left to avoid a loose finish.

The Deep Fix   60 feet   E2   (1979/1980)
1   60 feet. 5b. The obvious chimney crack a few yards right.

Vic 20   55 feet   Hard Very Severe   (12.11.83)
1   55 feet. 5b. Climbs the crack in the arête between The Deep
Fix and The Really Exciting Climb, finishing up the last few feet
of The Deep Fix.

★ **The Really Exciting Climb**   50 feet   Very Severe   (4.81)
1   50 feet. 4c. A pleasant route up the flake crack just right of
The Deep Fix.

★ **The Turquoise Tortoise**   60 feet   E3   (19.5.84)
A filler-in but the climbing is worthwhile. Start as for Space
Invaders.
1   60 feet. 6a. Climb to its first good ledge at 20 feet. Step up
left to a thread then go straight up the wall, avoiding easy
ground to the left, to a second thread. Step right then go straight
up the wall to another thread and exit left at the top.

Space Invaders   60 feet   E1   (1979/1980)
Start 10 feet right of The Really Exciting Climb.
1   60 feet. 5b. Climb up to a good ledge at 20 feet then follow
a vague groove up the wall above, over more small ledges,
bearing rightwards to finish.

Astro Blaster   60 feet   E4   (5.8.82)
Sustained and fairly serious. Start below a short black-stained
groove just right of Space Invaders.
1   60 feet. 6a. Climb the groove to its top, then move up right
to some flakes. Hard moves then lead straight up to finish over
a small roof.

Minas Anor   60 feet   E1   (1979/1980)
Start at a boulder just right of Astro Blaster.
1   60 feet. 5a. Step off the boulder and climb the groove for
about 20 feet. Climb the flake on the right traversing back left to
finish. A poor route.

About 30 feet right of Minas Anor is a white wall. The next routes
start here.

★ **Paradise**   50 feet   E4   (2.7.83)
Quite bold to start.
1   50 feet. 6a. Climb up and slightly rightwards, thread, then go
up to a small roof. Go over this on the left stepping back right
above. Finish straight up past a bolt.

The Bounty Hunters 50 feet E3   (2.7.83)
1 50 feet. 5c. Go up rightwards from the start of Paradise, thread, to a slim groove. Layback up this and finish over a small bulge past a thread.

The Boat of Millions of Years 60 feet, Hard Severe, 4b, (1979/80) is the obvious chimney about 15 yards left of the coastguard hut.

Eliminator 40 feet E4   (30.10.84)
1 40 feet. 6b. Starting as for Methylated Laughter, climb the wall, thin layback and headwall via a direct line and two bolts.

★ **Methylated Laughter** 40 feet E4   (21.10.84)
1 40 feet. 6b. Climb the ramp/groove left of Adequate Compensation past a thread and two bolts.

Adequate Compensation 40 feet E4   (21.6.83)
1 40 feet. 5c. Climb the right-hand of two slim grooves, left of the coastguard hut, past a peg at its top.

Go For Gold 50 feet E1   (29.3.81)
1 50 feet. 5a. Climb the open groove behind the coastguard station, finishing right then back left.

New Gold Dream 40 feet Hard Very Severe   (10.7.83)
1 40 feet. 5a. Starting 5 feet right of Go For Gold, go straight up the wall, thread, to the roof. Traverse right and pull over past a second thread.

Passionate Friend 50 feet E1   (8.81)
Good climbing. Start at a steep initial wall beneath an obvious flake.
1 50 feet. 5b. Go straight up for 10 feet then move left to twin cracks. Climb these to a good hold then move back right to finish up the last few feet of the next route.

Bruno His Wall 60 feet Hard Very Severe   (1979/1980)
1 60 feet. 5a. Climb the short, steep wall and flake crack above starting about 20 feet right of the coastguard hut.

Uaeba 65 feet E4   (27.10.83)
Start just right of Bruno His Wall.
1 65 feet. 6b. Hard moves lead over a bulge, thread, then go right into a groove. Move out right, and go straight up the wall to finish at the top of Sheik Yer Money.

★ **Sheik Yer Money** 60 feet E4   (11.6.83)
Start below the steep wall 10 feet right of Bruno His Wall.
1 60 feet. 6a. Go steeply up to a series of flake cracks on the left. Climb these and the short crack on the right at the top.

Variation
* **The Direct Start**   60 feet   E4   (1985)
A better, direct start climbing directly into the thin crack, passing
one thread.

Masada   50 feet   E5   (5.83)
Start 10 feet right of Sheik Yer Money below a scoop in the wall.
1   50 feet. 6b. Steeply gain the scoop and move up to its top.
Strenuous climbing then leads up and left to a thread just below
the top. Finish easily.

En Gedi   55 feet   E4   (11.6.83)
Start just right of Masada.
1   55 feet. 6a. Another steep start leads to a tricky move to gain
a ledge. Move right to a series of large flakes and follow these
trending leftwards to the top.

The Blood Red Game   60 feet   Hard Very Severe   (1979/1980)
Start just right of En Gedi.
1   60 feet. 4c. Climb the wide crack straight to the top.

Meanstreak   65 feet   E5   (5.11.83.)
The overhanging wall just right of the crack.
1   65 feet. 6b. Starting as for the Blood Red Game climb directly
up the wall past an in-situ thread to a peg. Move left onto a rib
to finish.

* **Homs' Punk**   75 feet   E5   (2.1.83)
Start just right of Meanstreak. Sustained.
1   75 feet. 6a. Climb straight up to a thread. Go up and right
then back left to a crackline. Finish straight up the crack.

** **Ward 10**   70 feet   E6   (1983)
Start 10 feet right of Homs' Punk below a slim groove system.
1   70 feet. 6b. Climb the first groove to undercuts at its top then
hard moves lead up left then back right to the base of the second
groove. Layback this strenuously to a ledge and peg. More hard
moves then lead straight up past the peg via a line of shallow
cracks to a tricky finish.

** **Fall Back**   70 feet   E5   (1983)
Start 5 feet right of Ward 10.
1   70 feet. 6b. Climb up to an obvious tiny flake at 15 feet. Pull
up over the bulge, quite awkward. Step right and go straight up
to a peg. Continue with difficulty up and slightly right over the
next bulge, bomber wire, to finish up a short incut groove.

★★ The Jehad   70 feet   E4   (12.5.83)
Start 5 feet right of Fall Back below a black wall.
1   70 feet. 6b. Strenuous climbing leads to good wires at 15 feet. Move up leftwards, crux, into a groove and climb up right to a peg. Go up left to finish up the final corner of Fall Back.

★★ Big Licks   80 feet   E3   (13.7.82)
A strenuous start leads to enjoyable, juggy climbing above. Start at an overhanging crack just left of the pill box.
1   80 feet. 6a. Climb the crack and make a hard move to gain the wall above. Move right then back up left into the open groove. Climb this exiting right at its top onto a ledge on Beachcomber, peg. The bulge above provides a finish.

★ Pil   80 feet   E1   (18.3.81)
Start on top of the old look-out post!
1   80 feet. 5b. Step off the roof using the thin crack. Go up this for 10 feet then step right and go straight up into Beachcomber. Ascend to the ledge on the left, peg and finish direct.

★ Yellow Belly   65 feet   E3   (11.5.83)
1   65 feet. 5c. Step off the pill-box and ascend the steep juggy wall direct to a ledge near the top of Beachcomber. Finish direct past a peg. Bold.

Primrose Walk   70 feet   E2   (5.83)
1   70 feet. 5c. From 15 feet up Beachcomber make a long rising traverse leftwards crossing Yellow Belly to finish up the final corner of Fall Back.

Beachcomber   80 feet   Hard Very Severe   (17.3.73)
Start 15 feet right of the pill-box at an overhanging crack.
1   80 feet. 5b. Ascend the steep initial crack then follow the large flakes to a ledge on the left, peg, just below the top. Descend under the overhang on the left to finish on the path. OR, better still, finish direct past the peg.

Pen Trwyn Pilots   70 feet   E4   (10.7.83)
Basically a direct finish to Pil.
1   70 feet. 6b. From the ledge 40 feet up Beachcomber enter the small niche above, hard and quite scary, and pull up left to an easier finish.

To the right of Beachcomber is a superb leaning wall. This contains some of the best routes on Pen Trwyn.

★ Foolish, Ghoulish   65 feet   E5   (8.3.85)
Tremendous climbing up the wall just right of Beachcomber. Start as for Mr. Olympia.

1 65 feet. 6b. From the thread on Mr. Olympia move out left, below the peg (on Mr. Olympia), on a prominent jug to the vague arête, bolt. Climb straight up on good small holds, bolt, then pull up left to a good flat hold and another bolt. Trend up rightwards on good holds to the break, bong, bolt belay above. Abseil off.

★★★ **Mr. Olympia** 65 feet E5   (1983)
Very sustained climbing with good protection.
Start about 20 feet right of the pill-box below a short crack with a thread at its top.
1 65 feet. 6b. Hard moves lead to the thread. Move up left to a peg then sustained climbing leads straight up to a sloping jug and small wire slot. Traverse 5 feet right to undercuts under an overhang. Surmount this and climb the juggy groove and bulge above to a bolt belay.

★★★ **The Chain Gang** 70 feet E5   (24.11.82)
The third in a fine trio of strenuous routes. Start just right of Mr. Olympia.
1 70 feet. 6b. Pull up onto a flake, then make a long reach for a good incut hold above. Traverse left to a poor resting place, then climb straight up for 15 feet until a hard move leads left to good undercuts below a small roof. Surmount this to a hand ledge then pull up left into a shallow groove. Climb this passing a thread on the right to a bolt belay.

Precious Time 70 feet E4   (3.12.82)
Start 10 feet right of The Chain Gang.
1 70 feet. 6a. Go up rightwards onto a block then step up to a small overhang. Undercut this leftwards to a jug on the lip, then hard moves lead left to pockets under a bulge. Go straight up then bear right to jugs at the base of a groove/crack. Climb this exiting right at the top to finish. Peg and nut belays.

Variation. E3, 6a,   (1983)
From the jug on the lip of the roof it is possible to climb straight up stepping left to the jugs at the base of the final groove. Slightly easier than the original.

Coiled Spine 70 feet E1   (21.6.82)
Start between Precious Time and The Stirrer.
1 70 feet. 5b. Go up over blocks into the shallow corner. Climb this until an exit right leads to the top peg on The Stirrer. Finish up that route.

★ **The Stirrer** 70 feet E2   (14.3.81)
Start right again from Precious Time.
1 70 feet. 5c. Ascend the obvious crack then step right to a flake. Move up onto the ramp, peg, then go up leftwards passing a second peg to the top.

Get on the Beam   60 feet   E2   (8.81)
1 60 feet. 5c. Girdles this area at about two-thirds height starting up The Stirrer and finishing round the arête of Pen Trwyn Pillar.

The open groove just before the arête gives two very enjoyable routes.

★★ **Kanly**   65 feet   E2   (11.6.81)
A bold but not technically hard route.
1 65 feet. 5b. Climb the groove until a move out left onto the ramp. Move up and rightwards to a small overhang. Pull over this and finish easily up the groove above.

★★ **Bauxed**   65 feet   E1   (1979/1980)
1 65 feet. 5b. Climb the groove until a pull out right onto the wall. Climb this on jugs then finish up leftwards.

Pen Trwyn Pillar   60 feet   E4   (27.10.83)
The right arête of the groove of Bauxed.
1 60 feet. 6a. Starting just left of the arête, climb up to a ledge and then a ramp above. Finish straight up the arête.

Reaving Slaying Conan   60 feet   Very Severe   (1979/1980)
1 60 feet. 4c. Climb the easy ramp and wide crack right of Pen Trwyn Pillar.

Once in a Blue Moon   60 feet   E3   (25.9.83)
Entertaining moves up the small wall right of Reaving Slaying Conan.
1 60 feet. 6a. Go up a corner to a ledge. Move up right then back left into the centre of the wall and climb straight up this, bolt, to finish via a short flake.

MONSTER BUTTRESS

Flying Lizard   35 feet   E2   (24.10.83)
Start at the foot of the descent gully.
1 35 feet. 5c. Climb the bottomless groove then move right past a thread, finishing direct.

Amnesia Seizure   30 feet   E3   (24.5.85)
1 30 feet. 5c. Start a few feet right of Flying Lizard and climb into the scoop. Move leftwards past a bolt to a layback finish through the top bulge.

Funky Dung   30 feet   E1   (24.5.85)
1 30 feet. 5b. Climb the crackline right of the last route, moving leftwards at the top.

★★ Up to the Hilt   70 feet   E6   (21.6.86)
A superb and very powerful problem which breaches the central
roof via the obvious weakness. Start on the ledge below the roof.
1 70 feet. 6c. Go easily up to the roof and cross it, bolt to a peg
on the lip. Pull around to gain the base of the groove above and
follow it directly to the top. Bolt belay. Walk off leftwards.

The Psychofant Roof   80 feet   E5   (22.7.83)
Start on a ledge below the central overhang.
1 80 feet. 6b. Climb up right to a bolt then traverse out right to
a second bolt at the lip. Surmount this with difficulty to a small
ledge below the upper scooped wall (possible belay). Climb the
wall past a bolt until it is possible to traverse out left onto the
arête. Go up right to bolt belays on the ledge. Walk off leftwards.

★ Krankenstein   70 feet   E5   (12.6.84)
1 70 feet. 6a. From the foot of the ramp on Gorgo step right
and climb the thin crackline and overhanging wall above to a
bolt belay. Lower off.

★ Gorgo   80 feet   E5   (14.6.83)
The main feature of this crag is a ramp-line trending rightwards.
Start below this.
1 80 feet. 6a. Climb the thin crack, peg, to gain the ramp. Follow
this, peg, until it steepens into a groove. Step right and climb
the wall, bold, to a huge finishing jug. Peg belays on left and
right above. Walk off leftwards.

★ Borogrove   70 feet   E6   (1986)
An extremely powerful problem tackling the large roof directly
underneath the ramp of Gorgo. Start at a rib just right of Gorgo.
1 70 feet. 6c. Go up to the roof and cross it rightwards past
several bolts and pegs pulling around onto the wall above.
Finish up Gorgo or go right and join Continuing Adventures etc
at the arête.

★★ The Continuing Adventures of Charlton Chestwig   80 feet   E4
                                                         (27.6.83)
Start below the right-hand arête of the crag, where a steep crack
rises from the right-hand side of the massive roof.
1 80 feet. 6a. Gain the crack from the right and jam it
strenuously to a bulge. Traverse out left, peg, to the arête and
climb this in a fine position, bolt, to the top. Peg belay. Walk off
left.

★ Charlton Chestwig (The World's Finest Climber)   80 feet   E5
                                                         (25.6.83)
More sustained, though not quite as good as its 'brother' route.
1 80 feet. 6b. From the top of the crack pull over the bulge to

a peg and poor resting place. Continue in the same line passing an in-situ wire 10 feet from the top. Peg belays. Walk off left.

★ Dive, Dive, Dive 60 feet E5   (17.8.84)
Sustained climbing up the steep wall right of 'Charlton Chestwig'. Start up on the ramp at a nut belay below the line of the next route.
1 60 feet. 6b. Climb up to a bolt then traverse left for about 10 feet. Go straight up to a jug then clip a second bolt above . Pass this on the right and move back left above it to a peg. Finish rightwards. Peg belays. Walk off left.

Crunchy Toad IX 35 feet E4   (24.8.84)
Start near the top of the ramp and directly below a thin crackline. Nut belays.
1 35 feet. 6a. Climb the wall and crackline to a bolt, pull past this onto a ledge. Finish direct to peg belays, OR, jump off the ledge and lower off the bolt!

The next route takes the fine white tower right of Monster Buttress.

★★ No Red Tape 65 feet E3   (7.8.83)
Start below the tower. A fine pitch.
1 65 feet. 6a. Climb a crack on the right to a peg then traverse left to a bolt above the break. Move up left then back right and up to the roof, bolt. Surmount this direct to a massive jug and climb a short groove above to a bolt belay. Abseil off.

YELLOW WALL
This is the broad yellow-coloured wall right of No Red Tape.

White Seam 60 feet E3   (15.10.83)
A faint white streak just left of Melkor.
1 60 feet. 5c. Climb the white streak with one move right near the top for protection. Move back left to finish on an easy ramp which leads to the belay bolt on the ledge.

★ Melkor 80 feet E3   (5.83)
Start on the grassy ledge below the left-hand side of the wall.
1 50 feet. 5c. Go up right to a thread then leftwards to a second thread. Go straight up stepping right onto the ledge and a bolt belay.
2 30 feet. 5b. The blocky overhang above is taken direct. Thread on the left.

★★ Pen Trwyn Patrol 50 feet E4   (25.6.83)
1 50 feet. 6a. From the first thread on Melkor go straight up to a bolt. Pass this to finish up a short groove. Bolt belay. Abseil off.

Craig Pen Trwyn – Monster Buttress and Yellow Wall

GREG GRIFFITH.

★★★ **The Pirates of Pen Trwyn**   50 feet   E4   (24.6.83)
Start 15 feet right of Pen Trwyn Patrol.
1   50 feet. 6a. Pull up onto a short ramp then go up, bolt, to a
thread just above a good hold. Go rightwards past this then
straight up to finish. Bolt belay. Abseil off.

★★ **String of Pearls**   50 feet   E3   (19.6.83)
Start just right of 'Pirates'.
1   50 feet. 6a. Go up a narrow ramp/groove to a slab and thread.
Pull up and left, thread, to a slim right trending groove, thread.
Follow this to the ledge and bolt belay. Abseil off.

★ **Pale Shelter**   50 feet   E1   (10.6.83)
Start 10 feet right of String of Pearls.
1   50 feet. 5b. Go up right then left to the foot of an obvious
groove. Climb this exiting left at the top onto a ledge. Bolt belay.
Abseil off.

Trivial Pursuits   50 feet   E4   (30.6.86)
The right to left girdle of Yellow Wall.
1 50 feet. 6a. Climb up Pale Shelter then move out left to the
first thread on String of Pearls. Pass this to the next thread on
the same route. Hard moves then lead left to the thread on
'Pirates' where a step down and moves left again gain the bolt
on 'P.T.Patrol'. Climb leftwards to finish up Melkor.

Second Sense   50 feet   E3   (17.7.83)
Rather scrappy. Start as for Pale Shelter.
1   50 feet. 5c. Move up right to the base of a shallow groove
and climb this, thread, with a blind move to gain holds on the
right. Pull up left to finish. Bolt belay. Abseil off.

Cool Water   50 feet   E1   (4.11.85)
1 50 feet. 5b. Climb the drainage groove right of Second Sense
passing a bolt at half-height. Bolt belay.

Just to the right again is a tiny wall with two obvious little lines.

Too Much, Too Young, Too Soon, E2, 5c, (1985) – The left-hand
line.

Too Little, Too Old, Too Late, E3, 5c, (1985) – The right-hand line.

THE BLACK WALL
This is the wall right again from Yellow Wall.

★ **Spine Chill**   50 feet   E4   (17.7.83)
Start below and to the left of an obvious right-trending crack.
1   50 feet. 6a. Climb straight up the wall to a bolt at 25 feet.

Move up left and use pockets to gain the bulge above. A long reach over this can be made to clip the bolt belay. Lower off.

★★ **Menincursion**   50 feet   E4   (2.7.83)
Start just right of Spine Chill.
1 50 feet. 6a. Climb straight up through the crack to a small thread. Trend up right to a bulge and bolt. Make difficult moves over this then move right to a bolt belay. Lower off.

★ **The Peppermint Pig**   50 feet   E3   (2.7.83)
Start 10 feet right of Menincursion.
1 50 feet. 6a. Climb the long slim groove to a bulge at 40 feet. Cross leftwards just below the top to the bolt belay on Menincursion. Lower off.

★ **Willowbrook's**   50 feet   E4   (8.7.83)
Start 15 feet right of the last route below another groove line.
1 50 feet. 6b. Move up to a bolt at 15 feet and pass it leftwards to shallow grooves in the wall. Go straight up these, thread, with a hard move to reach the thread belay. Lower off.

Storm Warning   50 feet   E3   (17.7.83)
1 50 feet. 6b. Pass the bolt as for Willowbrook's but step back right to the foot of a groove. Climb this direct to a peg belay. Lower off.

★★ **Drip, Drip, Drip**   50 feet   E3   (10.7.83)
Start 15 feet right of Storm Warning.
1 50 feet. 6a. Ascend to a thread then traverse left for 5 feet to a bolt. Go up right on small pockets to a ledge. Bolt belay 10 feet higher. Lower off.

★ **Captain Percival**   40 feet   E2   (16.2.85)
A good route up the groove line 20 feet right of Drip, Drip, Drip. Start beneath the groove.
1 40 feet. 5c. Climb an easy wall to a grassy ledge. Climb the groove, thread, past a large hold to a thread belay. Lower off.

Another Dead Christmas Tree   40 feet   E2   (2.2.85)
The thin crack right of Captain Percival.
1 40 feet. 5b. From the ledge on Captain Percival step right and climb direct up the wall into the faint crack. Follow this to good holds then move left to the thread belay. Lower off.
The obvious direct start has been climbed at 6a.

Salty Dog   60 feet   E1   (10.7.83)
Start 20 yards right of Drip, Drip, Drip, below 3 threads in the wall.

1 60 feet. 5b. Go straight up to the threads. Traverse left for 15 feet then go straight up via a slim groove to a bolt belay.

★ **Pure Mania** 60 feet E4   (10.7.83)
1 60 feet. 5c. From the tapes on Salty Dog step left and climb a narrow runnel to a bolt belay. (Dirty finish).

Let's Lynch the Landlord 60 feet E2   (10.7.83)
1 60 feet. 5b. From the tapes on Salty Dog go diagonally rightwards then straight up to finish. Bolt belay.

★ **Winterreise** 40 feet E2   (16.2.85)
Start 10 feet right of Let's Lynch the Landlord.
1 40 feet. 5b. Go easily up to a thread then step left to a grassy ledge. Move up right then direct to a thread. Continue in the same line to a bolt belay. Lower off.

★ **Secondhand Daylight** 40 feet E3   (16.2.85)
1 40 feet. 6a. From the first thread on Winterreise step right then go direct past 3 more threads and a bolt to a bolt belay. Lower off.

Dave's Rent a Drill Co. 60 feet E2   (12.6.86)
Start 10 feet right of Secondhand Daylight.
1 60 feet. 5b. Climb the ramp and wall to a thread at 25 feet. Go straight up to a crack and climb this to a bolt belay.

★ **Night-Time Rendezvous** 50 feet E3   (1985)
Start below a grey groove just right of Secondhand Daylight.
1 50 feet. 6a. Pull through a bulge and up to the groove, threads. Climb this passing two threads on the left with high steps at the top. Bolt belay. Abseil off.

★★ **Night Watch** 40 feet E4   (27.1.85)
Start at a bulge, below the arête, right of Night-Time Rendezvous.
1 40 feet. 6b. An awkward start via a faint groove and bulge leads to a thread. Move up, bolt, then left through the bulge to a bolt. A hard move then leads to a hidden hold and a bolt belay. Lower off.

The next routes start a further 60 yards along the Marine Drive, just before a bulging black wall containing three threads (The Thin Red Line).

2211 40 feet E4   (13.10.84)
1 40 feet. 6a. Starting 10 feet left of The Thin Red Line, climb the leftward leading bulging groove, thread, to a bolt belay. Lower off.

★★ The Thin Red Line   60 feet   E4   (3.8.83)
A fine route taking a line of pockets up the bulging wall.
1 60 feet. 6b. Go straight up to the first thread and pass it with
difficulty to gain easier ground. The next bulge is similar to the
first and has two threads. Nut belay. Lower off.

Farther right from The Thin Red Line is another overhanging bay
of rock. The first route takes a line up the wall just left of the left
arête of this bay.

The Eleventh Hour   30 feet   E3   (16.7.84)
1 30 feet. 6a. Climb a faint groove past a bolt trending right
above it past a peg to a small ledge and single bolt. Lower off.

The Thin Turquoise Line   40 feet   E3   (15.9.84)
1 40 feet. 6a. The thin crack between The Eleventh Hour and
Homo Sapien is climbed past three threads and a piece of metal
with a sling on it(!) to a bolt belay. Abseil off.

★★ Homo Sapien   55 feet   E5   (19.5.84)
A superb and very sustained climb. Start at the foot of the slab.
1 55 feet. 6a. Swing left past a thread. Hard moves then lead
up onto the slab above, bolt. Move up left to a hold on the arête
then continue just to its right, thread on the right, to a flake.
Move up right again to a good jug and peg. Pull over the bulge,
thread, on good holds and move left to a bolt belay. Abseil off.

★★ White Hopes   50 feet   E5   (16.8.84)
A fantastic companion to Homo Sapien. Start just up and right
of that route.
1 50 feet. 6b. Ascend the little groove on the left, thread, then
step out right to a bolt. Step right again then steeply up past a
second bolt to finish up a short groove, thread. Bolt belay. Lower
off.

★★ Snakes and Ladders   50 feet   E6   (1.87)
1 50 feet. 6c. Climb the wall between White Hopes and
Sèverine to join Sèverine at the top. 4 bolts.

★★ Sèverine   45 feet   E5   (1986)
A fine steep and fingery route. Start a few feet right of White
Hopes at a faint groove.
1 45 feet. 6c. Climb the groove, bolt, and swing left, bolt, and
up – crux. Move up and right bolt to a bolt belay. Abseil off.

★ After the Fact   65 feet   E3   (1985)
Start in the little bay just to the right of White Hopes/Sèverine
etc.

1   65 feet. 6b. Climb the hard bulging wall, thread and bolt, to a standing position at the top of the slab. Continue up the faint rib above, threads, past a good ledge, peg, to small holds. Continue more or less direct via a faint brown streak to a bolt belay. Abseil off.

The Gold Coast   60 feet   E2   (23.10.83)
Start just right of After the Fact.
1   60 feet. 5c. Climb the shallow corner, move right and climb the thin crack past two threads to a bolt belay. Abseil off.

Chock a Block   60 feet   E1   (1.2.85)
Start 20 feet right of The Gold Coast.
1   60 feet. 5b. A crackline runs the full height of the crag, climb this to a bolt belay on the second ledge.

Absolute Beginners   35 feet   E2   (7.5.86)
Start 20 yards right of Chock a Block.
1 35 feet. 6a. Climb the corner and ramp to a thread then go up right to a bolt. Climb the short left-trending groove above to the ledge. Bolt belay.

Michelle's Pillar   20 feet   E1   (20.10.85)
Start 25 yards right of Chock a Block.
1   20 feet. 5b. Go up to the tiny black pillar, step left, then go straight up to a bolt belay. Lower off.

Small Bore   25 feet   E3   (16.2.85)
Start 10 feet right of Michelle's Pillar at a small triangular wall.
1   25 feet. 6a. Climb the wall, bolt, to a jug and peg belay. Lower off.

The Cresta Run   70 feet   Very Severe   (1.11.85 though most
                                                  likely before)
Takes the gully right of Small Bore.
1   70 feet. Scramble up into the gully to an old peg (possible belay) then slide up the chimney to finish.

A further 30 feet right is a yellowish wall. A corner leads up to a yew tree on a ledge.

Lucky Eddie   60 feet   E2   (19.6.86)
Start 5 feet left of Helgar's Fury.
1 60 feet. 5c. Go past a bolt to the break and traverse 10 feet right to a crack. Climb up left then right to another break. Take the left-hand of the two crack/grooves above passing a thread to a fixed belay.

Helgar's Fury   50 feet   E3   (16.5.86)
Start 15 feet left of Hagar the Horrible.
1 50 feet. 5c. Climb to a bolt then go rightwards along a ramp then straight up to a ledge. The short corner above leads to the belay.

Hagar the Horrible   50 feet   Hard Very Severe   (19.1.85)
1 50 feet. 5a. Climb the corner via a layback crack to the tree. Abseil off.

The Benji Bee   50 feet   E2   (26.9.85)
The crack and groove line right of Hagar the Horrible.
1 50 feet. 5c. Climb the wall to a ledge, bolt. Enter the crack then go into the groove moving left to finish via a crack. Thread belay on the right.

Physical Abuse   50 feet   E5   (20.9.86)
Start 30 yards right of The Benji Bee beneath the front face of the roadside buttress.
1 50 feet. 6c. Climb the obvious nose of the buttress passing several pieces of fixed gear.

★ **Treat Me Like a Rag Doll**   50 feet   E2   (7.9.85)
Start a few feet right of Physical Abuse at the right-hand side of the roadside buttress.
1 50 feet. 5c. Climb the wall to gain the corner, peg. Go up and left, peg, trending left again using the arête to reach the break, thread. Trend up to the left side of the roof, thread, and finish out left. Bolt belay. Lower off.

★ **Reading Henry by the Road**   45 feet   E2   (4.9.85)
Start right of the last route at a flake.
1 45 feet. 5c. From the flake go rightwards up to a small roof, peg. Move slightly left and up the flaky wall above, peg, finishing direct past another peg. Bolt belay on the left. Lower off.

The Mile High Club   60 feet   E3   (15.7.86)
Around to the right and up above the road from Reading Henry by the Road is a clean wall capped by a roof. Gain this by a nasty scramble from the right.
1 60 feet. 6a. Climb the groove past a bolt to the break. Traverse left beneath the roof and pull up onto a ledge to finish.

LOWER PEN TRWYN
To reach the walls of The Lower Tier climb over the wall at the first roadside cave and descend a steep grassy gully to the boulder beach below. Walk left to the crag. The routes are described from left to right.

Lower Pen Trwyn

1	Statement of Youth	E7		5	The Jacuzzi Jive	E4
2	Rompsville	E5		6	Twisting by the Pool	E4
3	Night Glue	E5		7	Tokolshe Man	E2
4	Wall of Voodoo	E5		8	Voodoo Child	E4

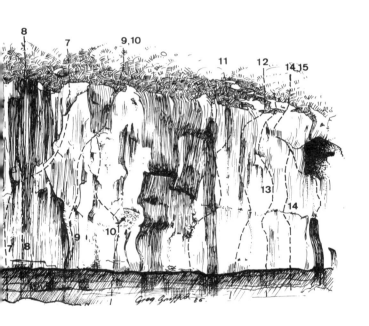

9 The Cynical Pinnacle
                          HVS
10 The Pink Pinkie Snuffs
   It   E4
11 La Bohème   E5
12 Libertango   E5

13 Mean Mother   E5
14 Face Race   E5
15 New Moon on Monday
                         E2

Under the Boardwalk   65 feet   E4   (28.8.84)
Start just left of a small cave at the left-hand end of the crag.
1   65 feet. 6a. Climb the initial wall, bolt, to good holds. Move
up right to the base of a shallow groove. Climb this until its
capping bulge. Surmount this and climb leftwards to a ledge and
bolt belay. Abseil off or scramble up over grass to the road.

To the right of Under the Boardwalk the crag steepens
dramatically. After 20 yards a roof at 40 feet guards access to a
series of rightward trending flakes.

★★★ **Statement of Youth**   75 feet   E7   (25.6.84)
A stunning line which gives one of the most sustained climbs in
the country. Start directly below the right-hand end of the
half-height roof.
1   75 feet. 6b. Pull through the initial bulge, bolts, then move
up left to a bolt at the start of the roof. Make a wild traverse left
along the lip to jugs at its end. Pull up and gain the start of the
flakes, bolt. Launch up these, and follow them to a bolt and the
start of a horizontal undercut crack. Go right along this for 5 feet,
bolt, then move up and left into a bottomless groove. This
provides a somewhat easier finish.

★★★ **Rompsville**   75 feet   E5   (19.9.84)
A fine route with a delicate crux sequence. Start as for Statement
of Youth.
1   75 feet. 6b. Follow Statement of Youth to its third bolt then
move right, bolt, then climb up rightwards, in-situ wire, to a
ledge. Pull over the bulge to a no-hand's rest above. Move up
left to another bolt and pass this finishing rightwards at the top.
Peg belay.

★★ **Night Glue**   70 feet   E5   (21.9.84)
To the right of Statement of Youth a curving overlap crosses the
initial wall. Start 10 feet from the right-hand end of this. Similar
in character to Rompsville.
1   70 feet. 6b. Pull over onto the slab, bolt, and move up left to
the overlap, bolt. Trend rightwards over this to a thread then go
up right again, peg, to a small ledge. The little groove above this
is climbed to a no-hands rest above and another bolt. Climb
diagonally up leftwards, bold and fingery to finish. Peg belay.

Wall of Voodoo   70 feet   E5   (4.10.84)
Start 15 feet right of Night Glue.
1   70 feet. 6b. Climb up to a bolt then hard moves lead up right
to a second bolt. Go straight up to a ledge and the next bolt.
Pass this onto a slab then straight up the front face of a vague
tower exiting left to finish. Peg belay.

★ The Jacuzzi Jive   70 feet   E4   (21.7.83/30.9.84)
A fine fingery route.
Start a few feet right of Wall of Voodoo.
1   70 feet. 6a. Ascend to a thread at 15 feet then go straight up
to the left-hand end of a small ledge at 40 feet. Climb flakes, bolt,
then go up the middle of the wall moving slightly rightwards at
the top.

★ Twisting by the Pool   70 feet   E4   (3.7.83)
Just right of Jacuzzi Jive is a vague groove. Start below this.
1   70 feet. 6a. Climb the brown wall on sharp holds first right
then up left into the groove. Pass the bulge above on the left
and step back right to a thread. Go straight up the headwall to
finish. Peg Belay.

Tokoloshe Man   75 feet   E2   (22.10.83)
Start just right of Twisting by the Pool.
1   75 feet. 5c. Climb straight up to a short rightward-facing flake.
Move up 10 feet into Twisting by the Pool at 25 feet then move
right to clip a bolt. Pass this, crux, to a ledge and thread. Follow
the rightward trending flakes above to finish. Belays up to the
right.

★ Voodoo Child   70 feet   E4   (2.10.84)
Thin climbing in its upper reaches.
1   70 feet. 6b. Climb the wall direct to the bolt on Tokoloshe
Man. Do its crux to the ledge then go directly up the wall above.
Peg belays.

The Cynical Pinnacle   80 feet   Hard Very Severe   (11.10.83)
Start a few feet right of Tokoloshe Man.
1   80 feet. 5a. Climb up to the left-hand side of the detached
pinnacle. Go up this then the groove above, rightwards, to finish
up a short corner. Peg and nut belays.

★ The Pink Pinkie Snuffs It   80 feet   E4   (25.8.84)
Start 15 feet right of The Cynical Pinnacle.
1   80 feet. 6a. Climb the wall, bolt, to where it steepens. Pull up
to another bolt then move left, thread, for a few feet then go up
for 10 feet onto a small ledge out right. Go straight up keeping
just right of The Cynical Pinnacle, but finishing as for that route
at the top.

★★ La Bohème   80 feet   E5   (28.6.84)
A tremendous route. Very sustained. Start 20 feet right of the
previous route below a thin crack.
1   80 feet. 6b. Climb the crack to a peg at its top then move out
right onto the wall and rock up left to a jug with a thread above.
Climb straight up past a bolt to another thread on the right. Move

right past this to a pocket/crackline which gives a direct and tricky finish.

★★★ **Libertango**   80 feet   E5   (15.6.84)
A beautiful route. Start 15 feet right of La Bohème.
1   80 feet. 6b. Climb straight up the wall on small flakes, bolt, to where it steepens slightly. Pull up to a second bolt runner then go straight up the wall above to a thread. Move 15 feet right and finish over the top on a hidden jug.

★★★ **Mean Mother**   80 feet   E5   (21.6.84)
Start just right of Libertango, beneath the streaked wall.
1   80 feet. 6b. Climb flakes up the wall, bolt, to a small niche and good nut runner. Clip the bolt above and pass it with difficulty to a little flake up on the right. Pull up left then straight up into another small niche with a good crack in it. Finish straight up. Excellent.

★★★ **Face Race**   80 feet   E5   (16.6.84)
A fine companion route to Mean Mother. Start a few feet right of this.
1   80 feet. 6b. Climb the wall to the first bolt via an obvious flake then go straight up to another bolt. Pass this on its left to the thread on New Moon on Monday and finish leftwards along the obvious line of New Moon.

★ **New Moon on Monday**   80 feet   E2   (9.6.84)
Start below the big cave up right of Face Race.
1   80 feet. 5c. Climb leftwards to the cave (possible stance) then move out left and follow the obvious traverse line, thread, across the wall then finish direct at its end.

Goodbye Mickey Mouse   80 feet   E2   (30.10.83)
Start just right of New Moon on Monday.
1   80 feet. 5c. Climb a thin crack until it closes then zig-zag up the wall to reach the cave. Leave the cave by the large undercut on its right to a crack. Climb this to belay on a large block 30 feet back.

★★ **Skin Deep**   70 feet   E1   (23.9.84)
An excellent route, one of the best of its grade on Pen Trwyn. Start about 40 yards right of the big cave.
1   70 feet. 5b. Climb to the break then swing left on big jugs and an undercut to a thread placement. Go straight up the wall on good holds to a thin break then move up left to a small corner. Swing back right and over the bulge on a prominent flake, thread, onto the slab. Climb this, thread, to the top.

★ Beauty is Only 70 feet E1   (21.2.85)
The centre of the fine wall right of Skin Deep.
1 70 feet. 5b. Climb direct on good holds to a thread placement then step right and go up a flake moving right again onto the slab at the top.

★ Skin Game 70 feet Hard Very Severe   (17.3.85)
Another excellent route. Start 15 feet right of Beauty is Only.
1 70 feet. 5a. Gain the break and bypass a steep section on the right to good holds. Continue direct up the face to a good ledge finishing up the slab on the left. Thread belay well back.

★ The Water Margin 550 feet (approx.) Hard Very Severe
                                                                (22.7.82)
A long, exciting sea-level girdle of the headland only gained at low tide. Start below the start of the horizontal break.
5a. Move up to the break and traverse along it, belaying as required, into a narrow zawn. Either go up the easy arête on the left and over grass to finish, OR:
5b. Climb the right wall of the zawn to re-gain the break and follow it around the corner into the next, similar zawn. Finish here. (Though an even more exciting finish is to make a long stride across onto the right wall of this zawn and climb delightfully straight up this to finish at 5b).

THE BLACK ZAWN
This recently developed area is actually Right-Hand Lower Pen Trwyn. From Paradise and The Bounty Hunters on the Upper crag cross the wall and walk down to the cliff edge. There is a bolt and thread belay point here. Abseil down to a bolt belay just above a sloping ledge at the barnacle level. A low-to-medium tide is neccessary to climb here.

★ Zawn Creature 110 fet E4   (7.86)
1 25 feet. 5c. Layback the strenuous flake passing a bolt to a ledge and thread belay.
2 85 feet. 6a. Climb the black wall above to a break. Go directly over the bulge above, thread, to easier ground and finish. Scramble of leftwards.

★★ Riders in the Chariot 120 feet E4   (7.86)
A fine route with good moves. Start from the same belay as Zawn Creature.
1 35 feet. 6a. Traverse right to a hole, bolt, and go up the black wall above to a stance. Thread belay.
2 85 feet. 6a. Go up to a thread then hard moves lead to a peg up left. Another difficult pull over the bulge above leads to easier ground, peg in a pocket. From a bolt above step right and up a shattered groove to finish.

★ **Orca**   120 feet   E4   (7.86)
To approach this route a low tide is necessary. From blocks 20
yards left (looking out) of the abseil point. Abseil down to two
threads at barnacle level.
1   35 feet. 6b. Traverse up left to a thread and stalactite. Pull up
past this to a steep slab. Step left then straight up to a flake
belay.
2   85 feet. 5c. Climb the steep wall past a peg to a poor break.
Lunge left to a good jug. Go over the bulge above to an easy
finish.

300 hundred yards before Middle Earth Buttress (at the number
1550 on the pavement) looking down to the sea is an obvious
roof.

Cockleshell Bay, Very Severe, 4c, (18.9.85) takes a rightwards
traverse through the roof.

★ **Adam's Roof**, E2, 5c, (23.9.85) takes the roof by Cockleshell Bay
direct passing three threads.

The next three micro-routes start just to the right.

The Green Sponge, Very Difficult, (23.9.85) takes the left-
trending ramp-line five feet right of Cockleshell Bay.

The Oyster Catcher, Very Severe, 4c, (23.9.85) takes a line up a
small corner 30 feet right of The Green Sponge and to the left
of a cave, onto a ledge via a rising leftwards line to finish.

Variation   Difficult   (23.9.85)
From halfway up the rising line move right into a cave finishing
up the wall on the left.

The next route is to be found on a new buttress located below
the Marine Drive near the summit turn-off. Approach the crag
by descending the grassy slope as for Cockleshell Bay/Adam's
Roof etc then walk left (facing out) for about 100 yards until
underneath the crag which is simply a slab topped by a leaning
headwall. The route takes the headwall at its centre.

★★ **. . . Future Days (Here's to . . .)**   50 feet   E5   (22.9.85)
A superb and strenuous route well worth doing. Start at a
hairline crack in the slab.
1   50 feet. 6b. Climb the slab to a flake. Move onto this from the
left then ascend to the top of the slab. Climb the headwall above
passing a thread and two pegs and pull onto a ledge, crux, with
bolt belays. Abseil off.

MIDDLE EARTH BUTTRESS   (R)
This crag is situated just before the summit road splits from the Marine Drive. Two jutting prows overhang the road.

The Silmarillion   45 feet   E3   (5.6.86)
Start 20 feet left of Gandalf's Groove below a steep wall.
1 45 feet. 6a. Go up left then right onto the wall. Bolt. Ascend this then go left to a ledge and thread. Go up again past two threads to a ledge and fixed belay.

Gandalf's Groove   35 feet   E3   (4.10.83)
1 35 feet. 5c. The obvious groove on the left of the buttress moving left round the roof, threads, to peg and bolt belays. Abseil off.

Hamburger Buttress   (R)

This crag is situated just above the road approximately half a mile before the lighthouse on the apex of The Great Orme.

Big Kazoo   60 feet   E4   (8.10.83)
The bulging wall up the centre of the left-hand buttress.
1 60 feet. 6b. Gain the break by awkward moves then climb the problematic wall, bolt and thread, to gain a groove above. Climb this, thread, to finish. Bolt belay. Go up right over grass to the top of the crag.

★ **Turn the Turtles, Turn**   60 feet   E4   (26.3.86)
Start 15 feet right of Big Kazoo.
1 60 feet. 6a. Climb the easy slab and an awkward bulge to below the obvious blue flake, bolt. Powerfully ascend this to a peg and make a difficult move onto the slab above. Bolt belay.

Turtle on Sight   65 feet   Hard Very Severe   (26.3.86)
Start below the big corner in the centre of the crag.
1 65 feet. 5a. Follow the corner stepping left at the top.

★ **The Turtle Run**   65 feet   E5   (9.5.86)
The wall just right of Turtle on Sight.
1 65 feet. 6b. From the ledge at the foot of the corner pull out right onto the wall and climb it past two bolts to gain a slim groove and crack. Climb the wall past a peg to finish.

★ **Heightmare**   65 feet   E5   (26.3.86)
Start beneath the roof 15 feet right of Turtle on Sight.
1 65 feet. 6b. Climb directly through the roof passing an in situ wire and two bolts then finish up the overhanging groove, peg, to a bolt belay.

★ **Turtle, Ring Your Mother!**   65 feet   E3   (26.3.86)
Start 5 feet right of Heightmare.
1 65 feet. 5c. Climb the bulging wall rightwards to a ledge then
up to a layback crack. Follow this to a thread and finish leftwards
through the bulge on jugs.

THE UPPER TIER   (R)
This is the compact wall above the right-hand buttress. It is
about 20 feet high and its main feature is two horizontal breaks
running the full length of the crag. The routes described are on
the face overlooking the road.

★ **Big Mac**   20 feet   Hard Very Severe   (8.85)
Starts roughly in the middle of the face where a crack runs the
full height.
1   20 feet. 5a. Follow the crack strenuously. Belay well back.

French Fries   20 feet   E3   (8.85)
Start right of Big Mac where a large undercut flake joins the
breaks.
1   20 feet. 5c. Climb the wall to the first break. Using the flake
gain the second break which is left by climbing a small groove
on the left past a peg. Belay well back.

THE CRINKLE CRAGS, SURPRISE ZAWN, WONDERWALL and PENINSULA WALL
A recently developed area of rock at sea level below Hamburger
Buttress. The routes are all about 50 feet in length and are
worthwhile. The area as a whole is non-tidal and approaches are
as follows.

THE CRINKLE CRAGS and SURPRISE ZAWN
Park beneath Hamburger Buttress at a gap in the wall (just after
the summit turning as the lighthouse comes into view). Walk
down the grassy slope keeping the large gully (Ogof Hafnant)
on the left (facing out) to the cliff edge.

For the Crinkle Crags walk left (facing out) into the gully and
scramble down this moving onto the wall at the bottom to gain
a platform (non-tidal). The routes are described from the far end
of this where a large block abuts an orange coloured wall.

For Surprise Zawn bear right (facing out) for approximately 100
yards to a narrow cleft. The left wall bears an obvious traverse
line – that taken by Fraggle Rock. All routes described from left
to right when facing the crag.

WONDERWALL and PENINSULA WALL
Beyond the previous parking spot a long straight terminates in a sharp right-hand bend. The grassy couloir above contains telegraph poles. Ample parking in the bend here.

Scramble down the gully and near the bottom go left (facing out) to a flat boulder containing the abseil bolts. The Wonderwall is below. Abseil diagonally right (facing in) enabling another block to be linked to the abseil rope. The platform at the foot of the crag is non-tidal.

For the Peninsula Wall traverse right (facing out) from the bolt and go down the gully onto a narrow peninsula. Abseil onto the platform beneath the wall, again this is non tidal.

SURPRISE ZAWN

Fraggle Rock   90 feet   Hard Very Severe   (1.7.84)
Start on the platform (above high water line) of the left-hand peninsula of the zawn (facing in).
1 60 feet. 4c. Step down and traverse the break rightwards across a corner to a ledge on the arête.
2 30 feet. 4c. Move back left to the corner and climb this to the top.

Winebar Wall   45 feet   E4   (1.7.84)
Start on the ledge at the end of pitch one of Fraggle Rock.
1 45 feet. 6a. Climb a vague ramp above the ledge until it peters out. The wall above provides an interesting finish.

'Tel Shady'   50 feet   E4   (1.7.84)
Approach as for Winebar Wall.
1 50 feet. 6b. Traverse right until it is possible to climb up to a bolt. Move left to another bolt then go straight up to a peg. Trend right from this to finish.

Primeval   60 feet   E5   (2.7.86)
Either abseil into the back of the zawn from a ring bolt or traverse in from the right at low tide.
1 60 feet. 6a. Climb the overhanging back wall of the zawn passing six threads.

The Dude's Rap   60 feet   Hard Very Severe   (4.7.84)
1 60 feet. 5a. Climbs the thin crack in the wall opposite 'Tel Shady'. Approach by abseiling to a ledge which is exposed from half-to-low tide.

THE CRINKLE CRAGS

★★ **Crinkle Crank**   25 feet   E4   (1986)
Takes the hanging wall of the block between the main buttress
and the rocky peninsula (known as Fisherman's Rock).
1 25 feet. 6a. Climb the wall via a black streak on bubbles and
pockets.

Amphibious Wreck   40 feet   E2   (6.84)
Start at the left edge of the platform beneath a groove in the
arête.
1   40 feet. 5a. Climb the wall to the groove. Follow this to a
ledge then climb the crack above.

Molasses Wall   40 feet   E1   (6.84)
Start just left of the large block which abuts the wall.
1   40 feet. 5a. Climb the wall direct to a crack in the roof. Ascend
this to the break then hand traverse this rightwards and finish
direct.

Glory Days   40 feet   E2   (20.6.85)
1   40 feet. 5c. Climb the wall right of Molasses Wall to a crack
in the roof. Pull over and climb the flake on the right to finish.

Identity Crisis   30 feet   Very Severe   (6.3.85)
1   30 feet. 4b. Climb the wall and cracks left of Owain's
Chimney.

Owain's Chimney   40 feet   Difficult   (5.84)
1   40 feet. Climb the obvious chimney either up the inside or
the outside edge (the latter is slightly harder).

Chasing the Dragon   40 feet   Very Severe   (1.7.84)
1   40 feet. 4c. Ascend Owain's Chimney to a ledge on the right
then climb the pocketed groove to the top.

Damn the Jam   40 feet   E2   (6.84)
1   40 feet. 5c. Climb the hairline crack to the right of the obvious
large block. Jam the upper wide crack to the top. (The wide
starting crack reduces the grade to Very Severe).

★★ **Crinkle Crack**   60 feet   E5   (1984/1986)
Start left of The Flim Flan Man below the obvious roof crack.
1 60 feet. 6b. A hard start then go easily to the roof and cross
this via the obvious crack, strenuous.

The Flim Flam Man   40 feet   E4   (6.84)
Start right of the jutting nose at a brown vertical seam.
1   40 feet. 6b. Climb the seam to a thread. Traverse left to a

niche. Make a series of hard moves past a bolt over the roof to an in-situ nut runner. The difficulties soon ease above.

Midnight at the Oasis 60 feet E2   (6.84)
1 60 feet. 5c. Follow the last route to its thread then hand traverse right for 10 feet and pull into a niche. Climb directly out of this to finish.

Ivan Skavinski Skavar 40 feet E3   (20.7.84)
Start right of the last route at a scoop left of Lazy Sunday.
1 40 feet. 6a. Climb the scoop moving left to a bolt. Make a long reach to the break. Climb the layback edge above moving right then back left to finish.

Lazy Sunday 40 feet Very Severe   (6.84)
1 40 feet. 4c. The vague left to right trending ramp with a curious hold at 10 feet is climbed moving rightwards then finishing direct.

Abdul the Bull Khamir 40 feet E3   (20.7.84)
Start at the scoop between Lazy Sunday and Strangers in a Strange Land.
1 40 feet. 5c. Climb the scoop direct on small holds past a peg to the break. Climb the groove above moving right to finish.

Strangers in a Strange Land 50 feet E2   (6.84)
Start 5 feet left of the scoop of Helter Skelter.
1 50 feet. 5c. Climb the wall direct to the break then move left to a crack up which the route finishes.

Helter Skelter 50 feet Hard Very Severe   (6.84)
1 50 feet. 5a. Climb over the roof into the black scoop. Follow this to the top.

Spirit in the Sky 40 feet Severe   (6.84)
1 40 feet. 4a. Climb the arête right of Helter Skelter.

Solo on Sight 40 feet Very Severe   (5.11.84)
Start 10 feet right of Helter Skelter.
1 40 feet. 4c. From the right-hand side of the flake traverse diagonally leftwards for 20 feet to the end of the flake then climb straight up to the top.

Morse 40 feet Very Difficult   (6.3.85)
1 40 feet. Ascend the shallow black corner right of Solo on Sight. Step left and finish up the wall above.

Grog on the Ground 40 feet Very Severe   (20.7.84)
1 40 feet. 4c. Climb the vague groove in the arête between Morse and No Comebacks, taking the left-hand crack at the top.

No Comebacks   50 feet   Very Severe   (1.7.84)
Start beneath the capped groove in the main arête of the crag.
1   50 feet. 4c. Climb the groove to the roof, move left to a ledge
and climb the crack above.

Jonathan Livingstone Seagull   60 feet   Hard Very Severe
                                                            (5.84)
Start 15 feet right of No Comebacks and to the left of a slim
groove.
1   60 feet. 5a. Climb the wall direct pulling over a small bulge
to finish.

Learning to Crawl   60 feet   Hard Very Severe   (6.84)
1   60 feet. 5a. Follow the slim groove just right of Jonathan
Livingstone Seagull.

X.P.D.   60 feet   E2   (5.84)
Start beneath a vague ramp rising rightwards to the break, a few
feet right of Learning to Crawl.
1   60 feet. 5b. Climb the ramp moving right along the break, pull
onto a flake in the headwall and finish with care.

Barracuda   60 feet   Hard Very Severe   (5.84)
1   60 feet. 5a. Climb the 'crinkly' wall right of X.P.D. finishing
up the obvious crack.

Ask Politely   60 feet   Hard Severe   (6.3.85)
1   60 feet. 4b. Climb the corner crack right of Barracuda then
continue straight up passing a flake crack to finish.

Luke Skywalker   65 feet   Very Severe   (6.5.85)
1   65 feet. 4b. Ascend the thin cracks in the wall right of Ask
Politely.

Ramp Romp   50 feet   Difficult   (5.84)
1   50 feet. Follow the leftward sloping ramp on the right edge
of the wall.

FLUTED WALL AREA
This is the wall opposite X.P.D. etc. Approach as for the Crinkle
Crags but traverse leftwards around the top of the deep cut zawn
heading for the seaward end to a block with a bolt belay on its
top. Abseil over the edge here and go down to a cave and a good
belay (thread) above high tide.

★ **Madness and Mayhem**   80 feet   E5   (19.8.86)
1   80 feet. 6b. A line of three threads marks the line to the left
of the belay cave. The crux is just above the third thread. All very
interesting!

PENINSULA WALL

Royal Sovereign   60 feet   E2   (5.84)
The obvious left-trending thin crack on the wall starting at a
capped corner.
1   60 feet. 5c. Climb the corner and pull round the bulge to gain
the crack above. Climb this moving left at the top.

Fly by Night   50 feet   E1
1   50 feet. 5a. Climb the wall left of Masochist's Chimney for 15
feet then move up left onto a ledge. Move back right to finish
up a crack.

Masochist's Chimney   50 feet   Very Severe   (5.84)
1   50 feet. 4b. Climb the chimney right of Royal Sovereign.
Traditional.

Man O' War   40 feet   Very Severe   (5.84)
1   40 feet. 4c. Climb the crack in the main nose of the peninsula.

WONDERWALL
The next route takes a line on the wall just right of the green
gully separating Wonderwall and Peninsula Wall. Approach by
abseiling from the bolts of Wonderwall well leftwards towards
the gully to another bolt in some grey rock. Clip this and abseil
straight down to a scoop at the base of the wall. There is an
excellent thread which is difficult to find. An alternative
approach is to traverse in leftwards from the terrace at Very
Difficult.

If I Die in a Combat Zone   80 feet   E3   (7.7.84)
1   80 feet. 6a. Climb the depression to a thread. Step left onto
the rib and a bolt and climb this moving right at the top to a
ledge, peg. Trend rightwards, avoiding a large flake and step
right to finish.

A Fine Time to Die   110 feet   E2   (15.5.84)
Start on the left-hand end of the terrace just right of a green
crack.
1   110 feet. 5c. Climb the wall to the break. Gain the groove
above and follow this moving leftwards at the top.

Touch the Dead   110 feet   E3   (15.5.84)
Start right of the last route at a right trending crack.
1   110 feet. 5c. Climb the crack to the break, thread. Move up
right from this and climb the bulge direct, thread, on the left.
Move up left to another thread and finish direct.

Sister of Mercy 100 feet E2   (6.7.84)
Start 5 feet right of Touch the Dead beneath a peg and sling on
the bulge.
1 100 feet. 5c. Climb to the bulge and pass the peg and threads
to reach the break. Move up right until level with another thread
out left. Move to this then finish direct.

Whispering Death 70 feet E3   (5.84)
Takes the bulge and the left-hand of two cracks left of the abseil.
Start on the subsidiary ramp beneath some slots in the bulge.
1 70 feet. 5c. Using the slots and a 'dinner plate' move up and
left across the bulge. Climb the left-hand crack to the top.

A Cry of Angels 70 feet E3   (5.84)
1 70 feet. 5c. As for Whispering Death but trend rightwards
through the bulge to the break. Move back left to the right-hand
crack which is hard to enter and leads to the top.

Sweet Dreams 70 feet E4   (15.5.84)
Start beneath the scoop.
1 70 feet. 6a. Climb up leftwards to a good jug and peg. Move
directly up from this to the break. Climb up left to a thread then
hard moves lead right to another thread. Move precariously right
then back left to finish.

*** **The Reflex** 70 feet E3   (15.5.84)
The best route in this particular area.
1 70 feet. 6a. Climb rightwards into the scoop which is then
followed to the break. Move left along this and pull up to a peg.
Climb rightwards from this to a bolt. Blind moves lead past
another bolt to the top.

* **Clowns of God** 70 feet E3   (15.5.84)
Start beneath the 'flute' in the leaning wall right of The Reflex.
1 70 feet. 6a. Climb rightwards to the first break. Move left and
up to the second break. Move right and up, thread until the flute
proper can be gained, thread. Climb this direct to the top.

Gibbering Wreck 70 feet Hard Very Severe   (1984)
Start at the black V-groove.
1 70 feet. 5a. Climb the groove until the corner on the left can
be gained. Climb this to the top.

Rainbow Warrior 70 feet Very Severe   (5.84)
1 70 feet. 4c. Climb the black V-groove as for Gibbering Wreck
and its continuation above to finish.

Time Gentlemen Please   70 feet   Hard Very Severe   (15.5.84)
1   70 feet. 5b. Climb the vague crack just right of Rainbow Warrior to a small corner. Ascend this to a large ledge. Finish direct.

Golden Goosed Creature   70 feet   E2   (15.5.84)
15 feet right of Time Gentlemen Please is a crack splitting the leaning headwall.
1   70 feet. 5b. Climb the crack to a ledge and finish direct.

★★ **Seaside Rendezvous**   150 feet   E2   (15.5.84)
A good girdle of the area. Start as for Touch the Dead.
1   150 feet. 5b. Climb the right-leaning groove to the break. Follow this with interest passing the line of Golden Goosed Creature to the large ledge. Belay here then finish direct.

CRAIG ARWAHAN   (R)
This crag is found just above the Marine Drive, before the entrance to the lighthouse. This totally detached crag is 60 feet high with a narrow ravine at its rear. This gives a safe and easy descent.

Gina   50 feet   Very Severe   (23.7.83)
The narrow left-hand face is split centrally at mid-height by a vertical crack.
1   50 feet. 4c. Gain the crack from below and follow it with good protection to the top.

About 10 feet right of Gina is a noticeable weakness in the overhangs which provides the next two routes.

White Linen   65 feet   Very Severe   (23.7.83)
1   65 feet. 4c. Ascend the left-hand crack and its continuation to an overhang. Move left and climb the arête to a ledge. Continue to the top by means of two corner cracks.

Patience   65 feet   Hard Severe   (7.83)
1   65 feet. 4b. Ascend the less-prominent cracks 15 feet to the right of the last route to an overhang at mid-height. Move left to gain a deep crack with a prominent chockstone. Follow the crack to finish.

Self Abuse   50 feet   E1   (6.85)
Start as for Patience at the wide crack.
1   50 feet. 5b. Climb the crack for about 20 feet until it is possible to move right along the wide break, thread, for a few feet. Pull up to a crack which is followed rightwards to a bolt and thread belay. Lower off.

★ **Squall**   50 feet   E3   (8.85)
1 50 feet. 6a. Climb the wall 10 feet right of Self Abuse to the break and thread. Climb the wall above passing a peg and thread to a bolt and thread belay. Lower off.

★ **Mystic East**   50 feet   E3   (6.85)
Follows the wall into the large niche at half-height. Start beneath the niche.
1 50 feet. 6a. Climb the wall just right of a small corner to the break, thread. Pull over the bulge moving rightwards into the niche. Climb leftwards out of this past a peg then go back right onto a ledge. Move up right to a bolt and lower off.

Central Passage   50 feet   Very Severe   (1983 – probably earlier)
The wide crack which splits the crag at its centre.
1 50 feet. 4c. Follow the crack passing jammed chockstones at half-height to the top.

★★ **Bodyworks**   50 feet   E4   (28.6.85)
Start in the middle of the depression 30 feet right of Central Passage.
1 50 feet. 6b. Climb the centre of the depression to the break, thread. Pull over a small roof to another one above, bolt, on the right. Pull leftwards through this, crux, then go back right to a sling. Finish up the juggy overhangs above. Bolt belay. Lower off.

★★ **The Brotherhood**   50 feet   E5   (8.85)
Desperate climbing. Start as for Bodyworks.
1 50 feet. 6b. Climb the depression to the break then go right along this until it is possible to pull into the scoop above on interesting holds and go up to the break (good runners). Pull over the first roof to a bolt then vicious moves lead over the second roof, thread to a good break and thread. Climb easily up the flake crack to finish. Thread belay. Lower off.

★ **Follow You, Follow Me**   40 feet   E2   (7.85)
10 feet right of the last route a slabby nose reaches the ground.
1 40 feet. 5c. Climb the left side of the slab to a crack splitting the roof. Pull over this, thread and climb the wall, bolt and groove above to a bolt belay. Lower off.

The Fall Guy   40 feet   E1   (7.85)
Start below the deep crack in the upper wall right of the last route.
1 40 feet. 5b. Climb the middle of the slab to the bulge. Enter the crack and climb it strenuously to its top. Nut and in-situ thread. Lower off.

Vaquero   40 feet   E4   (8.85)
Rather pointless but a good technical exercise.
1   40 feet. 6b. Climb the wall or the pinnacle to its top. Enter the
niche above and hand-traverse left under the roof, peg, and pull
onto the wall, bolt. Finish direct. Bolt belay. Lower off.

UN-NAMED CRAG   (R)
This crag lies at sea-level to the right of the lighthouse on the
apex of The Great Orme. From the entrance to the lighthouse
climb over the wall on the right and descend the wide grassy
gully on the right to reach a small path which leads down to
ledges below. These in turn lead past a small damp cave to the
platform at the foot of the crag. The crag consists of large
pinnacles with massive blocks at its foot. Note that this crag is
restricted during the bird ban. In the centre of the crag where
the blocks are the routes are described first rightwards the
leftwards from this central point.

Any Which Way But Loose   40 feet   E2   (25.8.84)
Start about 20 feet right of the blocks and 10 feet left of the
singular block, beneath a bulge just above the break.
1   40 feet. 5b. Climb the thin crackline to the break and pull over
to gain another crack. Follow this to the top. Scramble to the top
of the flake and descend down the rear of the flake on the right.

Captain Pugwash   40 feet   E1   (25.8.84)
A line up the scoop directly behind the block.
1   40 feet. 5b. Climb up to the traverse line beneath the scoop.
Move right then up left to finish up a crack. Scramble off left
then go back down the flake on the right.

Stormkeeper   40 feet   Severe   (25.8.84)
1   40 feet. 4a. Climb the wide crack opposite the block to a belay
on the right. Descend behind the flake.

Boltzmann's Constant   50 feet   E4   (25.8.84)
Start below the gently overhanging wall just right of the huge
flake.
1   50 feet. 6a. Climb the scoop to a bolt. Pass this direct then a
second bolt to a bolt belay. Abseil off.

Black Money   50 feet   E3   (28.8.84)
Start 5 feet right of the large flake beneath a vague groove
joining the two breaks.
1   50 feet. 6a. Ascend to the first break, bolt, then go up the
vague groove moving up right then back left to a good hold in
the top niche. Finish over the bulge. Abseil off (bolts).

Storm on the Sea   50 feet   E3   (28.8.84)
Start 5 feet right of Black Money beneath a bulge and a vague
crack.
1   50 feet. 6a. Climb the bulge to a good ledge then go up the
vague crack above, thread, with a hard but well-protected move
to finish. Abseil off (bolts).

Mr Nobody   50 feet   E4   (2.9.84)
Follows the thin right-trending crack right of Storm on the Sea.
1   50 feet. 6a. Climb the crack until it is possible to move right
to a ledge and bolt. Move back left then go up past a thread over
the top break to a niche. Go straight over the bulge above to the
abseil bolts.

The next routes start over to the left of this wall at another pile
of blocks.

★ **Hoe Down**   200 feet   E2   (7.78/30.1.82)
A good first pitch. Start behind the huge block in the centre of
the crag.
1   100 feet. 5c. Climb up leftwards to a peg. Pass this, crux, to
reach the break and traverse right and pull over the roof into a
wide crack. Follow this to a good ledge and belay.
2   100 feet. 5a. Ascend the wide crack behind the stance into a
short gully. Go up rightwards then back left to finish.

The Needles   170 feet   Hard Very Severe   (23.8.75)
Start at the furthest of the blocks.
1   95 feet. 5a. Step off the block and ascend steeply to a ledge
at the foot of a crack. Go up to a large jammed block on the left
and pass this to belay at the foot of a ramp.
2   75 feet. 5a. Climb the ramp to its top then go up to the top
of a large pinnacle. Step onto the wall and climb diagonally
rightwards to finish by a large block. Belay well back. A loose
pitch.

Flake Wall   160 feet   Hard Very Severe   (24.4.77)
Start left of The Needles.
1   80 feet. 4c. Climb the leftward-trending flakes then move
right on an overhanging flake into a crack. Ascend this to a ledge
and belays.
2   80 feet. 5a. Follow the large flakes on the left then finish up
the wall above.

The Rat   150 feet   Very Severe   (23.8.75)
Start left of Flake Wall beneath a left trending groove.
1   110 feet. 4c. Climb the groove up into a chimney. Ascend this
then go left to belay at the foot of a steep crack.
2   40 feet. 4c. Climb the crack to the top.

Chris Lyon on Old Sam, Great Zawn, Little Orme.

Dave Lyon

Mark Leach making the 3rd ascent of Statement of Youth.

Ritchie Brooks

Simon Berry—Down and Out at Pen Trwyn.

Andy Mutter

Little Corner   120 feet   Hard Very Severe   (23.8.75)
Start farther left again below a steep corner crack.
1   120 feet. 5a. Follow the corner to the top bulge. Enter the
chimney and climb up onto some large chockstones. Climb the
flakes and short wall above to finish.

To the left again is an obvious sea-stack. The side facing the
platform below the crag has been climbed:

Solid Reality   60 feet   Very Severe   (3.10.82)
1   60 feet. 4c. Climb the wall and curving crack to the summit.
Fixed belay and abseil point.

The Crack   220 feet   Very Severe   (4.77)
Just beyond the sea-stack is an obvious chimney.
1   100 feet. 4b. Climb the obvious chimney crack moving
rightwards and up the rib. Step back to the crack then follow it
until a step left can be made onto a broad ledge.
2   120 feet. 4a. Go up over ledges to the top. Belay well back.

The next route starts 100 feet farther left. Approach (tidal) by
walking around the buttress beyond the sea-stack to the foot of
a corner. Alternatively abseil (pegs) from a boulder at the top of
the crag.

The Sea Grave   150 feet   Hard Very Severe   (27.9.79)
1   150 feet. 5a. Climb the corner steeply to good ledges. Move
up into the chimney above and pull out of this into a crack. Finish
easily.

Castell y Gwynt

The most spectacular crag on The Great Orme. The climbing
virtually without exception is on superb, solid and very steep
rock and most of the routes contain a fair amount of fixed
protection. Situations are exciting throughout and though the
crag is not much more than 100 feet high the routes have that
'big feel' and plenty of atmosphere.

Approach by climbing over the wall just right of the lighthouse
entrance and follow the lighthouse wall until a narrow gully is
reached. Go down this to the bottom and traverse right. The crag
suddenly makes its presence known and is easily recognizable
by its sensational black and white striped prow – the line of
Psychic Threshold.

Demos   100 feet   Hard Very Severe   (1.76)
Start 50 feet left of the gully, just right of a cave and large
boulder.
1   60 feet. 5a. Enter the groove from the right and ascend this
until it steepens, then move onto the wall on the left. Ascend
this diagonally to a ledge and belay. OR, better, from blocks right
of the cave, ascend leftwards then go straight up to a flat ledge.
Belay on the right.
2   40 feet. 5a. Take the steep wall behind the stance making for
the groove and large flake then traverse right across the bulge
to a small ledge. Finish up the corner and slab above.

Variation
The corner above the belay has been climbed direct at 5c.

★★★ **Appian Way**   250 feet   E2   (3.77)
A fine route which girdles the crag below the top roof with good
protection and fine positions. Start as for Demos.
1   60 feet. 5a. As for Demos.
2   45 feet. 5a. Move up onto the arête on the left. Round this
onto the steep slab and traverse left under the roof stepping
down to the top belay on New Dimensions.
3   65 feet. 5b. Move left again onto the prow. Traverse left, peg,
above the groove of New Dimensions to a wide recess and huge
thread. Descend 15 feet to a bolt belay on the lower break.
4   80 feet. 5c. Move left to a scoop then follow the fault line,
thread to the arête. Go left again to a short steep wall (junction
with Psychic Threshold). Ascend this leftwards to finish up a
short easy groove.

Variation
★★ **Watling Street**   80 feet   E2   .   (3.77)
Start at the bolt belay at the end of pitch 3 of Appian Way.
1   80 feet. 5c. Climb back up to the huge thread under the roof
then traverse left around the steep prow into a scoop. Continue
left, thread and peg, to finish up the short final groove at the end.
N.B. The second thread contains a karabiner which should be
left in place as this is the belay and means of descent for
Sidekick.

★★ **Fosse Way**   250 feet   E3   (24.6.77/29.8.79)
A lower girdle than Appian Way giving fine, open climbing. Start
as for Demos.
1   60 feet. 5a. As for Demos.
2   50 feet. 5b. Step down to a line of footholds leading
leftwards. Traverse left to a hollow-sounding flake and step
down again, traversing left to the first belay on New Dimensions.
3   60 feet. 6b. Traverse left around the prow, make a long reach,
peg and then go up onto the ledge and bolt belay on Appian
Way.

4 80 feet. 5c. As for pitch 4 of Appian Way – the continuation break at this level – to finish leftwards across a short steep wall at the end.

★★ **Rude Awakening**   110 feet   E5   (19.7.80)
An eliminate line but the climbing is worthwhile and hard. Start as for Demos at the cave.
1 80 feet. 6b. Ascend steeply to the horizontal break then go up the overhanging cracks above to another break (Fosse Way). Traverse left to the base of a steep groove, bolt. Climb this, peg, to a bulge; surmount this, thread, and move up to the roof stepping left to the top belay on New Dimensions.
2 30 feet. 5a. Go up leftwards into the corner then ascend to a peg on the arête. Move onto the wall on the left and finish up this. (As for New Dimensions).

Alternative Three   130 feet   E5   (3.77)
A rather out-dated route since the creation of Rude Awakening. Start as for Demos at the cave. Usually dirty on pitch 1.
1 60 feet. 5c. Ascend steeply to the horizontal break and traverse this, thread, leftwards to the groove on New Dimensions. Follow this to the stance.
2 40 feet. 6b. Traverse right and go up to the groove. Climb this (Rude Awakening) moving left to the top stance on New Dimensions.
3 30 feet. 5b. Climb the corner above the stance to the roof. Cross this rightwards, peg, then go straight up to finish. OR, the roof directly above the steep groove can be combined with Pitch 2.

★★ **Good Taste!**   125 feet   E5   (28.8.84)
A superb test-piece taking the ridiculously steep groove above and to the right of the first belay on New Dimensions.
1 65 feet. 5c. As for New Dimensions.
2 60 feet. 6b. Enter the groove, bolt, and bridge up it passing a further two bolts to reach the break. Step right to the top belay on New Dimensions and finish as for this.

★★ **New Dimensions**   140 feet   E3   (11.10.75/1976)
The original classic of the crag – sustained and spectacular. Start from a small cave at the foot of the buttress. Huge thread belays.
1 65 feet. 5c. From the cave climb out by a crack in the roof and step right onto a steep slab above a thread. Go up to a roof, peg then right again and up a bulging groove to an old peg. Swing right to the foot of a steep groove and climb this, hard at its top, exiting left to a small stance and bolt belay (good threads up right).
2 45 feet. 6a. Move left to the foot of a steep black groove. Climb this, bolt and peg, over a couple of bulges to the roof then

traverse right, peg, under the roof to a ledge and good belay beneath a corner.
3 30 feet. 5a. Go up leftwards into the corner then up to a peg on the arête. Move onto the wall on the left and finish up this.

★★ **Plas Berw**   215 feet   E5   (29.8.79)
An exciting first pitch which takes the magnificent hanging arête left of New Dimensions.
1 70 feet. 6a. Climb New Dimensions to the steep slab on the right, then climb leftwards to a peg at the base of the arête. Climb wildly up this to a bomber nut at its top, moving right to belay on New Dimensions.
2 50 feet. 6b. Traverse left, peg, to the lower stance on Appian Way. (This is Fosse Way pitch three.)
3 65 feet. 6a. Move right onto the wall then climb flakes up and rightwards to the roof. Traverse right under this to the belay on New Dimensions.
4 30 feet. 5a. As for New Dimensions.

★★★ **The Bittersweet Connection**   110 feet   E5   (6.9.79/14.9.82)
A strenuous problem first pitch leads to a sensational finish over the top roof. Start as for New Dimensions.
1 70 feet. 6b. From the steep slab on the right traverse left underneath the roof and pull over by a prominent jug on its lip to a thread. Climb the wall above to a bulge and bolt. Pass this, crux, on the left with a long reach or on the right, sustained and sloping, to gain holds leading to Fosse Way. Follow this leftwards to the lower stance on Appian Way.
2 40 feet. 6a. Climb up to the roof and a huge thread. Step left and surmount the roof on huge undercuts to jugs on the lip. Pull round, peg onto the top wall, and finish up this.

★★★ **Telegraph Road**   240 feet   E5   (10.8.86)
An excellent low-level girdle of the crag taking the obvious horizontal break from New Dimensions leftwards to finish up the fine wall of Opal Moon. Start as for New Dimensions. Thread belays.
1 80 feet. 6a. Climb New Dimensions to gain the break (as for Bittersweet). Traverse this leftwards for 50 feet to twin threads and a hanging belay. Two Friends 3s needed.
2 50 feet. 6b. Continue the traverse, thread passing Blast Peru and Sidekick, and move down slightly to the thread over the roof on Psychic Threshold. Go left again past the thread on Teenage Kicks to a bolt belay on the arête.
3 110 feet. 5c. Climb the superb wall above, this is Opal Moon, first on the left then back right into a vague groove past three threads. Scramble off leftwards then go back right to belay.

Central Pillar   120 feet   E6   (25.9.72/1983)
An audacious route climbing directly up the magnificent central
wall. Start at the foot of the obvious grey pillar in the centre of
the face.
1   80 feet. 6c. Ascend the left-hand side of the pillar to a monster
thread then go up the steep wall above to the roof and a bolt.
Pull over the roof leftwards to a thread then go up right to a line
of obvious pockets and holds. Follow the line of these to the
ledge on Appian Way. Bolt belay.
2   40 feet. 6a. Climb up to and over the top roof as for The
Bittersweet Connection.

Blast Peru   120 feet   E5   (24.8.1984)
An exhilarating route up the obvious hanging white pillar in the
middle of the wall. Start as for Central Pillar.
1   80 feet. 6b. Climb Central Pillar past the thread and go up to
the roof. Move left a few feet and pull up leftwards, bolt, over
the bulge and move up to the base of the hanging pillar. Climb
this, bolt, to a huge spike at the top. Ascend the juggy wall above
to belay on the right as for Appian Way.
2   40 feet. 6a. Go up to the roof, thread, and surmount this to
finish (as for Bittersweet).

Sidekick   120 feet   E6   (26.8.84)
A big, intimidating pitch taking a parallel line just to the left of
Blast Peru. Start as for Psychic Threshold.
1   120 feet. 6a. Climb out of the cave as for Psychic Threshold
and move up to the thread just above. Go right to a bolt below
a slender rib on the wall. Sustained climbing leads straight up
the wall for about 30 feet until a move right gains holds leading
direct to the break on Appian Way. Go straight up the wall to a
thread under the top overhang. Abseil from this, OR, traverse 15
feet left and finish easily.

Psychic Threshold   120 feet   E5   (3.8.77/5.81)
A phenomenal route taking the continuously overhanging prow
of the buttress. Start at a short arête leading up to an obvious
cave.
1   120 feet. 6b. Trend up right then move left onto the arête.
Climb this, peg, to huge threads in the back of the cave (possible
stance – not recommended). Climb rightwards through the roof
past two slings to a bolt and go up again to a thread and good
shake-out. Move up leftwards to a line of good pockets which
lead to a large niche and thread. Pull over the bulge on the right
and move up left with difficulty to another sling. Gain the thin
crack in the steep wall above this and follow it, thread, to the
break of Appian Way. Climb the short wall above trending left
to an easy finishing groove.

*** **Teenage Kicks**   140 feet   E6   (28.8.84)
A really mean route, with continuously bold and pumpy
climbing. Start as for Psychic Threshold.
1   140 feet. 6b. Climb out of the cave as for Psychic Threshold
and move up to the thread. Traverse left, across Psychic
Threshold to a small ledge and thread, then go up and
rightwards for about 20 feet to a flake crack just above a slight
bulge. Step left to a thread then pull straight up on small holds
moving up leftwards to a big pocket. Easier climbing leads up
rightwards to the break of Appian Way. Finish leftwards up the
top wall.

*** **Opal Moon**   125 feet   E4   (3.8.86)
An excellent route – well worth the approach. Abseil to a thread
belay in a corner/cave 30 feet left of Psychic Threshold from
about 30 feet left (looking in) of the bolts on the terrace above
the crag.
1   125 feet. 6a. Climb rightwards to the arête – thread and pull
over the bulge above on good holds to the bolt and a junction
with Telegraph Road. As for this route to the top.

Spacewalk   80 feet   E4   (17.9.77/6.11.79)
The route follows the obvious flake on the steep wall left of Opal
Moon after a very spectacular abseil approach.
1   80 feet. 5c. Climb the thin flake crack to the roof. Pull over
rightwards, peg and continue in the same line until a step left
can be made into a groove. Climb this to finish.

POINT FIVE BUTTRESS (R) and UPPER CRAIG PEN GOGARTH (R)

This is not a particularly popular pair of crags. Approach as for
Castell y Gwynt to the base of the narrow gully and traverse left.
Point Five Buttress is directly above. Not a lot is known about
the quality and grades of the routes here and the descriptions
are the original ones written up by the first ascensionists. The
buttress peters out as one travels rightwards only to reappear
in the shape of Upper Craig Pen Gogarth – a steep crag with a
prominent arête – the line of Hang Ten – probably the most
worthwhile route on these walls.

POINT FIVE BUTTRESS (R)

Oceanside North   140 feet   E3   (5.77)
A girdle crossing the crag below the top roofs. Start at the
left-hand side of the buttress halfway down the gully.
1   120 feet. 6a. Traverse right into the chimney on Memphis.
Climb up to the roof then go right to a sling. Continue the
traverse, around the prow, to belay at the far end.
2   20 feet. Straight up the easy gully to finish.

Memphis   65 feet   E1   (5.77)
Approach the route from the gully on the left and belay beneath
the first groove.
1   65 feet. 5b. Climb the groove to a narrow chimney below the
roof. Step out left then go up to the roof. Move right into another
groove and climb this to finish.

King Ja Ja   65 feet   E2   (5.77)
Supposedly the best route on this buttress. Start 15 feet left of
Zero in a small bay.
1   65 feet. 6a. Climb the short slab to a cave. Traverse right from
one crack to another on the arête. Climb up to the roof then
traverse left to a good undercut hold. Move out over the roof,
peg, then go up the wall above to finish.

Huntington   80 feet   E2   (5.77)
Start as for Zero.
1   80 feet. 5c. Ascend to the cave, then go up to another cave.
Move up into a sentry box on the right then on to a flake. Move
up and left on to the arête and follow steep cracks to the roof.
Go over this to finish.

Zero   65 feet   Hard Very Severe   (5.77)
Start at a ledge 20 feet up from the foot of the buttress.
1   65 feet. 5a. Climb the short slab to a cave then go rightwards
to some steep cracks just before the gully. Ascend these and
step right into another crack. Climb this to finish.

UPPER CRAIG PEN GOGARTH   (R)

The Vice   170 feet   E2   (1pt. aid)   (19.4.75)
Start about 100 feet along the path from the base of the gully.
Scramble up a short gully to belay beneath the obvious chimney.
1   120 feet. 5c. Move up onto a small ledge then enter the first
chimney. Make an awkward move into the smaller chimney
above. From the top of the chimney a small thread can be
arranged through a small hole under the overlap. Use this for
aid to gain a crack and layback this passing a further two threads
to a peg. Move right then go straight up the crack to a ledge and
peg belay.
2   50 feet. 5a. Climb up rightwards and enter the groove above.
Finish up this.

Hang Five   190 feet   E1   (21.6.75)
A steep route with some loose rock. Start farther along the path
from The Vice near a large boulder.
1   60 feet. 5a. Climb the groove (easier than it looks) to the roof
and thread. Traverse right to a small ledge and belay.

St. Tudno's Buttress Upper Tier

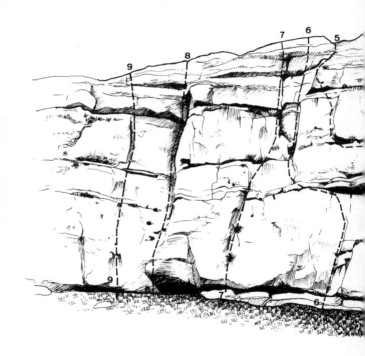

1	Puerto Rican Harlem	E4
2	Tales of Future Past	E4
3	Goliath	E3

| 4 | Limestone Lemur | E2 |
| 5 | Gritstone Gorilla | E3 |

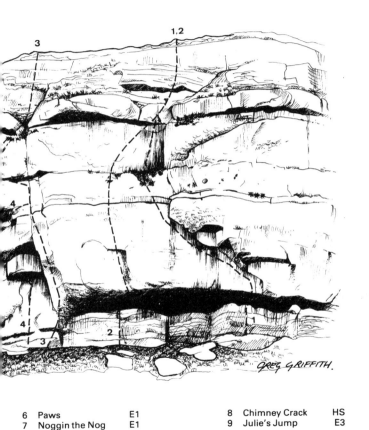

| 6 | Paws | E1 | 8 | Chimney Crack | HS |
| 7 | Noggin the Nog | E1 | 9 | Julie's Jump | E3 |

2 130 feet. 5a. Climb the groove for 15 feet then swing left around the arête. Traverse left again then go straight up until a move right onto the arête can be made. Climb this then the groove on the left to the top.

★ **Hang Ten** 155 feet E3   (3.77)
A strenuous route up the grooves in the arête of the buttress. Start as for Hang Five. It has been compared with Big Groove on Gogarth.
1 60 feet. 5a. As for Hang Five.
2 95 feet. 5c. Climb the left wall of the groove then move onto the right wall. Ascend this steeply to a small roof. Move back to the groove on the left wall and climb it to a peg. Step back right on to the arête then go leftwards into the groove again. Finish up this to the right of the roof.

ST. TUDNO'S BUTTRESS
A pleasant place to climb with no access problems and generally firm, clean rock. Just past the lighthouse entrance is a car park on the right. This is the site of the Rest and be Thankful tea shack. A little farther on is a wide, grassy gully with a scree slope in it. Go down this gully. The Upper Tier is on the right and is about 60 feet in height. For the main buttress descend a little further and follow the path below the crag which gets progressively bigger as one travels below it. All routes on these crags are described from right to left.

UPPER TIER

Thank You Johnny 30 feet E2   (27.4.86)
Not a particularly inspiring climb taking the wall right of Pile Driver.
1 30 feet. 5c. Ascend to a flake then go up right to a sloping ledge. Climb up past a peg to finish leftwards.

Pile Driver 45 feet E1   (1979)
1 45 feet. 5b. Climb the bulging wall directly above the remains of a fence-post at the right-hand end of the crag, leftwards to an easy finishing groove.

Fool's Paradise 50 feet E2   (27.6.82)
Start 15 feet left of Pile Driver.
1 50 feet. 5b. Pull over the bulge to a thin crack. Climb this then traverse right to finish up an easy corner as for Pile Driver.

And All Hell Broke Loose 60 feet E2   (17.4.84)
Takes the thin crack and groove 10 feet left of Fool's Paradise.
1 60 feet. 5c. Climb the thin crack to a ledge on the right. Ascend the groove on the right to the roof then step left to a

peg. Climb the bulge above and continue in the same line to the top.

Rest and be Thankful   60 feet   E2   (23.8.82)
Farther left is a wide crack. Start just left of this.
1   60 feet. 5c. Climb the thin crack direct past a thread at 25 feet.

Farther left again a large roof guards access to a left-trending ramp/flake.

⋆ **Puerto Rican Harlem**   60 feet   E4   (10.6.82)
A very hard problem.
1   60 feet. 6c. Go easily up to the roof and reach right to clip a peg over the lip. Gaining a standing position, by using two 'dinkies' left of the peg, is the crux. The ramp and undercut flake present no problem and lead to a short finishing corner. If the crack over the roof can be reached and used to surmount the overhang then probably 6b is correct.

⋆ **Tales of Future Past**   45 feet   E4   (1982)
Another vicious roof problem starting 15 feet left of the last route.
1   45 feet. 6c. Pull over the roof with great difficulty and climb the short flake and wall above, past a peg to finish.

Goliath   65 feet   E3   (1981)
A safe and strenuous route. Start below the steep finger crack in the right arête of the corner, just left of Tales of Future Past.
1   65 feet. 6a. Steeply climb up to the crack and follow it to a ledge at 45 feet. Finish up the loose groove on the left.

Limestone Lemur   65 feet   E2   (8.10.77)
Start below the corner just left of Goliath.
1   65 feet. 5c. Climb the corner to the first roof. Cross left then go straight up to the top roof, peg. Traverse right to the arête and pull up onto a ledge. Finish up the short loose groove on the left.

⋆⋆ **Gritstone Gorilla**   65 feet   E3   (20.9.77)
An excellent route crossing the roof left of Limestone Lemur. Very strenuous.
1   65 feet. 5c. Go up to the top roof as for Limestone Lemur, peg. Swing left and pull over the lip into a short flake crack. Climb this to the next roof, peg. Traverse left and finish up the wide crack just left of the arête.

Paws   60 feet   E1   (14.2.78)
Start 20 feet left of Gritstone Gorilla below a slim groove.
1   60 feet. 5b. Ascend the steep wall leftwards to the arête then

go up the wall on the right stepping into the wide crack on the left at the top.

Noggin the Nog   60 feet   E1   (1983)
1   60 feet. 5b. Climb the groove left of the arête of Paws.

Human Erosion   60 feet   Hard Very Severe   (17.4.85)
1   60 feet. 5a. From the arête left of Noggin the Nog go up rightwards into that route 10 feet from the top.

Chimney Crack   40 feet   Hard Severe   (1980)
1   40 feet. 4b. Takes the obvious chimney 20 feet left of Noggin the Nog.

Julie's Jump   40 feet   E3   (13.10.85)
Start just left of Chimney Crack.
1   40 feet. 6a. Climb the crack then the steep pocketed wall, passing a peg to the break. Finish up the broken crack above.

The Ramp   40 feet   Severe   (1980)
Start 40 feet left of Chimney Crack at a right-trending ramp.
1   40 feet. 4a. Follow the ramp to a ledge then move up to the overhang. Step left the go straight up to finish via a short groove.

Variation
The Direct Start   40 feet   Severe   (1980)
1a   40 feet. 4a. Climb twin cracks to the ledge then continue as for The Ramp.

Ankle Attack   50 feet   E3   (17.8.85)
Start just left of The Ramp.
1   50 feet. 6a. Follow the obvious crack to the roof, peg and thread. Pull over leftwards then climb direct to finish.

The Corner   40 feet   Very Severe   (1980)
Start 50 feet farther left at the foot of a corner.
1   40 feet. 4b. Climb the corner over a triangular overhang at 10 feet and go straight up to finish.

The Groove   40 feet   Severe   (1980)
Start 30 feet left again below a groove capped by an overhang.
1   40 feet. 4a. Climb the groove to a ledge at 10 feet then go up to a roof. Traverse left below this then go straight up to finish.

ST. TUDNO'S BUTTRESS
A popular crag with several good routes. Some of the in situ protection is now rather old so some care is needed.

★★ Speed Livin' 70 feet E2   (13.7.86)
A fine climb on excellent rock. On the right-hand side of the crag
is a vague crack with a cave/hole at half-height. Start below and
slightly right of this beneath an obvious flake.
1 70 feet. 5b. Climb to the flake, peg on left. Gain a standing
position on the wall above then go right and up left to the right
edge of the hole. Pull round the bulge rightwards to jugs then
go up the wall and arête to finish.

★★ Red October 70 feet E3   (13.7.86)
Start directly below the hole. Again very good and well-
protected.
1 70 feet. 5c. Climb the crack direct moving left at the cave. Finish
direct.

★ Invisible Touch 80 feet E2   (3.8.86)
1 80 feet. 5c. Climb the vague crack left of Red October the crux
being at half-height. Friend 2 essential.

Stretcher 120 feet E1   (10.3.72)
Takes the crackline right of St. Tudno's Chimney. Start at a large
embedded flake just right of the base of the chimney.
1 120 feet. 5c. Climb up the slab then traverse right to a flake
below the roof. Pull over the roof, peg, and step left onto a small
ledge. Go up to another ledge below a steep crack. Climb the
crack stepping left for the last few moves. Belay well back.

St. Tudno's Chimney 120 feet Very Severe   (14.1.72)
A rather scrappy but pleasant route. Start as for Stretcher.
1 45 feet. 4b. From the top of the flake climb the thin crack to
a short wall. Ascend this then go left to belay at the foot of the
chimney.
2 75 feet. 4b. Climb the chimney and crack, over a bulge, to the
top.

★ Oceanside 440 feet E2   (12.6.72)
A very good route girdling the crag from right to left. Start just
left of Stretcher.
1 125 feet. 5b. Cross to the ledge on the left and step down to
the horizontal break. Hand-traverse this passing several pegs to
the arête. Continue the traverse, 2 pegs, until a step down can
be made to a good niche and peg belays.
2 80 feet. 5c. Climb leftwards to the roof and continue the
traverse to the bulge. Move round this, 2 pegs, and go up onto
the fault-line. Step left into a groove, then descend to the break
again. Traverse this, peg, to a peg belay in Ivy Wall.
3 60 feet. 5a. Traverse left to a thread then step down left onto
a ledge. Regain the break above and follow it to another peg.
Step down to a good ledge and peg belay.

St. Tudno's Buttress

GREG.GRIFFITH.

4 150 feet. 5a. Ascend leftwards into a long, open groove. Follow this to a loose ledge on the right after about 100 feet. Climb the crack, or move 10 feet right to climb a shallow groove (better) up to the arête on the left. Go straight up to a cave and bolt/stake belay.
5 25 feet. 5a. Bridge up over the roof and go up a short easy gully to finish.

Fugitive 240 feet E1   (8.1.72)
An enjoyable route taking a diagonal line across the crag. In the centre of the crag is a large vertical crack. Start just right of this.
1 70 feet. 5a. Climb up the slab and step right to a faint crackline slanting up rightwards. Follow this to a good niche and peg belay (on Oceanside).
2 70 feet. 5b. Move up to the break and traverse right for 10 feet. Go up to a flake and follow this awkwardly onto a long loose ledge. Move leftwards to belay (peg high on the wall).
3 100 feet. 5a. Traverse right for about 30 feet and pull over the bulge onto a steep slab. Climb up rightwards to some steep cracks. Ascend these then go straight up to finish.

The Paranoid Schizoid 100 feet E5   (7.9.86)
Start as for Fugitive.
1 100 feet. 6c. Follow Fugitive for 30 feet until a faint corner on the left leads to the break/roof on Oceanside (poor gear). Pull directly over the roof into a groove then up the wall above to a bolt. Move left past this to gain better holds which lead to a good belay (on Freudian Slip). Traverse left and abseil off as for Man on the Run.

Freudian Slip 230 feet E1   (10.3.72)
A good steep route on firm rock. Start as for Fugitive.
1 130 feet. 5c. Climb up to the obvious wide crack and follow it rightwards as it dictates, to the roof. Traverse left around the bulge, 2 pegs and go up onto the fault line. Step left then climb the groove to a good ledge. Belay on the right.
2 50 feet. 5a. Traverse the ledge rightwards to a steep wall. Climb the wall, peg, to the overhang. Step right then go up into a cave.
3 50 feet. 4c. Climb the wall just right of the cave trending rightwards to the top. OR, from the cave go left and straight up the wall to finish.

★★ Man on the Run 100 feet E3   (3.8.86)
Climbs the wall between Freudian Slip and Ivy Wall.
1 100 feet. 6a. Climb Freudian Slip until a step left along a ledge can be made. Climb the wall to the break via a thread on the right. Climb the small slab above to a peg then move into the scoop above where good holds lead to a bolt belay. Abseil off.

★ Ivy Wall   165 feet   E2   (10.6.72/28.1.81)
A fine route on steep, solid rock. Strenuous but with good protection. Start at the large ivy root left of Freudian Slip.
1   140 feet. 5c. Ascend leftwards over easy rock to gain the steep flake and follow this to its top, peg. Traverse left into a crackline and follow this, peg, onto a ledge at 100 feet. Go up the crack on the left to a cave. Belay. (Bolt/stake).
2   25 feet. 5a. Climb up over the cave finishing up the easy gully as for Oceanside pitch 5.

Fresco   245 feet   E1   (4.4.72)
Start left of the ivy at the foot of the wall.
1   70 feet. 5b. Ascend the wall leftwards at first, then move back right to a ledge. Go straight up to a good ledge and peg belay. (As for Oceanside).
2   150 feet. 5a. Trend up leftwards into the long open groove and follow this to a loose ledge on the right after about 100 feet. Traverse right for 10 feet then climb the left-leaning groove to the arête. Ascend straight up over easy rock to a cave, bolt and stake belay.
3   25 feet. 5a. Climb up over the cave finishing up the short gully above.

SEAL POINT
This crag is located at the bottom of the grass slope as one approaches as for Red Sentinel/Astrodome etc.

Abseil 80 feet from a large block as the path cuts back from the point.

The Crigyll Outlaws   70 feet   E1   (8.1.87)
1   70 feet. 5b. From the platform (low-half tide) climb the obvious groove to the top moving right by a small roof to a belay at the abseil point.

Craig Pen Gogarth   (R)

A large crag, usually covered in birds but holding vast potential for future generations.

Approach by descending the gully as for St. Tudno's Buttress. Go to the very bottom of the grassy slope and over the edge to some hidden steps. Go down these and follow the path rightwards, facing out, round an overhung damp cove and onto the long rock terrace. At the far end of this terrace and just beyond the huge open corner of The Red Sentinel are some large roofs. Astrodome and Hippodrome take parallel lines up this buttress.

Just along from the start of the terrace a stepped roof has been
climbed on aid. Several wooden wedges show the way.

The Red Sentinel   140 feet   Hard Very Severe   (25.9.74)
The huge corner, at the time of writing contains much vegetation
and several birds nests. If cleaned however the route is
apparently well worthwhile.
1   140 feet. 5a. Climb broken rock right of the corner then go
left to a roof. Surmount this to a peg, then go up the corner
making a minor detour onto the right wall half-way up. Go back
to the crack then up steeply to finish by a traverse left to a ledge
and peg belays.
WAY OFF. Continue to traverse the ledge and go up the gully
beyond. OR: from the belay go straight up over loose rock to
the lighthouse.

Around to the left of The Red Sentinel is a shattered pillar. The
next route starts here.

★ **Astrodome**   230 feet   A3/Very Severe   (1.78)
A very direct line up the cliff. All bolts are in place but few pegs
so a good selection is advisable. Also many nuts are required
ranging from wires to 9/10 hexes. 'Friends' were not used on
the first ascent but have proved useful on subsequent ascents.
Skyhooks are essential, as is a 3-foot cheating stick.
1   100 feet. A3. Climb up over two roofs, peg and bolts, to a bolt
over the lip. Gain the crack under the next roof and move up left
to another roof. Traverse left along the lip to a spike. Take the
crack under the next roof and move onto the wall above, bolt,
moving right into a flake crack. Climb this on nuts, (pegs would
possible remove it) to a thread at its top, then step left to a bolt
belay.
2   130 feet. A1/4b. Move up and with the aid of three bolts gain
a traverse line leading right. Follow this free to a friable scoop,
thread. Ascend the easy but loose groove to a large break. Go
left along this to a crack in the headwall directly above the
stance. Aid up this on to a ledge then traverse left into a gully
and go up this to finish at the foot of The Upper Tier.

★ **Hippodrome**   285 feet   A3/Very Severe   (8.5.72)
Another long difficult aid route through the impressive overhangs left of The Red Sentinel. Start over left from Astrodome
at large blocks on the terrace.
1   65 feet. Go up to the roof and cross this, three bolts, to the
lip. Move round onto the wall above. Ascend to the roof then go
rightwards over another roof to a short wall. Traverse left then
up to a good thread-hanging belay.

2 70 feet. Traverse left to a crack and follow this until it steepens, then peg up to the roof above. Good belays under the roof.
3 100 feet. Traverse right to a blind crack crossing the roof. Aid across the roof onto the wall above. Move right then free climb into a shallow groove, which is climbed, pegs, to the roof. Go right into a corner then use a bolt to gain a foot traverse. Peg belays at the far end of this.
4 50 feet. Ascend the headwall to the steep grass. Traverse left into a short gully and finish up this to reach the path below the Upper Tier.

THE HORNBY CRAGS (R)
A series of buttresses about 100 feet in height. The climbing is generally not that good, the majority of the routes being rather scrappy. However the crags do hold a certain charm and the situation is one of peace and tranquility.

From the car-park just beyond the lighthouse entrance go left facing out, along the top of the cliffs to the fourth gully along; this is just before a coastguard lookout post. Go down the gully and turn right at its base. The first buttress, on the right is Crescent Buttress, with Central Buttress and Observatory Buttress farther left. The routes are described from right to left as one heads back towards the car park. Complete grades are not available for all the routes here.

CRESCENT BUTTRESS
On the extreme right-hand edge of the buttress is an obvious crack and chimney. The first route starts at the foot of this.

Ergon 110 feet Hard Very Severe   (13.6.71)
1 80 feet. 5a. Approach the crack from the right and make a hard move to reach it. Go straight up the chimney above past some ledges to belay in a crack.
2 30 feet. 4b. Move on to the wall on the left and climb the first thin crack to the top. Pleasant.

Ending of the Day 110 feet   Very Severe   (18.9.71)
Well to the left of Ergon is a vegetated gully.
1 80 feet. 4c. Climb the left wall of the gully then go up the crack to gain some fingerholds above. Traverse right to a ledge at the foot of a crack. Belay.
2 30 feet. 4b. Ascend the crack to the top.

Trooping the Colour 130 feet   Very Severe (5.78)
Midway between Ending of the Day and Initiation is a 20-foot right-trending easy-angled buttress.

1 110 feet. 4c. Climb the buttress and step right at its top to a broken crack. Follow this to a ledge.
2 20 feet. Move left then ascend back up right to the top.

Initiation 95 feet   Hard Very Severe   (21.4.71)
Just left of the centre of the face are two large boulders. This route follows the slanting groove above.
1 55 feet. 5a. Start up the crack, peg, and make a difficult move on to the ledge above. Continue more easily in the same line to a ledge and belay.
2 40 feet. 4b. Negotiate grass and rock to finish up a steep crack in the wall above. Pleasant.

CENTRAL BUTTRESS
This buttress is made up of three separate faces – termed, for convenience, Right, Middle and Left.

RIGHT-HAND SECTION

Slanting Groove 110 feet   Very Severe   (22.9.71)
Near the middle of the face is a right-trending groove.
1 45 feet. Climb the groove, keeping right until it meets a crack. Belay.
2 40 feet. Ascend the crack to where the face steepens then traverse right to a ledge and belay.
3 25 feet. Step back left and follow the slanting crack to the top.

Hot Gossip 120 feet   Very Severe   (7.78)
Start as for Slanting Groove.
1 45 feet. As for Slanting Groove.
2 75 feet. 4b. Climb the crack and an obvious line above, moving right to a flake, then go up to a peg belay. Finish up the ivy-covered wall on the right.

Crack Rampant 125 feet   Very Severe   (6.71)
Left of Slanting groove is a ramp leading up to a crack-line.
1 45 feet. Climb the ramp and crack on the right to a ledge and good thread belays.
2 50 feet. Ascend the crack above to a recess then make a difficult move right to gain the ledge above. Traverse right then go up to the next ledge – peg belay.
3 30 feet. Ascend directly up the wall behind the stance.

MIDDLE SECTION
Round to the left of Crack Rampant and high up is a white wall with a grassy slope leading up to it. This wall provides three fine routes.

⋆ Zero 1   100 feet   E2   (13.7.80)
A fine steep route on solid rock. Start at a shallow cave at the foot of the right-hand side of the wall.
1   100 feet. 5c. Bridge up over the cave and trend leftwards to a ledge. Move up to a hollow-sounding flake then traverse right to a short crack and thread. Climb the crack then go leftwards to a good large hold. Go straight up the wall above, thread, to the break and enter the short corner above. Ascend this exiting rightwards to a ledge at the top.

⋆ The Enemy   120 feet   E2   (28.9.79)
A good route taking a line up the centre of the wall. It is strenuous but has better protection than Zero 1. Start on the right-hand side of a rib to the left of the centre of the face.
1   20 feet. 5a. Climb the rib on poor rock to a good ledge below and to the right of the open corner on the left-hand side of the face.
2   100 feet. 5c. Ascend rightwards, peg, to a steep crackline in the middle of the wall. Make a hard move up to a small thread and continue up the steep firm cracks above, finishing up an obvious groove above.

⋆ System 6   130 feet   E2   (13.7.80)
Start as for The Enemy.
1   20 feet. 5a. As for The Enemy.
2   100 feet. 6a. Enter the corner on the left and climb it strenuously, bolt and peg, to the top.

To the left of this wall is a vegetated buttress. A poor route **Grott Buttress**, Hard Very Difficult, (1971) meanders its way up here.

LEFT-HAND SECTION
The following routes start at the left-hand end of this buttress at the foot of an obvious crack. However over to the right of this is a clean, vertical groove with a peg at 20 feet. No details are known about this groove.

Goliath's Crack   110 feet feet   E1   (18.9.71/23.1.82)
Start at the foot of the crack. A pleasant climb.
1   60 feet. 5b. Climb the crack, or easier, the wall on its right to a niche. Go up over broken rock to the main crack and climb it to a ledge. Belay.
2   50 feet. 4c. Using the crack and wall surmount the huge block then step left and go straight up over easier rock to the top.

Looser   120 feet   Very Severe   (8.9.71)
As its name suggest the route is a scrappy line on poor rock. Start beneath a crack-line on the face just this side of the sky-line arête of this section.

1 60 feet. 4b. Climb the crack onto a ledge. Either go straight up or left and back right, then straight up to another ledge. Follow the wall and crack above to a belay.
2 60 feet. Climb the crack to the left of the block above then ascend over easy rock to the top.

Round the arête from Looser and before the next main gully is a short wall.

Ocean Girl 100 feet   Very Severe
Start at a thin crack about 50 feet right of Grand Finalé.
1 100 feet. 5a. Climb the thin crack and slab finishing up the obvious overhanging crack above.

Grand Finalé 100 feet   Hard Very Severe   (25.9.71/27.5.80)
In the middle of the wall a thin crack gives access to wider cracks on the left and right.
1 100 feet. 5a. Climb steeply up the initial crack to the horizontal break. Traverse right on poor rock and move up to the base of the wide crack. Follow this until a difficult move leads left, then go back right to the wide crack above. Climb this more easily to the top.

Perilous Journey 120 feet   Very Severe
To the left of Grand Finalé is an obvious large scoop.
1 60 feet. 5a. Climb up into the scoop, peg then traverse right out of it and climb the crack to a ledge.
2 60 feet. 4c. Follow the chimney above moving left at the top.

Gardener's World 100 feet   Very Severe   (22.9.71)
Start just up the gully left of Perilous Journey below a large vertical overlap.
1 100 feet. 4c. Climb the wall right of the overlap to a large ledge. Finish up the groove on the left.

OBSERVATORY BUTTRESS
The next buttress along is probably best reached by descending the wide gully as for St. Tudno's Buttress and turning left at the bottom to a path under the crag. The routes start left of the foot of the gully at the right-hand side of the buttress.

In the centre of the wall, beneath a small roof at 10 feet is an obvious split block. The first route starts 15 feet right of this.

★**Alien Forces** 130 feet   E3   (9.84)
1 80 feet. 5c. Climb out over the small roof and go up the crack in the arête for a few feet, peg. Move left and climb the pocketed wall above direct past a peg and thread to an obvious belay.
2 50 feet. 4c. Trend up right then go direct to a loose finish.

Elder Flower Wine   130 feet   E1   (31.10.77)
Start just left of the split block.
1   130 feet. 5c. Climb into the groove, peg, then step right and
go straight up the wall to an easier finish.

Hom Day Wall   70 feet   E1   (1.1.85)
Start between Elder Flower Wine and the groove of Phalanges.
1   70 feet. 5a. Climb the wall 15 feet right of the groove moving
into this at 50 feet. Trend rightwards to finish.

Phalanges   110 feet   Hard Very Severe   (27.5.75)
Start 20 feet left of Elder Flower Wine at a leaning block.
1   75 feet. 5a. Climb the crack in the wall then traverse right over
broken rocks to thin cracks. Ascend these to a ledge.
2   35 feet 4c. Go left then straight up to finish

Aphasic   100 feet   Hard Very Severe   (7.5.77)
Start below a groove, 15 feet left of Phalanges.
1   100 feet. 5b. Climb the crack on the right to the top of the
pinnacle then cross left into a small groove. Climb this, peg, and
the steep finishing slab.

★ Wind and Worrying   80 feet   E3   (6.9.85)
A sustained pitch taking the big open groove which overhangs
the path at the apex of the crag.
1   80 feet. 6a. Climb into the groove, peg, to reach a thread.
Move leftwards over solid rubble to a bolt. Climb the little groove
above, thread, to a good ledge. Pull back left and climb the crack
in the arête to the top — good ledge and belay.

★ Life's a Joke   80 feet   E4   (11.9.85)
Start at the groove in the wall 15 feet left of Wind and Worrying
at a thin crack.
1   80 feet. 6b. Climb the crack to the roof, peg and thread. Pull
rightwards around the roof via a series of painful and technical
moves to gain the break, thread. Move left then back right over
solid rubble to the next break and thread. Pull up the wall and
climb the groove above to finish. Scramble upwards to the top.

★★ When the Lion Feeds   80 feet   E5   (1.9.85)
Sustained and reasonably well-protected. Start 6 feet left of
Life's a Joke at a small corner.
1   80 feet. 6a. Climb the corner, move left under the first roof
and pull up to holds under the second roof, thread. Pull over the
roof rightwards, bolt, to a good break. Climb the wall above, bolt
and surmount the bulge to a ledge. Climb the wall and bulge
above, bolt, crux, moving left to finish. Abseil from two poor
pegs.

** Watcher in the Woods   80 feet   E4   (1.9.85)
Start 10 feet left of the last route at an overhanging groove.
1 80 feet. 6a. Climb the thin crack to gain the groove proper,
thread. Follow the groove, thread, until it is possible to move
out rightwards to a good ledge. Climb the small capped groove
above, peg, moving left then back right above the bulge to gain
the continuation of the main groove. Follow this with increasing
interest and two threads to the top. Abseil from two poor pegs.

Phalanx   100 feet   Hard Very Severe   (29.5.75)
Start left of Watcher in the Woods at a corner and vegetated
groove.
1 100 feet. 5a. Climb the corner and groove, left of the
vegetation where possible.

Josey Wales   100 feet   Hard Very Severe   (15.5.77)
Start at a short crack in the arête of the buttress.
1 70 feet. 5a. Climb the crack to a flake then traverse right along
the break until a move up gains a small stance.
2 30 feet. 4c. Finish straight up the cracks above the belay.
Pleasant.

** Opus Pistorum   85 feet   E4   (30.8.85)
A fine route. Start as for The Teal.
1 85 feet. 6b. Follow The Teal for 25 feet then traverse out right
on good flakes for 10 feet and move up to a small cave and
resting position (thread out left on a flake). Pull up past a bolt
and make fingery moves to gain the break and a peg. A final
mantel leads to the top. In-situ belays.

* The Teal   70 feet   E1   (6.62/27.5.80)
A good route on steep, solid rock. Start below the large
left-facing flake/crack overlooking the gully (obvious from the
road).
1 70 feet. 5c. Move up to the start of the crack and follow it past
several jammed chockstones to its top. Move left and go up
through the bulge then up the steep wall to a little ledge on the
left. Move back right and climb the thin crack, peg, to finish.
In-situ belays left and right.

Tips   80 feet   E3   (3.10.83)
Start 10 feet left of The Teal.
1 80 feet. 6a. An easy start leads to a hard bulge and thin crack,
peg and thread, which leads up right to a junction with The Teal
at its top crack. Climb this, peg, to finish. In-situ belays.

Silent Voices   80 feet   E3   (2.10.83)
Start 10 feet left of Tips.
1 80 feet. 6a. Climb a thin crack then the wall above passing a

peg and thread, to peg and bolt belays on a ledge at the top of the buttress.

Space Hunter   70 feet   E3   (3.12.83)
Start below an obvious series of grooves left of Silent Voices.
1   70 feet. 5c. Climb the wide groove to reach the break (runners on the right). Go left into another groove and up to a better hold in a hole. Ascend the steep crack to the top finishing past a good jug. Scramble off.

CREIGIAU COCHION   (R)

Creigiau Cochion is a long band of cliffs of between 50 and 100 feet in height lying on the north-west shoulder of Great Orme's Head above the Marine Drive road.
The cliffs may be split up into four distinct buttresses separated by grassy gullys or bays of easy broken rocks. The main features of these crags are the long horizontal erosion bands which tend to form deep uniform cave-like ledges and long bands of overhangs.

Facing the band of cliffs A Buttress is the farthest left, higher up the hill than the others. It is very broken with a steep overhanging nose around the middle of the crag. B Buttress, the most impressive section is clean and steep with good rock. The main feature here is the band of ivy on the left and the obvious yellow groove in the middle of the buttress. The principal features of C Buttress is the dense section of ivy and the huge overhang in the centre, whilst D Buttress, the farthest right, is not so high, broken but with some excellent problems.

Note: Due to the area's position above the road, climbing should not be developed any further here. The routes are included purely for the record.

A BUTTRESS

Little Buttress   60 feet   Very Difficult   (8.3.86)
Start at the extreme left-hand end of the crag at the toe of the obvious little buttress separated from the main crag by a wide gully.
1   30 feet. Climb the steep cracked wall to good jugs then an overhanging crack above to a ledge. Belay.
2   30 feet. The clean slabby wall leads to the top.

Footloose   70 feet   Very Severe   (15.12.85)
Start directly below a prominent overhanging nose dominating the highest section of the cliff.
1   30 feet. 4c. Climb steeply to a ledge at 15 feet. Continue direct up past a small tree to another ledge and peg belay.

2 40 feet. 4b. Move steeply up left over a loose band to gain a good crack. Ascend this to the overhang moving left up another crack to the top. Peg belay.

B BUTTRESS

Biceps   30 feet   E2   (6.57/1979)
Start at the extreme left-hand side of the crag below the overhang seamed with four cracks. This climb takes the second crack through the roof.
1 30 feet. 5c. Climb the wall to the roof then the crack-line to the top.

Triceps   30 feet   E3   (6.57/1979)
Start about five feet right of Biceps.
1 30 feet. 6a. Climb up and around the overhang using the fourth crack past an old peg.

Bigwig   90 feet   Hard Very Severe   (12.10.85)
Start 35 feet right of Triceps, just left of an ivy-covered overhang.
1 40 feet. 5b. Layback up a sharp finger-crack to gain the steep wall, peg. Continue up the steep groove, peg to a good ledge (called Hare Street) peg belay.
2 50 feet. 4a. Continue rightwards up broken walls to the top or carry on straight up the corner. Peg belay.

Beanstalk   100 feet   Very Severe   (9.10.85)
Start 15 feet right of Bigwig at an obvious break in the ivy.
1 50 feet. 5a. Climb the crackline between huge ivy trunks moving left at the top. Traverse delicately right across a smooth slab for a few feet then ascend directly up past a peg to a belay on the ledge.
2 50 feet. 4b. Traverse 15 feet right to gain a short corner. Climb this moving left to below a bulging overhang seamed with a wide crack. Ascend this to the top. Peg belay.

Boldstreet   85 feet   E1   (12.10.85)
Start 20 feet right of Beanstalk below the first overhang of Yellow Groove.
1 40 feet. 5a. Climb the black overhang, peg, to the ledge above. Crawl six feet left to below an overhanging groove. Peg belay.
2 45 feet. 5b. Lean out awkwardly to gain access to the groove above, peg. Climb this to a small ledge and continue up a crack past a small tree finishing left of a small overhang. Peg belay.

Yellow Groove   90 feet   Hard Very Severe   (6.53/10.85)
Start below the black overhang directly below the prominent
yellow coloured groove; As for Boldstreet.
1   40 feet. 5a. Climb the black overhang, peg, to the ledge
above. Traverse right to a peg belay below the groove.
2   50 feet. 4c. Climb the yellow wall, peg, to the top of the cliff.
Peg belay.

Christmas Crawl   95 feet   Hard Very Severe   (1 pt. aid)   (12.65)
Start 50 feet right of Yellow Groove below a roof with black
stains.
1   55 feet. 5a. Climb leftwards under the overhangs to gain a
deep overhung ledge. Crawl along this for 20 feet leftwards to a
peg and possible belay beneath an ochre-coloured slab. Climb
the slab, peg for aid, to a ledge and peg belay.
2   40 feet. 5a. Move right then back left to a steep crack, peg.
Ascend the crack to the top. Peg belay.

Moulfess   80 feet   Very Severe   (24.11.85)
Start 30 feet right of the last route below the obvious vegetated
break. The route seeks to avoid the vegetation.
1   80 feet. 5a. Climb the steep crack leading to another, steeper
one above. Ascend this to a good ledge then move left and
continue up the corner, peg, and finish steeply. Peg belay.

C BUTTRESS

Brutus   70 feet   A2   (9.59)
This climb follows the prominent large overhang right of the
huge bands of ivy.
1   70 feet. A2. Climb up to a ledge to the right of the ivy to a
peg and possible belay. Climb out over the first lip, pegs, to gain
an impressive crack under the outer lip. Follow this crack right
until a crack leads out around the roof, pegs.

TOLL GATE CRAGS, GREAT ORME   (R)
These crags are situated on the west side of Great Orme's Head
and lie directly above the Toll Gate Lodge.

Pigeon Buttress is the right-hand of the two cliffs and has a
distinctive dark cleft-like chimney which splits the face down the
middle (Pigeons Chimney).

Tower Buttress is easily identified by the huge towering nose
reminiscent of a Dolomite peak in miniature. This impressive
tower is bounded on its right by a steep gully (Dark Gully) and
on its left by broken vegetated cliffs containing a detached
pinnacle standing high above a vegetated rake.

The rocks on both of these crags tends to be very loose and friable and in consequence only the steeper, harder routes are of merit and Pigeons Chimney although an excellent climb is spoiled by the pigeons and their droppings.

Both crags are easily reached from the top and a decent via a grassy bay between the two buttresses. Access from below is now a little difficult due to erosion problems and the local council has at present fenced off the lower approach. **Note:** The crag should be avoided at certain times – see Pen Trwyn.

PIGEON BUTTRESS
This buttress stands above the south toll gate of the Marine Drive (as one leaves the Orme). Its main feature is the huge black chimney that splits the face.

Pigeon's Chimney   80 feet   Very Difficult   (6.50)
Walk to the back of the chimney.
1   80 feet. Bridge up the back of the chimney finishing up the dark rear or by climbing out onto one of the retaining walls.

Colin's Groove   80 feet   Very Severe   (8.52)
Start 30 feet right of the chimney at the foot of an obvious groove.
1   80 feet. 4c. Climb the corner on excellent rock, peg, and step out left at the top.

TOWER BUTTRESS
This buttress is dominated by the huge towering nose with a detached pinnacle on its seaward face.

Pinnacle Route   100 feet   Very Difficult   (6.51)
Start below and left of the nose at the foot of an obvious leftward slanting rake.
1   100 feet. Climb up the rake past a steep little corner to the foot of the detached pinnacle. Chimney up behind this until one can stand on top and step onto the wall behind and so to the top.

Pinnacle Direct   100 feet   Very Severe   (7.58)
Start much lower down than the last route, directly beneath the face of the pinnacle.
1   100 feet. Climb the broken wall, steepening at 30 feet, then go straight up the face of the pinnacle on small holds to its top. Loose.

The Kite   100 feet   Difficult   (1949)
Start 40 feet left of the last route, to the left of some ivy. A broken
traverse line leads to the right.
1   100 feet. Climb rightwards on a rising traverse over large
holds to a vegetated bay in the middle of the cliff. Finish straight
up.

Dark Wall, Severe, (8.52) takes the left wall of the big gully
behind the towering nose of Tower Buttress.

The Little Orme

The Little Orme is the huge, complex headland situated at the east end of the Llandudno promenade. The crag is made up of several buttresses and faces some of which are not visible from the promenade. It is unfortunate that many of the routes on The Little Orme grass over rather quickly and hold a fair amount of birds' nests. In particular Auk's Buttress, The West Buttress of Detritus and The Allotment. None of these crags is a particularly pleasant place to climb on but on the rest of The Little Orme there are many fine routes. The crags are described from right to left starting with Manor Crag and the three tiers of Craig y Don.

Upper Craig y Don offers probably the best introduction to climbing on this headland — with no access problems and compact, clean rock. The longest and most dramatic routes are to be found around the hidden side of the headland — in the exciting Great Zawn. Once again, the routes here do contain some grass but are far cleaner and much better than their appearance may foretell. This zawn is an incredible place in which to climb being a sheer, almost featureless slab of unique rock rising straight out of the sea, similar to but much larger than Wen Slab on Gogarth.

Indeed situations on this part of the cliff are most dramatic and on the more committing routes where abseil approaches are necessary it is recommended that the abseil rope be left in place as a means of escape in the event of failure, rain or whatever. In the case of the Great Zawn Amphitheatre the rope provides a back-up to the main belay. Please note that access is restricted on certain buttresses on The Little Orme. Also, don't be too put off by epic tales outlined in the historical section of this guidebook. They could happen on any crag! Couldn't they?

MANOR CRAG
This crag is situated above the main road over The Little Orme. It is a long strip of crag consisting of two tiers. All the routes are on the Upper Tier. This Upper Tier consists of three areas; The Far Left, Middle Left and Far Right areas. On the whole the routes are just short problem type climbs.

Approach by taking the tourist path onto The Little Orme (the crag is directly above and over to the left). Follow the path up then left along beneath the Upper Tier to its far end. The routes are described rightwards from here.

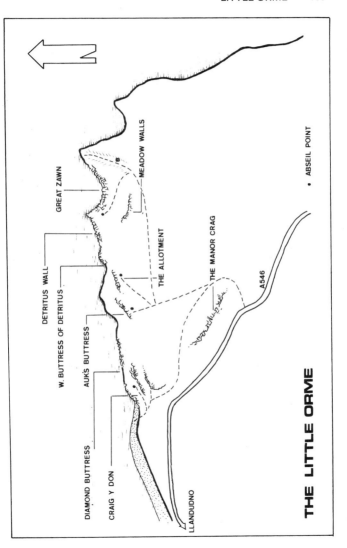

THE LITTLE ORME

FAR LEFT
Bounded on the left by a cleaned groove and on the right by a huge flake which forms a step up in the path. As is apparent all the routes here are very strenuous.

Walk of Life 70 feet   (4.86)
1 70 feet. 5c. This route girdles this section of the crag using the upper break – spectacular. Climb the groove at the left-hand side of the crag to reach the second break. Follow this rightwards until it is possible to step down to the ground again.

The Fat Man 5c   (1986)
Start just right of the corner at a small right trending ramp. Climb direct to a peg then rightwards to a thread. Climb the twin cracks above to a ledge. Climb the thin groove in the arête above to finish, peg.

Condition Red 6a   (1986)
Start as for The Fat Man. Climb along the ramp until it is possible to move up to the roof, thread. Climb the small corner above, peg, to a ledge. Climb the flake crack above, thread, to finish.

Field of Blood 6b   (1986)
Start at a slot and peg 10 feet right of the last route. Pass the peg and a bolt to the break. Climb the wall above, thread, to the second break. The headwall is climbed past three threads to horizontal bliss!

Anno Domini 6a   (1986)
Start beneath the suspended corner 5 feet right of Field of Blood. Use a slot to gain better holds leading to the break. Enter the corner above and climb it finishing up a crack in the headwall.

Shimdahir 5c   (4.86)
Climb the left side of the huge flake to its top. Step onto the wall above and climb direct to gain a large hole. Move left to finish.

MIDDLE LEFT
The next obvious feature is a slab capped by a roof and a corner on its right-hand side.

It's a Kind of Magic 5c   (3.86)
Climb the left edge of the slab to the roof. Pull leftwards around the roof and finish up a short groove.

Black Dog 5c   (3.86)
Climb the slab just right of the corner to the roof-thread. Go straight over this to finish.

Lost Lens Corner   4a   (4.86)
Climb the corner past assorted contact lenses to the top.

Trilogy   5c   (4.86)
Start 30 feet right of the last route and 10 feet left of a hole in
the ground. Climb the wall then the crack through the bulge
above moving right to finish.

Xexu   5b   (6.4.86)
Start at the hole in the ground. Climb the shallow groove to a
thread. Swing over the bulge above and surmount the next
bulge past a peg and finish direct.

The Bear's Tears   6a   (4.86)
Start just right of the hole. Climb the rib to the thread on Xexu.
Move right and up into a shallow groove and layback the crack
above then undercut rightwards, thread, and climb direct to
finish.

Fun in the Sun   5b   (4.86)
Start on a pillar right of the hole. Climb the wall above the pillar
to a deep crack. Climb this, thread, to its top then swing up left
to finish.

Thanks   6a   (5.86)
Start in a cave to the right of the pinnacle. Climb the crack in the
left side of the cave to a ledge. Climb the bulge above past a peg
to gain better finishing holds.

The next two routes climb the large detached nose split by two
cracks.

Sorrowing Wind   5b   (4.86)
Start beneath a hole at 10 feet at the right end of the nose. Gain
the hole then another above, thread. Climb leftwards to a second
thread beneath the nose proper. Gain the left-hand crack and
follow it to the summit. Bolt belay on the terrace behind.

Take It or Leave It   5b   (4.86)
Climb as for Sorrowing Wind but take the right-hand crack to
finish.

FAR RIGHT
The only route here is situated in the grossly undercut bay of
quarried rock, bounded on its left by an ivy covered wall.

Pale Rider   6a   (4.86)
Start beneath a large crack which splits the undercut wall
towards its right-hand side. Climb the crack and swing onto the

Craig Y Don

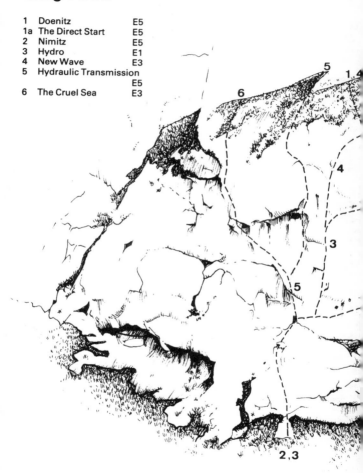

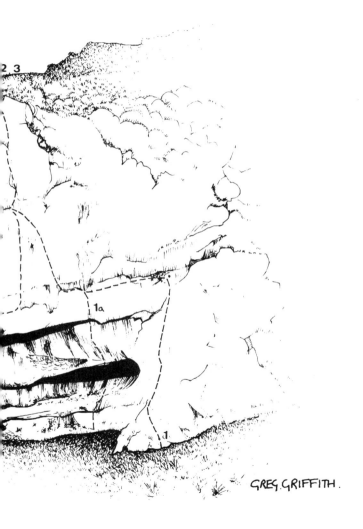

2 3

1a

d

GREG.GRIFFITH.

face above, peg. Move left and up to a bolt and pass this to a peg then the top.

CRAIG Y DON

The crag is split into three obvious tiers. The Middle and Upper Tiers can be approached at all states of the tide by walking along the boulder beach to a rocky spur and scrambling up this, over grass to the Middle Tier, the routes being at the left-hand side on this section. A further short scramble brings one to the Upper Tier – an attractive buttress with a large central overhang. Alternatively take the tourist path (see map) onto the Orme. The path goes up right to a small hollow at 150 yards then bear up left and walk over the field, through a steel fence then on to a path descending rightwards along to the foot of the Upper Tier.

For the Lower Tier, abseil approaches are described in the relevant sections.

UPPER TIER

Hydrofoil   130 feet   Hard Very Severe   (28.6.74)
Start just right of the arête, right of the huge cave.
1   60 feet. 5a. Ascend rightwards to a ledge and belay.
2   70 feet. 5a. Step down and move into a small corner then traverse up leftwards to finish.

** **Doenitz**   130 feet   E5   (2.6.82)
A brilliant route taking a diagonal line leftwards across the buttress. Start at the foot of the arête just left of Hydrofoil.
1   130 feet. 6b. Climb the rib to reach a peg on the obvious traverse line. Go left over a large block to a niche and resting place. Fingery moves lead straight up, bolt, to better holds then move left and up to a peg. Go straight up to another peg at the end of Hydro's traverse and reverse this leftwards to another peg. Enter the slim groove above and climb it finishing leftwards up the top wall to a peg belay.

Variation
** **The Direct Start**   100 feet   E5   (24.2.86)
1   100 feet. 6c. From the back wall of the cave climb the overhanging wall with a series of callisthenic contortions and utilizing a long pinch hold gain good holds and an excellent thread. Layback through the roof above to join Doenitz in the resting niche. Finish as for Doenitz.

** **Nimitz**   120 feet   E5   (3.7.85)
An excellent route with sustained and fingery climbing. Start just right of the arête, left of the cave.

1   120 feet. 6b. Go straight up the white wall and move right into the niche (as for Hydro). Drop down and go rightwards past three large pockets to a thread. A hard finger-traverse then leads right to a good foot ledge. A hard move up, bolt, is followed by small holds up the shallow overhanging groove. There are good holds near the top of this which allow a vertical slot to be reached. Move up past the peg on Doenitz to reach the end of Hydro's traverse and finish up Hydro's top cracks.

✶ **Dough'Nutz** 140 feet E5   (16.7.85)
A superb piece of climbing. Start as for Hydro.
1   140 feet. 6b. Climb straight up to the bulge then move right over this to the ledge that Nimitz traverses. From the thread climb the wall above to a peg. Move right onto a flake then hard moves up left lead to the peg on Hydro. Finish up the top groove and wall of Doenitz.

✶ **Frozen Moment** 100 feet E4   (7.7.85)
A good eliminate. Start as for Nimitz.
1   100 feet. 6a. Climb up to the niche then go up the right side of the bulge above to a square hold. Climb onto this to reach a horizontal slot. Rugosities allow sloping holds to be reached with a final hard step up to the Hydro traverse. Move right to the top groove on Doenitz, peg, and finish up this. Peg belay.

✶ **Hydro** 130 feet E1   (3.10.73)
A fine route on excellent rock. Start at the foot of the arête on the left-hand side of the cave. The original classic of the buttress.
1   30 feet. 4c. Climb leftwards across the wall then go up to a small ledge and peg belay.
2   100 feet. 5b. Descend onto the arête on the right and climb up into a niche. Climb the groove on the left to the obvious traverse line leading rightwards. Follow this, pegs, and step up onto a small ledge at its end. Follow the cracks above the ledge to finish. Peg belays on the left.

Variation
✶ **New Wave** 90 feet E3   (27.6.85)
A delightful direct finish. Start as for Hydro.
1   90 feet. 6a. Follow Hydro to the start of the long traverse, threads. Climb the right arête of the shallow depression above to reach a good pocket and thread. Move diagonally rightwards on pockets to finish up the last few feet of Doenitz.

✶ **Hydraulic Transmission** 90 feet E5   (26.6.85)
Fierce climbing on perfect rock. Start as for Hydro.
1   90 feet. 6b. Follow Hydro to the belay then move into the cave above, thread. Go right and up, bolt, then to another thread in a break. Layback the crack above, fixed wire, to reach a good

vertical slot, bolt out right. Hard moves back left are followed by difficult pulls in a crozzly crack to reach better holds and a thread on the left. Finish easily.

★ **The Cruel Sea**   100 feet   E3   (28.6.85)
A quality route. Start as for Hydro.
1   100 feet. 6a. Follow Hydro to the belay. Step left then go up to a diagonal break. Move left to a thread in the bulge above. Climb the bulging wall just right of this passing two more threads to a grassy bay and thread out left. Exit left moving back right to belay at a small rib.

Road to Nowhere   60 feet   E4   (1985)
A curious route.
1   60 feet. 6b. Follow Nimitz to the foot ledge and continue traversing to reach the niche on Doenitz (clipping any bolts within reach). Reverse the initial traverse of Doenitz then go over the block and lower off the peg at its end. The leader then swaps ends with the belayer who reverses the route (the safest way to follow!).

Changeling   120 feet   Very Severe   (3.10.73)
Start 15 feet left of the start of Hydro.
1   120 feet. 4c. Climb the rib for 20 feet then cross to a ledge on the left. Move left and up to another ledge then straight up passing left of an overhang to finish at a grassy ledge.

Variation
Changeling Direct   120 feet   Hard Very Severe   (14.3.74)
1a   120 feet. 5a. Climb the rib as for Changeling then go up leftwards to a ledge below a steep wall. Climb the wall exiting up the crack just right of the overhang to finish.

Tradesman's Entrance, 120 feet, Very Severe, 4c is a poor route up the buttress 90 yards left of Changeling.

Scoop Route   140 feet   Very Severe   (22.9.73)
A poor route. Start about 100 yards left of Changeling at an obvious slab.
1   90 feet. 4b. Ascend the slab to its top then move onto a ledge on the left. Traverse left under a bulge to a ledge on the far side of a small groove.
2   50 feet. 4a. Go up the wall for a few feet then trend up leftwards to the top.

MIDDLE TIER
Three very worthwhile routes on the slab towards the left end of the tier. Follow the path below this tier until 15 feet after a step down a fang of rock is reached. Nut belay. The routes are described from right to left as one approaches under the tier.

Just Along for the Ride   60 feet   E2   (20.4.85)
The hardest of the trilogy. Start from the left end of the cave
system just before the step down to Crab Slab.
1 60 feet. 5c. Pull directly out of the left end of the cave and
climb direct just left of vegetation to a left-facing flake. Step left
then go direct to a bucket via small pockets. Move left to a peg
belay. Lower off.

The Get Along Gang   65 feet   E1   (20.4.85)
A very good route taking the central line of the slab. Start as for
Just Along for the Ride.
1 65 feet. 5b. Traverse left along some grass out of the left end
of the cave to a thread in the centre of the slab. Pull around the
bulge, thread, then climb direct on good slots and jugs passing
another thread to the peg belay shared with its neighbouring
routes. Lower off.

Crab Slab   70 feet   E2   (20.4.85)
A delightful route up the left edge of the slab. Good clean rock.
Start at the fang of rock below a faint pillar leading onto the main
upper slab.
1 70 feet. 5c. Pull over the bulge and go up via the faint pillar,
threads, then move diagonally rightwards across the slab past
a further two threads to the peg belay. Lower off.

LOWER TIER
At low spring tides the routes can be approached by a walk along
under the crag. However, at other tides the means of access is
by abseil and there are two fixed points above the crag. For the
routes on the Right Side, approaching from below Hydro go
down to the right (facing out) and continue beneath the right
side of the Middle Tier (looking in) to about 20 feet beyond a
rock step. Drop down there onto grass and move back right
along ledges beneath a small undercut wall to twin bolts. From
there abseil 150 feet going slightly rightwards (facing in) to a
small ledge just above the high water mark. Thread belay. The
first route takes the striking slanting crack (obvious from the
beach).

RIGHT SIDE

Exocet   145 feet   E3   (7.7.85)
1 145 feet. 5c. From the thread move left past a deep pocket,
thread, and onto the arête. A hard move around this leads to the
crack just below a triangular pocket (runner). Follow the crack
which gets progressively easier to a bulge which leads to ledges
and shallow caves. From the right-hand side of the cave step out
and make a few hard moves up the continuation crack to easy
ground. Go up the grassy depression above to twin bolt belays.

E.C.M.   145 feet   Hard Very Severe   (10.7.85)
Basically a variation on Exocet but worthwhile in its own right.
Start as for Exocet.
1   145 feet. 5b. Climb the wall above the ledge to the roof. Move
left along the exposed traverse line to reach Exocet just below
the bulge. Continue as for that route.

The chimney over to the right has been climbed. **Game for a
Laugh**, Hard Severe, (1985) is the first chimney when approaching from the beach.

LEFT SIDE
Follow the path along underneath the Middle Tier as for Crab
Slab etc. At the end drop down to a flat rock ledge. From a bolt
and wires abseil 140 feet down to a small ledge at the base of a
rightward trending crack-line crossing the concave buttress (this
is the first pitch of Moon Shadow).

Peace Train   250 feet   E1   (24.5.74/1.4.81)
Start at the foot of the abseil.
1   70 feet. 5a. Follow Moon Shadow until the crack steepens
then make a descending traverse rightwards across the slab until
it is possible to move down onto a long ledge. Belay at the
right-hand end of this.
2   120 feet. 5b. Climb the corner crack above onto the slab, then
traverse right, past a scoop to the foot of a slim groove. Climb
this with good holds on the left wall to its top then step left to
a large perched block. Traverse left to a ledge and peg belay.
3   60 feet. 4c. Ascend the slab above the belay and go over
steep grass to belay on the approach path.

Variation
The Original Start   E1   (1974)
1a   5b. At low tide the slim groove can be gained directly from
the beach by climbing a thin crack 150 feet from the end rocks.

Shazam   250 feet   E3   (17.5.68/30.4.81)
A technically interesting route with one very hard section. Start
at the foot of the abseil.
1   70 feet. 5a. As for Peace Train.
2   120 feet. 6a. Step off the ledge about 20 feet left of the corner
crack on the right and climb the wall to a large scoop. Ascend
the arête on the right, peg, to another scoop and peg. Pull over
the roof rightwards, peg, onto a slab, peg, then ascend the wall
leftwards to a ledge. Climb the wall above to a small corner. Peg
belay.
3   60 feet. Go up over steep grass rightwards to finish on the
path.

★ Moon Shadow   210 feet   E4   (9.4.74)
A steep route with technical climbing. Start at the foot of the abseil.
1   100 feet. 5a. Climb the right-slanting crack in the slab. Move right onto a ledge then go up into a shallow cave. Peg belay.
2   110 feet. 6a. Move round the arête on the right into a shallow corner. Ascend this, peg, into a scoop. Climb leftwards into another scoop, then go diagonally rightwards to the break. Traverse left along this onto a ledge then up leftwards over poor rock to the abseil point.

★★ Moonshine   180 feet   E5   (12.10.86)
An excellent route with two fine and differing pitches. Start 40 feet right of Moon Shadow and directly below the cave on that route.
1   80 feet. 5c. Climb the thin crack moving right into another crack. Directly up from here over ledges leading to the cave. Peg belay.
2   100 feet. 6b. Exit from the cave via the groove to a roof. Surmount this, peg, to a good ledge. Move 5 feet right and climb the headwall to an exposed finish.

Moon Madness   145 feet   E5   (30.11.86)
A serious and direct line. Start at the foot of Moon Shadow.
1   145 feet. 5c. Ascend straight up the wall with hard moves to the overlap, peg. Pull through this, peg, then go up leftwards to the stance on Midnight Blues, continuing as for that route.

★★ Midnight Blues   210 feet   E3   (18.4.74/10.85)
An exposed and exciting route up the obvious curving corners left of Moon Shadow. Protection is good. Start at the foot of the abseil.
1   60 feet. 4c. Follow Moon Shadow for 20 feet then traverse left across the slab to a small ledge and belay.
2   80 feet. 6a. Move up left to the corner and climb this to the large roof and a peg. Cross the roof rightwards, peg, and pull round into a long flake crack. Follow the flake to an old peg at its top then step back down and traverse right, crux, to a small stance and peg belay.
3   40 feet. 5c. Climb the crack above, peg, steep at its top to a ledge and belay.
4   30 feet. 4c. Go rightwards over poor rock to the abseil ledge.

The Diamond   535 feet   XS/A2   (9.71)   (R)
A long intimidating route with fine positions. Start as for Moon Shadow at the foot of the abseil.
1   60 feet. 4c. As for Midnight Blues.
2   40 feet. 5a. Move left into the corner. Climb up onto ledges on the arête on the left and traverse left to belay beneath a seeping crack.

Lower Craig y Don — Lower Tier

Greg. Griffith.

3   140 feet. A2. The route is heading for a small slab in the middle of the huge overhanging wall on the left. Climb the seeping wall on the left to a narrow slab and crack. Follow this for 15 feet and move onto the wall on the left. Using skyhooks follow the blind crack out on to the wall until a peg can be placed higher up. From this ascend left on pegs, bolts and skyhooks to the foot of the slab. Make a hard move onto the slab and free-climb pleasantly to its top. Bolt and peg belay.
4   145 feet. Climb up into the corner on the right, make an awkward move out of the corner and ascend leftwards to a wide crack. Climb this, then go rightwards over grassy rock to a ledge.
5   150 feet. Traverse left for 20 feet then go up onto another ledge. Climb the bottomless groove on the right (some loose rock) to finish on top of the crag.

THE DIAMOND BUTTRESS   (R)

This is the gigantic, black overhanging buttress to the left of the Lower Tier of Craig y Don. It is bounded on its right by a huge ramp – the line of Gemstone. Approach as for the Lower Tier but descend from the foot of the abseil to the beach and walk leftwards. Just right of Gemstone is a long wet and not very inspiring climb.

Rhiwledyn   440 feet   Very Severe   (17.5.68)
Start at the foot of the ramp as for Gemstone.
1   70 feet. 4c. Climb up to the start of the ramp, then move right and round to a peg belay down on the right.
2   90 feet. 4c. Ascend the wall for 15 feet then go right into a seeping crack. Follow this with disgust to a ledge.
3   100 feet. 4c. On the left is a groove. Climb this up to a bulge and step left. Climb the slanting groove above to a stance and peg belay.
4   120 feet. 4c. Climb the wall behind the stance then traverse left into a gully. Follow the arête on the left to a cave.
5   60 feet. 4c. Enter the chimney above and climb this until a traverse left just short of the top leads to a grassy bay.

★ **Gemstone**   500 feet   E2   (23.10.73)
A long delicate route in an exciting situation. Start at the foot of the ramp. Often damp.
1   145 feet. 5c. Gain the slab and move up to meet the wall. Follow the crack to a loose block. Carry on past a large flake until the ramp narrows and step right onto a small ledge.
2   145 feet. 5b. Move left again onto the ramp and using the wall for handholds move up to a shattered pillar. Continue in the same line to a flat-topped flake and go up the crack on the right into a chimney.
3   60 feet. 4c. Take the short wall on the left (loose) and on to a ledge on the left.

4 150 feet. 5a. Traverse left for 20 feet then go up to another ledge. Climb the bottomless groove on the right (some loose rock) to finish on top of the crag.

★★ Wall of the Evening Light 500 feet Hard Very Severe/A2
(2.4.72)

A magnificent outing mainly on firm rock taking a direct line up the middle of The Diamond Buttress. One of the longest aid routes in Britain. At present most of the aid pegs are in place so about eight hours should be sufficient, although escape is virtually impossible except by abseil. About 80 karabiners and a good selection of pegs and nuts are required. Skyhooks should also be carried. Start at the foot of the huge ramp of Gemstone.
1 80 feet. A2. Go up into the cave and follow a line of pockets over the roof to the first of four bolts. Follow these then move right to a hanging belay.
2 130 feet. A2. Go straight up then diagonally rightwards for about 50 feet. Move up and follow the thin crack leftwards to a ledge and bolt belays.
3 100 feet. A2/VS. Ascend to the top of the slab then go up again, traversing left on poor rock to the arête. Ascend rightwards to a shallow groove then left onto a small slab. Peg belays in the middle of the slab.
4 90 feet. HVS. Climb up the slab to the steep wall and ascend it, peg, and the groove above. At the top move left onto a ledge.
5 100 feet. VS. Behind the ledge are two large grooves. Take the right-hand one which is broken twice but leads to the top. Belay to the left of the prow at the top. Way off – go right and up ledges to the top.

Beyond the Grave 410 feet Very Severe/A2 (12.76)

A companion aid route to Wall of the Evening Light up the left-hand side of the buttress. Start below some large caves high up on the face, to the left of Wall of the Evening Light.
1 100 feet. A2. Go up the short wall to a roughcast cluster below a large roof. Move over this trending leftwards to a blunt flake crossing the wall. Go up right then up again to a point 10 feet below the first cave. Move left then straight up to the left-hand side of the cave and a large stance.
2 70 feet. A2. Move out left then go up to the second cave. Follow a diagonal crack through the 30-foot roof above to a short wall and an earthy exit onto slabs and belay.
3 140 feet. VS. Climb the earthy slabs to a wall at 70 feet, peg. Ascend the wall, then more grassy slabs lead to a cave and belay.
4 100 feet. VS. Go up for 10 feet then traverse left off the wall. Climb up then traverse back right to a grassy bank above the overhangs. Belay. Traverse right to escape as for Wall of the Evening Light.

RUBBLE BUTTRESS (R)
This route is included purely for historical interest.

The Easy Way Off 460 feet Hard Very Severe   (20.4.68)
A totally unique climb involving three grass fields.
1 200 feet. The First Grass Field. Climb the left-hand side of the
buttress to reach the repulsive plateau on top, known as The
Seagull's Fish and Chip Shop.
2 40 feet. Over on the very right is a pinnacle. Climb this by the
layback crack on its left side.
3 70 feet. The Second Grass Field. Climb straight up then left
on rock to a grass overhang. Surmount this and move right to
a stance in a grass cave.
4 150 feet. The Third Grass Field. Move right on tension, with
direct aid from the cabbages and then finish up the grass to a
belay.

AUK'S BUTTRESS (R)
Probably the worst and least climbed on crag on The Ormes.
Much vegetation and birds' nests coupled with an appalling
surface layer of rock are enough to put all but a very few people
off its routes. Approximately 270 feet high the routes are said to
stick to solid rock as much as possible though this is a bone of
contention. For those interested, approach by taking the tourist
path onto The Orme (see map) and go right to the small hollow
at 150 yards. Go straight on here, through a small steel fence
and out onto the wide grassy col beyond then bear leftwards
around the bluff to a path running along the top of the crag.
Abseil from the region of a boulder below the path to a ledge
(The Rockery) then again from here (or join two ropes – better)
to land on the stinking Rubble Buttress – this area is known as
'The Seagull's Fish and Chip Shop'. The routes are described
from right to left. Complete grades are not available.

Thule 280 feet Hard Very Severe   (20.4.69)
Start to the right of the foot of the abseil at the prominent
buttress capped by an overhang.
1 140 feet. Climb the groove on the left for 20 feet then cross
to the roof on the right. Follow the crack then move on to the
wall. Make some hard moves up to gain holds leading leftwards
to a big ledge.
2 140 feet. Go up the wall behind the stance to a crack and
follow this over the roof. Follow the break rightwards then steep
grass leads to a belay 30 feet farther on.

Vertex 260 feet Hard Very Severe   (3.71)
Start at a large pinnacle in the centre of Rubble Buttress.
1 140 feet. On the right of the pinnacle is a left-leading ramp.
Follow this then go straight up and across the short wall to a

steep crack. Ascend the crack and loose groove above to a ledge and belay, pegs required.
2   120 feet. Traverse left to a shattered pillar. Go up the wall on the left then left again into a crack. Move back right to the overhang. Go right again, around a fang of rock, and up the other side. Traverse right then go up to the top.

Auk's Route   350 feet   E1   (2 pts. aid)   (2.4.71)
Supposedly a worthwhile route. Start near some large blocks round to the left of Vertex.
1   140 feet. Climb up onto the blocks then traverse the ledge leftwards to a small slab. Climb this then get into a niche on the left wall. Ascend the loose crack, sling for aid, to a peg. Use this to gain the roof on the left. Climb this to a traversing line leftwards and belay beneath a groove.
2   120 feet. Climb the groove and step left to the foot of an imposing wall. Go up this rightwards to a niche, peg. Surmount the overhang and follow the crack above into a groove. Climb rightwards to a ledge.
3   90 feet. From the shattered pinnacle in the middle of the ledge traverse left for 15 feet and climb a groove. Move left into a niche then go left again and straight up passing a shallow groove to a mantelshelf. Climb the left-slanting groove to finish.

THE WEST BUTTRESS OF DETRITUS   (R)
As seldom visited a part of the cliff as Auk's Buttress for the same reasons. Again for those brave enough to climb here approach by a further walk along the beach from the foot of The Diamond Buttress, around the headland of Rubble Buttress to reach this vast face. Note that the boulder beach is submerged at high tide. All the routes finish in The Allotment so it is neccessary to do one of the routes to get out or to return to the beach by a very long abseil (not recommended). As with Auk's Buttress complete pitch grades are unfortunately unavailable as the author has repeatedly failed to find any information, other than original first ascent manuscripts to these climbs.

The Sickle   320 feet   Hard Very Severe   (19.4.69)
Start beneath the left-hand side of the obvious pinnacle.
1   110 feet. Climb up over loose rock to the foot of the crack on the left and belay.
2   80 feet. Take the right-slanting crack then the vertical crack above to belay on top of the pedestal.
3   130 feet. Climb rightwards to a scoop and go up over the overhang above onto the wall. Trend rightwards over poor rock and exit left onto the large terrace of The Allotment.

Variation
Right-Hand Sickle   320 feet   Hard Very Severe   (5.68)
A poor route mainly on loose rock, although supposedly the
better way to do The Sickle.
1   100 feet. Go up over loose rock to belay on the right-hand
side of the pedestal.
2   60 feet. Climb the chimney crack above to the belay ledge of
Sickle. Follow this to The Allotment.

Sea Crack   200 feet   Very Severe   (10.4.69)
Start 50 feet left of The Sickle.
1   120 feet. 4c. Climb the left-slanting crack and enter the
vertical crack above. Ascend this then step onto the arête at the
top. Peg belays.
2   80 feet. 4c. Traverse 10 feet left then go up over ledges to the
top. Tree belay well back.

The Needle's Eye   230 feet   Very Severe   (29.6.74)
Start 50 feet farther left from Sea Crack.
1   90 feet. Gain the right-hand side of the huge pinnacle and
climb up to its top. Go left then climb up to a cave.
2   40 feet. Traverse right around the corner then go up to grass
ledges. Belay.
3   100 feet. Climb the wall then finish up the crack on the right.

Wall of Caves   200 feet   Very Severe   (4.9.73)
Start below a line of caves, left of Sea Crack.
1   30 feet. Ascend straight up to a large ledge.
2   120 feet. On the left is a ramp. Follow this and the steep wall
above up to some large blocks. Move left then go diagonally
rightwards into a cave.
3   50 feet. Climb the corner crack above to the top and poor
belays.

THE ALLOTMENT   (R)
Not as horrific a proposition as climbing on Auk's or the West
Buttress of Detritus but nevertheless not much more popular.
Approach as for Auk's Buttress to the wide grassy col, then
instead of going left around the bluff go down rightwards to a
grassy gully with a small cave at its top. Abseil 50 feet from the
rock ledge at the foot of this gully into the huge vegetated area
below. This is The Allotment and the routes start over to the
right (facing in) of a spectacular and futuristic overhanging wall.
Complete grades are again unfortunately not available.

Rapunzel   240 feet   E1   (22.2.71)
At the far right-hand end of The Allotment is a small rib. Start
just right of this.
1   70 feet. 5a. Climb the short corner above then traverse right
and go up the short slab above to a ledge.

2   150 feet. 5b. Move right and climb up to the right-hand side of the long overlap. Surmount this on good holds to a ledge. Climb the groove above moving left then back right to a niche at its top. Climb the groove on the left to a narrow corner and belay.
3   20 feet. 4c. Climb the corner above. Belay far back on the right.

Easy Rider   190 feet   Very Severe   (17.5.72)
Start just left of Rapunzel.
1   70 feet. Climb the rib then traverse left. Climb up rightwards to a peg belay on a small ledge.
2   100 feet. Move round to the left and climb diagonally rightwards to big ledges, then back left to a ledge. Belay.
3   20 feet. Climb the crack and easy rock to the top.

Gillies Groove   140 feet   Hard Very Severe   (4.69)
Start just left again from Easy Rider near some large embedded blocks.
1   100 feet. Climb the shattered pillar then move left to good holds. Go straight up then left to the base of a crack.
2   40 feet. 5a. Climb the crack to the top.

Kitties Groove   125 feet   Hard Very Severe   (6.4.69)
Start over left of Gillies Groove at the foot of a short steep wall.
1   90 feet. Make a hard move up to a good hold at 10 feet. Go up for 15 feet then leftwards on to the slab and ascend this to another slab. Traverse left past some blocks and move up to the foot of the large open groove above.
2   35 feet. Climb the groove to the top.

The abseil wall has been climbed left to right from its base. **The Garden Wall**, Hard Very Severe, 5a and:

Red Herring   45 feet   E4   (6.2.87)
1   40 feet. 6a. Climb the left-hand side of this wall past three threads.

The Bender   135 feet   E3   (4.10.69/1982)
At the far left-hand end of The Allotment is a long roof. Start just left of the arête on the left of the roof.
1   100 feet. 5c. Climb the face of the arête, peg, and move up into the groove on the right. Follow this and the crack above to the roof. Traverse right for 30 feet under the roof to a small niche. Belay.
2   35 feet. 6a. Move up and right, peg, then step onto a ledge on the right. Ascend to a stance. A long roped scramble leads up over easy rocks to the top.

Loose Exit   120 feet   Very Severe
This is an old 'escape route' from The Allotment.
1   120 feet. 4c. From the foot of The Bender go diagonally out leftwards over poor rock and follow the easiest line to the top.

DETRITUS WALL AREA   (R)
The Detritus Wall – the largest on all of The Ormes – is the end wall visible from the promenade and contains just a few routes. Follow the tourist path as for Auk's Buttress and The Allotment to the wide grassy Col then go rightwards into a large grassy field with an old lookout post at its far end. This lookout post can also, and more easily, be reached by approaching through the housing estate on the Rhos on Sea side of The Little Orme and following the track, through some old quarry workings, up onto the top to the lookout. Just left (looking out) of this lookout is a path running down rightwards, then back left into a large sloping field containing a scree slope halfway down. This is The Meadow and has several points of access starting from it. For the Detritus Wall, walk down left to the top of a rock peninsula then traverse left to a convenient ledge. A 110-foot abseil then leads to a small ledge just above the high water mark. The three routes on this wall all start from this point. Alternatively, climb or abseil down the peninsula to a ledge at its foot. From there a single Hard Very Severe traverse leads rightwards, around to a cave at the foot of the obvious corner of Atlanta. This traverse can only be completed at low tide but is worthwhile when possible.

Atlanta   110 feet   E1   (29.6.74)
Start either from the foot of the abseil or the cave at the end of the traverse. In the latter case the crack is reached direct.
1   110 feet. 5b. Traverse left into the corner and ascend it to the top moving rightwards to belay at the abseil point. The crack only becomes dry after a long period of good weather.

Uranus   145 feet   E3   (29.6.74)
Thin sustained climbing up the wall right of Atlanta with spaced protection. Start as for Atlanta at the abseil ledge.
1   145 feet. 6a. Reach the crack of Atlanta and climb it for 15 feet. Traverse right until a move up can be made onto another vague traverse line, peg. Go right again and make a hard move up on small pockets then continue traversing to a flake and resting place. Ascend straight up to a peg then step left and go straight up the wall to finish.

∗∗ Detritus   550 feet   E5   (4 pts. aid)   (3.70/15.10.85)
This magnificent old aid route now goes almost free with two difficult and quite different crux pitches. Start at the foot of the abseil.

1 50 feet. 5a. Climb up for about 10 feet then move right past an alcove to the first of a mass of fixed gear. Hanging stance.
2 150 feet. 6b. Follow the obvious traverse line for 25 feet to a good pocket and continue with difficulty to a bolt just before some hanging tat. Rest. Continue for another 25 feet to another rest just past a vertical crack. Very sustained and bold climbing then leads down rightwards to a good flake (stance when aided). Climb this then move up left into a steep groove. Climb this to a spike at its top. Belay.
3 150 feet. 5b. Climb leftwards over poor rock into an obvious groove-line. This leads to an exit rightwards into a large cave and bolt belays.
4 60 feet. 6a. Climb the corner on the left to the bulge and use two pegs for aid to move round this, then traverse strenuously right along the overlap to the vertical crack going through the roof. Pull over here with difficulty to an exposed stance on the left.
5 90 feet. 5a. Climb the groove, peg, then grassy rock leads to a huge cave.
6 50 feet. Go right from the cave and scramble up to the top.

** **Against All Odds**   550 feet   E3   (5.9.86)
A totally committing route taking a massive sweeping line across the Detritus Wall. A tremendous expedition of exceptional character in very impressive surroundings. Start from the Detritus abseil point.
1 90 feet. 5a. Move down to a traverse line below the stance. Follow this rightwards for 70 feet to reach a cluster of pegs. Belay (Shared stance with Detritus).
2 50 feet. 5b. Descend 5 feet and make a committing move across the wall to re-join the traverse line, pegs. Follow this and move round the arête, peg, to gain the next stance. Bolt and thread.
3 40 feet. 5c. Cross the wall on the right to a hidden peg. Climb rightwards to easier ground and traverse the ledge to a thread low down, belay.
4 130 feet. 4c. Climb across the rib on the right to gain the traverse once more, peg. Follow this until a move around the arête, bolt, brings easier ground into sight. Traverse right to a cave and fixed belay.
5 200 feet. Easy scrambling leads rightwards into The Allotment.
6 30 feet. 5a. Escape up The Garden Wall.

The Meadow Walls

At the head of The Meadow is an obvious cave bounded on its right-hand side by a broad pocketed wall. The cave itself provides a gynaecologically interesting experience (!) while the meadow walls give three worthwhile routes.

★★ **The Hole of Creation** 60 feet E3   (19.7.83)
1 60 feet. 6a. Bridge up the back of the cave and bypass a weird bulge to good holds. Bridge up once more to a huge thread then finish direct.

Karma 60 feet E4   (1973)
A line up the grey rock at the left-hand side of the wall.
1 60 feet. 6a. Gain threads at 15 feet and climb straight up above them for a further 15 feet. Step left then go up to the overlap. Pull rightwards over this to finish.

★★ **Slime Crime** 75 feet E5   (4.85)
A difficult route taking the centre of the wall.
1 75 feet. 6b. Gain the first bolt at 15 feet then with difficulty move up rightwards passing the second bolt to reach some flakes on the right. Go straight up and over the bulge strenuously finishing rightwards.

Back to the Egg 80 feet E4   (9.83)
Start to the right at a slab.
1 80 feet. 6b. The easy slab leads to a steep section at 30 feet below a small niche, bolt. Climb above the niche to a second bolt then a hard move leads to a resting position. Finish rightwards. Peg belay (quite difficult to find). There is also a bolt belay 15 feet farther back to the right.

GREAT ZAWN – THE AMPHITHEATRE
The Great Zawn gives the most dramatic situations on the whole of The Ormes. Sound rock, comparatively easy access and no ban on its main area. For routes in this area — the right-hand side of the zawn — descend from The Meadow (see Detritus Wall Area) to the rock peninsula and descend this to the ledge at the bottom. From there a 300-foot traverse, described below, leads to a non-tidal rock bay (on the right of the huge slab) known as The Amphitheatre. Alternatively, and best, abseil from a ledge at the top of Mur yr Ogof: Follow the path to The Meadow then traverse back right, facing out, to the abseil point which is at the right-hand end of the long overlap at the top of the zawn. There is a large bolt and also thread and nut placements. A 45 metre rope is sufficient to reach The Amphitheatre from this point.

Mephistopheles   520 feet   Hard Very Severe   (21.4.73)
A high girdle crossing the top of the zawn linking all the existing routes. Only the last pitch is new however. Start at The Amphitheatre abseil point. Bolt belay.
1   120 feet. 5a. Climb leftwards to the overlap and traverse this to the belay of Quietus.
2   150 feet. 5a. Ascend to the overlap and traverse left for about 120 feet to join The Big Flake (this is Tartarean's Left Traverse). Carry on in the same line to a grassy belay on Genesis.
3   40 feet. 4c. Climb up to another overlap (as for Genesis).
4   60 feet. 4c. Reverse the traverse of Rabble Rouser to belay around the arête on the left.
5   150 feet. 5a. Move up to the roof on the left and follow this until the crack peters out. Step down onto a ledge on the left and follow the grassy arête to belay higher up.

The Entry Traverse   300 feet   Very Severe   (24.4.70)
1   150 feet. 4c. From the foot of the rock peninsula traverse left across the slabs to a damp hollow. Cross to the arête on the left and belay a few feet lower down this.
2   150 feet. 4c. Cross the slab on the left to a wide recess. Traverse left again and move up onto a large rock platform sloping down left.

The first routes start at the obvious chimney/cave at the left-hand end of this platform.

★★ **Ride Across the River**   100 feet   E2   (17.8.86)
Takes a line to the right of Hot Space and at its grade provides a good introduction to this zawn. Start 10 feet right of Hot Space.
1   100 feet. 5b. Climb the wall trending rightwards to a ledge at 30 feet. Climb straight up past a second ledge continuing in the same line to the top. Bolt belay. Scramble off rightwards.

Hot Space   140 feet   E3   (10.7.83)
Takes the pocketed wall right of the chimney/cave. Start below a large slot 15 feet right of the chimney.
1   140 feet. 6a. Go up to the slot then follow pockets and finger-slots rightwards until they peter out. Make a series of fingery moves first up right then back left into a groove. Climb this to join Mur-yr-Ogof in its upper crack. Finish up this.

★★ **Mur yr Ogof**   140 feet   E3   (27.7.80)
An excellent route on steep firm rock. Start below the cave/chimney.
1   140 feet. 6a. Climb up into the cave then go up to the roof above. Pull out onto the wall on the right and ascend steeply to the foot of a corner. Ascend the corner to a good ledge and belay on the right at the top.

Great Zawn

Greg Griffith.

Quoin   150 feet   E1   (4.71)
Start as for Mur yr Ogof.
1   150 feet. 5b. Climb up to the cave then ascend leftwards to a
flake then back up right into a crack. Climb the crack until it ends
at about 100 feet. Climb rightwards to end on the abseil ledge.

Tartarean   270 feet   Hard Very Severe   (24.4.70)
Start as for Quoin and Mur yr Ogof.
1   150 feet. 5a. Climb to the top of the flake on Quoin. Step up
then trend up leftwards. Go straight up to belay below the long
overlap.
2   120 feet. 5a. Traverse up to the right-hand end of the overlap.
Carry on in the same line and pull over at its weakest point.
Straight up to finish on the path. Very grassy.

Variation
Tartarean's Left Traverse   150 feet   Hard Very Severe (24.7.70)
A long unusual traverse across the overlap at the top of the
zawn, containing much grass.
2a   150 feet. 5a. Climb up to the roof and make a long traverse
left for 120 feet to join The Big Flake. Pull over the overlap and
belay in the crack on the right. Or from half-way along the
traverse, pull over the overlap and follow the smaller overlap
above (as for Quietus) to finish at the same point (better and
cleaner).

★ **Father John**   300 feet   E3   (17.7.80)
A bold and delicate line up the slab left of Quoin. Start at The
Amphitheatre belay.
1   150 feet. 5c. Move left and go up to gain a horizontal crack
directly beneath a small overlap at 50 feet. Climb direct to the
overlap, 2 pegs, then go straight up to some thin cracks above.
After a further 20 feet there is another peg. From this move left
towards good holds on The Girdle then go up to a peg belay.
2   150 feet 5b. Climb straight up to the overlap and surmount
it directly. Ascend the short wall above to finish on the path. Bolt
and thread belays on the left.

★★ **Quietus**   320 feet   E2   (4.4.71)
An excellent route up a slim hidden groove left of Father John.
Start on a small ledge down on the left of The Amphitheatre.
Fairly bold.
1   150 feet. 5c. Step of the left end of the ledge and ascend
leftwards under a long open groove. Move up right to a peg at
the base of the groove. Climb the groove to a peg at its top then
straight up to another peg. After a further 10 feet traverse left
for 15 feet then go straight up to a small ledge and peg belay.
2   50 feet. 4c. Ascend straight up to belay beneath the overlap.

3 120 feet. 5a. Climb up leftwards to the roof and pull over onto the slab above. Follow the secondary overlap leftwards into a small gully and belay in the crack on the right.

★ Old Sam   250 feet   E3   (13.6.81)
A superb route taking a very direct line up the centre of the huge wall. Start as for Quietus.
1 50 feet. 5b. Step off the ledge and ascend leftwards to two very good holds. Descend slightly and traverse left to a small recess and belay (good nut on the left).
2 100 feet. 5c. Climb straight up for 20 feet then move right to the base of a thin crack, crux. Ascend this past a thread until level with the top peg on Quietus. Climb a second crack slightly leftwards then go up to join Quietus at the belay.
3 100 feet. 5b. Ascend straight up to the overlap (as for Quietus) and pull over right onto a rib. Climb up this and go over steep grass to finish on the approach path. Bolt and thread belays on the left.

★ The Glass Wall   390 feet   E2   (24.8.74)
A fine route taking a line farther left and in a more committing position than Old Sam. Start as for Quietus.
1 50 feet. 5b. As for Old Sam to the recess.
2 100 feet. 5c. From the recess climb straight up for about 15 feet then move up left into a crack. Climb this and the groove above to a small roof. Go over this and up the wall above to a small ledge and poor belay.
3 120 feet. 5b. Ascend straight up above the belay to some small pockets at about 20 feet. Move right across a shallow groove then go rightwards on better holds and climb straight up to a small ledge and belay beneath the overlap (as for Quietus).
4 120 feet. 5a. As for Quietus.

★ Tunnel of Love   350 feet   E4   (24.9.81) (R)
A magnificent route. The main pitch is sustained and bold and the whole route requires total commitment from both the leader and second. Definitely a bold leader's pitch. Start as for Quietus. Expect some guano on the slab beneath the stance.
1 50 feet. 5b. As for Old Sam to the recess.
2 150 feet. 5c. Make a couple of moves up then traverse left to a vertical slot. Go up and left then traverse steeply left, descending slightly, to a vague crackline. Climb this until it is possible to cross leftwards to a peg. Go straight up to an overlap and pull over to another peg. Awkward moves lead to an undercut crack above (junction with The Girdle). Go straight up the wall above, loose, to a peg belay on top of The Big Flake itself.
3 150 feet. 5a. As for The Big Flake.

GREAT ZAWN — LEFT-HAND SIDE   (R)

For the routes on this side of the zawn approach as follows: From the old lookout on top of the crag go rightwards, facing out, to the edge of the field and scramble down a long grassy peninsula which is quite difficult to locate from above, to ledges at its base. The routes on this side of the Zawn share the same traverse to start.

★ **The Big Flake**   580 feet   Hard Very Severe   (22.4.70)
A good route at this standard, mainly on sound rock in a fine position. The final pitch often contains some grass. Start at the foot of the steep grassy arête.
1   100 feet. Easily traverse right and move up onto a ledge. Belay at the far end at an iron spike.
2   110 feet. 4a. Traverse right and into a groove. Descend this for 5 feet. Cross the slab on the right, step down and traverse right to a good ledge and belay.
3   70 feet. Traverse the easy ledge to belay below an obvious crack.
4   150 feet. 4c. Climb the crack then traverse right, peg and move up to the foot of the huge flake. Climb up the left-hand side of this and traverse right at the top, peg, to a peg belay at the end.
5   150 feet. 5a. Climb up right to a peg. Move up then leftwards and go straight up to a peg just short of the overlap. Surmount this and belay in the crack on the right.

Genesis   600 feet   Hard Very Severe   (2.11.72)
A long interesting route which unfortunately grasses over very quickly. Start at the end of the third pitch of The Big Flake.
4   100 feet. Climb up left to two big scoops, then go up in the same line to the long vertical overlap. Traverse right then go up to a belay on the left.
5   100 feet. Take the traverse line to the right then go diagonally up the wall to belay below the last steep section.
6   120 feet. Ascend straight up to the steep wall then follow easier ground to meet the end of Rabble Rouser's traverse. Belay. Traverse right again and go over steep grass to an easy exit.

★ **Rabble Rouser**   640 feet   Very Severe   (20.4.70)
A long route in a fine position. Often grassy. Start at the end of pitch 3 of The Big Flake.
4   90 feet. 4c. Climb the obvious deep crack on the left to a peg belay.
5   150 feet. 4c. Climb the wall behind the stance then traverse right under an overhang to the foot of a 50-foot groove. Climb this to the roof then step round the arête on he left to a small ledge and peg belay.

6 120 feet. 4c. Step back into the crack and move up to the roof. Traverse right under the roof to the end and descend over large blocks to a ledge and belay.
7 50 feet. Scramble across rightwards to the path.

★ **Girdle of The Great Zawn** 650 feet E2   (25.4.74)
A fine route of great character taking a huge sweeping line across the zawn. Start at the end of the third pitch of The Big Flake.
4 40 feet. 4c. Climb the crack behind the stance then traverse right (as for The Big Flake) to a peg and belay.
5 100 feet. 5b. Traverse right and step down to a line of holds leading to a groove and crack under the overhang. Follow this until it peters out then move up on small holds then go up left to a peg belay on top of the huge flake.
6 80 feet. 5b. Descend slightly then make a long traverse right, ascending and descending slightly, passing the top peg of Quietus. Climb straight up to a peg belay at the foot of the grassy slabs.
7 30 feet. 5b. Traverse right and follow Tartarean in reverse to the shallow groove. Belay.
8 120 feet. 5a. Go straight up to the roof, traversing rightwards and pulling over at its weakest point. Ascend straight up over steep grass to the top. OR, from the right-hand end of the overlap descend rightwards onto a ledge and bolt belay (The Amphitheatre abseil point). Or again, 5b, go straight up to the roof and finish as for Father John – to avoid the grassy final pitches of the original route – better –

The slabs above the iron spike at the end of the first pitch of The Big Flake have been climbed: **The Exploding Rabbit Thing**, 120 feet, VS, 4b.

BOULDERING — GREAT ORME
The two main bouldering areas are the road side caves 100 yards along the Marine Drive and the superb Pigeon's Cave which offers some of the best bouldering in North Wales. It is situated at sea level below Yellow Wall and is mainly tidal. Though problems are hundred fold in both areas several notable test pieces have been done and are described below.

Parisella's Overhang 40 feet 6b   (1983)
From the lowest point of the first roadside cave follow flakes diagonally left to a difficult move over the lip. Move right and finish up a loose corner.

Clever Beaver 6c, (1983) goes directly into this corner by dynamic moves from the initial holds of Parisella's Overhang.

Muscular Obscurity   65 feet   6b   (1983)
From the very back of Pigeon's Cave cross the huge roof (5 feet above the ground) to finish on the break 10 feet above the lip.

Another problem has been done from half-way out of this roof. Starting on the left wall and joining the above route before the lip.

Problems abound on the steep retaining walls of the cave. **Gorilla's Delight** the overhanging corner crack 20 yards right of Pigeon's Cave is E2, 5c, (1983).

Just below Once in a Blue Moon is a small overhanging buttress where several problems have been done. The central groove is 6a. The wall left of this is 6b and 6a and a left-to-right low level girdle is 6b.

Another good bouldering area is Bodafon Buttress behind the primary school south of The Little Orme and is clearly visible from that end of the promenade.

The right arête of the concrete ramparts 100 yards before the toll gate has been climbed – **No Boring Holds**, E4, 6b (1984).

BOULDERING — CRAIG Y FORWYN
The best areas for bouldering are the steep walls at the foot of Scalar and Burgess Wall.

Outlying Areas

THE GREAT ORME

CRAG ABOVE THE TRAM STATION

Swordfish Trombone   60 feet   E3   (27.10.85)
Start 10 feet right of The Three Musketeers.
1   60 feet.   5c.   Go awkwardly up to a rightward trending pocketed crack and follow it to sloping ledges beneath a double bulge. Climb the first bulge on the left traversing right to a drilled thread. Reach left over the next bulge to small holds then pull over to jugs and the top.

The Three Musketeers   70 feet   E2   (16.1.82)
Nice moves on reasonable rock. Start near the right-hand side of the crag, below a large smooth wall and between two large patches of ivy.
1   70 feet.   5c.   Go directly up the wall and up to a niche on the left. Pull out right and finish steeply up a flake.

A few minor routes have also been climbed on this crag.

A route has been climbed near the left-hand end of this crag taking a line just left of a cave. However, **Bananarama**, HVS, 5a 30 feet (1982) is not very pleasant.

CRAG ABOVE THE EMPIRE HOTEL

This crag is the one clearly visible from the main shopping street in Llandudno (Mostyn Street). The main features of the crag apart from the caves along its foot are a large sentry box one third of the way along from the left, and a wide depression/ groove just left of centre. The second pitch follows this depression. Start under the overhangs well to the right of this where a rib penetrates the roofs. Gain the rib from the right-hand side, pull through and go up to a good traverse line. Go left for 20 feet to a ledge and poor peg belays (not in place). Climb the depression, pulling round a roof direct to finish. This route is very loose and the protection uninspiring. Definitely not recommended, but included here purely for the record. The name **Fallen Empire** has been proposed.

★ **Lost Empires**   130 feet   E5   (7.1.87)
Start at a rib just right of ivy at the left end of the crag.
1   80 feet. 6a. Climb the rib, pull up and right past the roof, bolt, move right again then back up left, bolt, to a slight ramp. Ascend this then go up rightwards, bolt, past a shot-hole to a good bolt stance.
2   50 feet. 5c. Climb straight up above the belay to a small roof and good wires. Climb up left into a groove past a bolt then pull right into a corner. Finish up this.

First Ascents

The number of any aid points known to have been used on a first ascent is given in brackets after the route name. (AL) indicates Alternate or Varied Leads.

1949	**The Kite** (Gt. Orme) B Goodey, C Goodey
	Climbed to retrieve a child's kite that was caught high on the cliff face.
1950 July	**Pigeon's Chimney** B Goodey, C Goodey
1951 June	**Pinnacle Route** C Goodey, D Williams
1952 Aug	**Colin's Groove** and **Dark Wall** C Goodey, D Williams
1953 June	**Yellow Groove** (1) C Goodey, D Williams
	First free ascent by C Goodey in October 1985. This was thought to be the second ascent. Interestingly the same climber made both ascents – with a 31 year interval in between.
1957 June	**Biceps** (2) C Goodey
	First free ascent by C Lyon, D Lyon, 1979.
1957 June	**Triceps** (2) C Goodey, M Butler
	First free ascent by C Lyon, D Lyon, 1979.
1958 July	**Pinnacle Direct** A Davies, C Goodey
1958 Sept	**The Y-Chimneys** (L+R) C Goodey, D Thomas (bach) (AL)
	The first known routes at Forwen.
1958-1960	**Elephant Cave Ceiling** and others (aid)
	Many unrecorded peg climbs were done during this period by C Goodey, A Davies, M Butler, H Groom and D Birchley.
1959 May 16	**Ivy Sepulchre** C Goodey, D Thomas (bach)
1959 June	**Mojo** (aid) F Corner, B Thompson
	This line was pegged in September 1959 by C Goodey, D Thomas thinking the line to be new.
	First ascent probably as above as no pegs or wedges were in place on Corner/Thompson's ascent.
	First free ascent by R Edwards, N Metcalfe May 12 1975.
	Direct Finish by M Owen, H Watkins July 19 1979.
1959 Sept	**Brutus** (aid) C Goodey, D Thomas (bach)
1959 Oct	**The Shadow** (some aid) C Goodey, D Alcock
	Now obsolete since the disappearance of its top pitch.
1959 May-1962	**Castle Inn Quarry Routes 1, 2, 3** C Goodey, A Davies, D Thomas, H Groom, M Butler
	All on a top-rope. Route 2 was led by C Goodey with A Davies in 1959.
1960	**Quick Step** (aid)
	Both Frank Corner and Colin Goodey independently pegged the line in the very early Sixties. Barry Brewster did the climb using much less aid in the spring of 1962. The original line broke out of Mojo at the huge roof and finished up the thin crack at the top. First completely free ascent and climbed as described by P Livesey, J Lawrence in May 1975. The final thin crack was climbed free by R Fawcett in March 1979 as part of Tears of a Clown – a route now superseded by Space Case. Soloed by A Pollitt on May 5 1982.

1960 June	**Demolition** and **Twisting Chimney** F Corner, B Forder	
1961 June	**Penelope** (1) A Davies, H Groom	
	First free ascent by A Pollitt, T Freeman (AL) on October 23 1979.	
1962-1963	**Scalar, Sinister Chimney, Stretch** and **Route 66** D Patrick, C Bartlett	
1962 June	**Scalar Direct** D Thomas (bach) C Goodey	
1963	**Stripper** D Patrick, D Lynton	
1963	**Titus** F Corner, B Thompson	
1964 April 15	**Thatch** N Sherry, D Williams	
1964 Sept	**Rocker** D Patrick, N Sherry	
1964	**Wacker** (aid) D Patrick, N Sherry	

Pitch 1 climbed free and pitch 2 (1) added by R Edwards, L Holliwell on June 8 1975 to produce Wackeroo. First free ascent unknown. Direct Finish by A Pollitt, D Hall, N Clacher January 17 1982.

1965 April 22	**Grotty Arête** D Williams, D Patrick	
1965 April 25	**Ivy Union** N Sherry, D Williams, D Patrick	
1965 April	**The Arête** N Sherry, D Patrick	
1965 June	**The Teal** (2) A Davies, D Alcock, D Thomas (bach)	

First free ascent by A Pollitt, T Freeman on May 27 1980.

1965 July 17   **Fido's Redemption** N Sherry, D Williams

Pitch 1 added by L Holliwell, R Edwards in January 1974 as the original start was up the gully on the left. The gully had been climbed as Fido's Folly by D Williams, R Roberts on May 14 1965 – so called because of the presence of a dog's skeleton near the top. Climbed as described by A Ingham, K Farrimond on July 1 1983.

1965 July 30   **Square Cut Chimney** N Sherry, D Williams

Originally climbed as 'Chimney and Corner' but since renamed.

1965 Sept	**Glade Arête** D Williams, G Faulks	
1965 Dec	**Christmas Crawl** C Goodey, D Williams	
1965	**Top Cat** D Patrick, N Sherry	
1965	**Ivy League** D Patrick, N Sherry	

A route since disappeared under vegetation. The route being an easier version of Street Stroller.

1967 June   **The Flue** C Goodey, D Williams

The route was cleaned on a rope – much ivy and rubble being removed before the route was led.

1967 Oct 14   **Great Wall** (aid) C Goodey, P N Dilly

Many climbers had made attempts to peg this fine wall. Those who tried included C Goodey/D Thomas, C Goodey/B Brewster, F Corner/B Thompson and J Amatt. The wall finally went to Goodey and Dr. N Dilly. Corner and Thompson got the second ascent. Brewster climbed about half-way up the wall free after several attempts. Rumours of a free attempt by P Littlejohn and J Perrin in the early Seventies probably prompted R Edwards to pre-place several pegs and threads for an attempt. However, on turning up on the day he found Pete Livesey and Jill Lawrence on the climb. It was then done with two yo-yo's by Livesey March 1975. The route was first soloed by A Pollitt on April 27 1982.

1967 Nov 19	**Softly Softly** D Williams, C Goodey	
1967	**Zig Zag** C Goodey, P N Dilly	

1968 April 20   **The Easy Way Off**   F E R Cannings, T I M Lewis
The first route climbed on The Little Orme.
A variation was climbed by R Isherwood, K Wilson in August of the same year.

1968 May 17   **Rhiwledyn**   F E R Cannings, T I M Lewis

1968 May 17   **Shazam** (3)   P Biven, M Springett
It later transpired that the route had been named Thorfin Skullsplitter but Shazam now seems to have 'stuck'.
First free ascent by A Pollitt, P Bailey on April 30 1981.

1968 May   **Right-Hand Sickle**   R Isherwood, K Wilson
The first route to breach this central wall.

1968 Sept   **Pterodactyl**   F Corner

1969 April   **Gillies Groove**   R Edwards, C Phillips
Edwards's first route in this area which he was to develop almost single handedly over the following six years.

1969 April 6   **Kitties Groove**   R Edwards, C Phillips (AL)

1969 April 10   **Sea Crack**   R Edwards, C Phillips

1969 April 19   **The Sickle** (L.H. start)   R Edwards, C Phillips (AL)

1969 April 20   **Thule**   R Edwards, C Phillips

1969 Oct 4   **The Bender** (1)   C Phillips, L Brown
Aid point eliminated by M Lyndon, D Towse in 1982 but the pitch was not completed. First complete ascent by S Haston, P Williams sometime later.

1969   **The Fox** (Un-named Route 2)   D Archer, R Newcombe

1969   **Chatterley** (Clem)   R Newcombe, D Archer, J Whittle

1969   **Beeline** (aid)   R Newcombe, M Hallway
The top part of which had previously been climbed by R Newcombe, D G Peers in 1967, though it also was climbed as part of Quick Step even earlier.
Later free-climbed by R Fawcett to give Tears of a Clown. (See Space Case.)

1970 March   **Detritus** (aid)   R Edwards (solo)
Several other climbers were involved in cleaning and climbing some parts before Edwards's solo ascent: L Dickinson, N Horne, P Minks, B Molyneux, C Phillips. On the old pitch 3 aid reduced to 1pt. by A Pollitt, C Lyon December 7 1980. Pitch 2 free by T Freeman in 1982. On October 15 1985 P Littlejohn and J de Montjoye climbed the route splitting the first pitch with a hanging belay and utilizing a further two rest points. On the cave pitch two pegs were used to surmount a difficult bulge. A fine achievement.

1970 April 20   **Rabble Rouser**   R Edwards, R Harris

1970 April 22   **The Big Flake**   R Edwards, R Harris

1970 April   **Wall and Groove** (3)   R Edwards and party
Possibly climbed by D Yeats in the 1960's.
First free ascent by A Pollitt, T Freeman (AL) October 23 1979.

1970 April 24   **Tartarean** and **The Entry Traverse**   R Edwards, R Harris

1970 May   **Knightsbridge**   R Newcombe, D Robinson
Pre-dates an ascent by R Edwards in 1974.

Originally known as D R in memory of Robinson who was later killed on the Matterhorn.

Knightsbridge Variation possibly by R Shepton, if not then by A Pollitt, D Prendergast September 15 1979.

1970 July 24	**Tartarean's Left Traverse** R Edwards, R Harris	

"Tartarean's left Traverse was done on the same day as we did Tartarean itself. We actually did the initial pitches and the left traverse as one and then came in from the side to do the right finish. It was put down in the form it is now because it made a better line", R Edwards.

1970   **Thatcher Traverse**   R Newcombe, R Peart

Pre-dates an ascent by R Shepton in 1976.

1971 Jan   **Jugular Start**   J Whittle, D G Peers

1971 Feb 6   **The Neurotic Woodpecker**   D G Peers, P Jardine

1971 Feb 22   **Rapunzel**   R Edwards, T Claire, P Kershaw

1971 Mar   **Vertex**   R Edwards, J Connor

Pitch 1 had been climbed by R Edwards in 1969 when first exploring this crag.

1971 April 2   **Auk's Route** (2)   R Edwards, K Toms

1971 April 4   **Quietus**   R Edwards, K Toms

A fabulous discovery – the scene of a nasty fall when rain transformed the slab into a 'sheet of glass'.

1971 April   **Quoin**   R Edwards, K Toms

Climbed with a slightly different finish by R Edwards, R Shepton on a later ascent.

1971 April 21 **Initiation**   R Shepton, D Wragg (AL) R Wallis

1971 May   **Hooter**   R Newcombe, D Archer

1971 May   **Brer Rabbit** (1)   R Newcombe, D Archer

1971 May 2   **The Flake Wall** (5)   D G Peers, J Whittle

First free ascent later by R Edwards, L Holliwell (see The Snake).

1971 June   **Crack Rampant**   R Shepton, D Wragg (AL) A Thornley

1971 June 12 **Arian**   C Goodey, D Williams

The Direct Finish by A Pollitt, N Clacher on May 9 1981. Wall Finish by F Simpson, D Ramsay July 17 1984.

1971 June 13 **Ergon**   R Shepton

1971 June 13 **The Groan** (1)   D G Peers, J Whittle

"Dave, John and Rick Newcombe all tried the top pitch but could find no protection and backed off. Dave and John came back a few weeks later, abseiled to place a peg then climbed the whole route." R.N. First free ascent Unknown.

1971   **Man Alive**   R Newcombe, G Ashton

Pre-dates an ascent by J Moran and M Crook.

Direct start by A Pollitt, N Clacher, T Freeman July 3 1982.

1971 Sept   **The Diamond** (aid)   R Edwards

Climbed with K Toms and M Smith they finished up the top chimneys of Rhiwledyn due to fading light. It now has a better and more direct finish – that of Gemstone.

1971 Sept 8   **Looser**   R Shepton, J Innes

1971 Sept 15 **Grott Buttress**   A Thornley, G David

1971 Sept 18	**Goliath's Crack** (1) R Shepton, R Wallis *First free ascent by A Pollitt, P Bailey and direct start added January 23 1982.*
1971 Sept 18	**Ending of the Day** R Shepton, N Richter
1971 Sept 22	**Slanting Groove** G David, A Thornley
1971 Sept 22	**Gardener's World** R Shepton, R Wallis
1971 Sept 25	**Grand Finalé** (aid) R Shepton *First free ascent by A Pollitt solo on May 27 1980.*
1972 Jan 8	**Fugitive** R Edwards, C Jones, A Moulam
1972 Jan 14	**St. Tudno's Chimney** R Edwards, C T Jones, A J J Moulam
1972 Jan 14	**Zig** and **Zag** R Edwards
1972 March 10	**Freudian Slip** (1) and **Stretcher** (1) R Edwards, M Martin, B Molyneux *Possible First free ascent of Stretcher by A Pollitt, A Boorman October 24 1980. Or the Lyons earlier.*
1972 April 2	**Wall of the Evening Light** (aid) R Edwards, F Harvey *The final 'push' took 16 hours.*
1972 April 4	**Fresco** R Edwards, M Martin (AL)
1972 May 8	**Hippodrome** (aid) R Edwards, M Martin (AL)
1972 May 17	**Easy Rider** R Shepton, J Innes
1972 June 10	**Ivy Wall** (1) R Edwards, M Smith *First free ascent by A Pollitt, C Lyon January 28 1981.*
1972 June 12	**Oceanside** (5) R Edwards, F Harvey *Aid reduced to 3pts by A Wild, P Boardman. First free ascent by R Edwards sometime later.*
1972 Sept 25	**Central Pillar** (aid) R Edwards, F Harvey *The start and the whole top pitch were climbed free as part of **The Bittersweet Connection** (1) by J M Redhead and K Robertson on September 6 1979. R Fawcett freed the aid point on this on September 14 1982 and the pitch was climbed as described by A Pollitt, B Moon August 19 1983.* *R Fawcett then returned to completely free the original Central Pillar in July 1983 – a major achievement.*
1972 Nov 2	**Genesis** R Shepton, J Innes *Cleaned by students at Shepton's school – or so the story goes.*
1972 Nov	**Mayfair** (aid) R Edwards *First free ascent using siege tactics by A Pollitt, J Moffatt March 16 1980.*
1972 Nov	**Oyster** (aid) R Edwards *Aid reduced to 1pt by A Pollitt, T Freeman August 8 1982.* *First free ascent by J Moffatt August 1983 – another major achievement.*
1972 Nov	**Connor's Folly** (1) J Connor and party *First free ascent by A Pollitt N Clacher August 6 1982.*
1973 March 17	**Beachcomber** R Edwards
1973 April 21	**Mephistopheles** pitches 1-3 J F Kerry, P R Prior (AL) *Pitches 4 and 5 added by J F Kerry, C Dale (AL) on April 25 1973.*
1973 Aug	**Plumbline** R Edwards

1973 Sept 4	**Wall of Caves** R Shepton	

The second failed to follow resulting in a rescue by the inshore lifeboat.

1973 Sept 22   **Scoop Route** S Johnstone, E Craig
Possibly Tradesman's Entrance is the line climbed by this party – facts are unclear.

1973 Oct 3   **Hydro** R Edwards, M Creasey

1973 Oct 3   **Changeling** P Boardman, O Knowles

1973 Oct 23   **Gemstone** R Edwards, M Creasey

1973 Nov 21   **Sangfroid** R Edwards, L Holliwell
This utilized the 1st pitch of The Shadow – a route that exits no more.
Direct Finish by A Pollitt, J Moffatt January 30 1981.

1974 Jan   **Freedom** R Edwards, L Holliwell
Direct Start (2) added by T Hodgson, M Wilson August 19 1982.
First free ascent by A Pollitt, M Donnan Aug 25 1982.

1974 Jan   **The Snake** R Edwards, L Holliwell
Free-climbs The Flake Wall.
This originally climbed a huge flake on pitch 2 which formed part of The Shadow climbed by C Goodey and party in June 1959. This later fell down.
New pitch 2 by A Pollitt, J Moffatt and alt pitch 2 by J Moffatt, A Pollitt January 30 1981. More variations have been climbed since.

1974 March 14   **Changeling Direct** R Edwards, I Pomfrett

1974 April 9   **Moonshadow** R Edwards, R Shepton

1974 April 18   **Midnight Blues** (5) R Edwards, C Graham
Aid reduced to 1pt by A Pollitt, P Bailey on 12 December 1980.
First free ascent P Littlejohn, S Bishop, S Briggs October 1985.

1974 April 25   **Great Zawn Girdle** R Edwards, P Trower

1974 April   **Sunset Strip** R Edwards, P Meads
Free climbs The Bat (3) which was climbed by D Williams, F Corner, C Goodey.
Direct Start by A Pollitt, P Bailey, N Clacher 11 March 1982 – probably done before.

1974 May 24   **Peace Train** R Edwards and party
Climbed via the Direct Start. First climbed as described by A Pollitt, N Clacher April 1st 1981.

1974 June 28   **Hydrofoil** R Shepton, A Dutton

1974 June 29   **Atlanta** and **Uranus** R Edwards, I Pomfrett

1974 June 29   **The Needle's Eye** R Shepton, A Dutton

1974 Aug 24   **The Glass Wall** R Edwards, I Pomfrett

1974 Sept 25   **The Red Sentinel** R Edwards, I Pomfrett

1975 April 19   **The Vice** (1) R Edwards, C Graham

1975 May 27   **Phalanges** R Shepton, D Trollope

1975 May 29   **Phalanx** R Shepton, P Dyer

1975 June 21   **Hang Five** R Edwards, N Metcalfe

1975 Aug 23   **The Rat**, **The Needles** and **Little Corner** R Edwards, T Jepson

1975 Oct 11   **New Dimensions** (3) R Edwards (N Metcalfe partly) T Jepson
In 1976 on the 3rd ascent J Moran and P Williams free-climbed the 2nd pitch having used 1pt aid on the first pitch. R Edwards returned to make a completely free ascent 2 weeks later.

1975-1976	**Great Whaler** P Livesey, R Fawcett (AL)	
1975-1976	**Hedera Wall** R Fawcett, C Gibb	
1975-1976	**Yam** R Fawcett, P Livesey, P Gomersall	
1976 Jan	**Demos** R Edwards	
1976 April	**Burgess Wall** D Jones	
1976 Nov 5	**Scalar Arête** R Edwards	

1976 Nov 5   **Scalar Arête** R Edwards
Soloed with a back rope but the grade was found to be far harder on subsequent ascents.
A similar line was climbed (as described) by R Fawcett, G Birtles late 1970's.

1976 Nov   **Little Neb** R Edwards

1976 Dec/ 1977 Jan   **Beyond the Grave** (aid) M Brady, P Temple, B Courtney
Climbed over 5 days.

1977 March   **Appian Way, Alternative Three** and **Hang Ten** · R Edwards, G Perry

1977 March   **Watling Street** R Edwards, F Smith

1977 March   **Goliath** R Edwards and party
An aid route used for practising pegging.
Edwards claimed a later ascent free at a low grade. Repeated and found much harder by A Pollitt, M Griffiths on June 16 1981.

1977 April   **The Crack** J Frost, C Lyon

1977 Spring   **Purple Haze** N Shepherd, W Wayman, T Jepson
Pitch 1 had been climbed on aid previously.

1977 April 24   **Flake Wall** A Bailey, D Lyon (AL)

1977 May 7   **Aphasic** A Bailey, J Frost

1977 May 15   **Josey Wales** D Lyon, C Lyon

1977 May   **Zero, Huntington, King Ja Ja, Oceanside North** and **Memphis** R Edwards, G Perry

1977 Jun 24   **Fosse Way** (1) R Edwards, G Perry
Free-climbed as a part of a new route: Plas Berw by J M Redhead, K Robertson on August 29 1979.

1977 July 7   **Human Menagerie** M Owen, P White

1977 Aug 3   **Psychic Threshold** (2) R Edwards, P Williams
Aid reduced to 1pt by J M Redhead, K Robertson on August 15 1979. First free ascent by K Carrigan, D Hall in May 1981. A fine achievement.

1977 Sept 17   **Spacewalk** (1) R Edwards, P Williams
First free ascent by J M Redhead, K Robertson on November 6 1979.

1977 Sept 20   **Gritstone Gorilla** P Williams, R Edwards
A fine popular discovery.

1977 Oct 8   **Limestone Lemur** R Edwards, P Williams, D Roberts

1977 Oct 31   **Elder Flower Wine** A Bailey, D Randell

1977 Dec 26/27   **Fallen Empires** C Lyon, P Elliot (AL)

1977/1978   **Sea Goat** and **Ocean Girl** M Gill, A Gill

1978 Jan   **Astrodome** (aid) C Lyon, D Lyon (AL)

1978 Feb 14   **Paws** R Edwards

1978 May   **Trooping the Colour** P Leavers, W Ramsbottom

1978 July   **Hoe Down** (1) D Lyon, C Lyon
Aid Point eliminated by A Pollitt, P Bailey January 30 1982. The team traversed off above the crux due to wet.

1978 July	**Hot Gossip**	A Monument, M Routley, J Tearsley
1979 Feb 18	**Hairline**	A Pollitt, A Boorman
1979 March 4	**Coulombe**	A pollitt, A Boorman

Pre-dates an ascent by T Hodgson, I Jones.

1979 March 14	**The Crunge**	K Robertson, M Owen
1979 August 29	**Duchess**	G Gibson, D Beetlestone

Variation by G Gibson, C Smith March 3 1982.

1979 Aug 29 **Plas Berw** J M Redhead, K Robertson

Pitch 3 was added on 2 October 1979.

1979 Sept 27	**The Sea Grave**	D Lyon, C Lyon
1979 Sept 28	**The Enemy**	C Lyon, D Lyon
1979 Oct. 2	**Banana Moon**	M Owen, H Watkins
1979	**Pile Driver**	P Williams, H Walton
1979	**Squatter's Rights**	H Watkins, G M Williams, H Jones

Possibly done by C Jones even earlier.

1979-1980 **Uriah's Neck, The Stairs of Cirith Ungol, Into a Game, Jivin' Around, The Exodus of Plastic Penguins, The Deep Fix, Minas Anor, The Boat of Millions of Years, Bauxed** and **Reaving Slaying Conan** G Roberts, T Cunningham

1979-1980 **Cruise Missile** and **The Men in the Jungle** T Freeman, G Roberts, N Radcliffe

Cruise Missile Direct by T Freeman solo July 20 1982.

1979-1980	**Ozymandias**	G Roberts, B Roberts
1979-1980	**Space Invaders**	G Roberts, H Williams, S Troop
1979-1980	**Bruno His Wall**	G Roberts, H Williams
1979-1980	**The Blood Red Game**	G Roberts, G Bream
1980	**Chimney Crack, The Ramp** (& var) **The Corner, The Groove** (Gt Orme) P Leavers	
1980 Jan 20	**Spike Driver** (free)	A Pollitt, A Boorman, P Bailey

Previously climbed as an aid route by M Smith.

1980 Feb 9	**One Step Beyond**	A Pollitt, T Freeman
1980 May 28	**Swinger** and **Snotty Arête**	J Moffatt, P Leavers
1980 July 13	**System 6** and **Zero 1**	D Lyon, C Lyon (AL)
1980 July 17	**Father John**	D Lyon, C Lyon
1980 July 19	**Rude Awakening**	M Jones, W Wayman
1980 July 27	**Mur yr Ogof** (1)	D Lyon, C Lyon

First free ascent by M Owen, D Cowans.

1980 Nov **Zonesthesia** W Parker, S Reid

Zonesthesia being a fear of girdles!

1981 Jan 10 **High Steppa** (1) A Pollitt, P Bailey

Pitch 2 climbed previously by A Pollitt and T Freeman. Rest point eliminated by A Pollitt January 31 1981.

1981 Jan 31 **Sour Grapes** J Moffatt, A Pollitt

Pitch 2 added by S Melia, A Ingham on April 27 1984.
So named by Moffatt due to the inacceptance of his 'ascent' of Tremadog's Strawberries.

1981 March 6 **Book of Dreams** A Pollitt (unseconded)

The Magnum Opus start added by G Gibson, S Melia on April 17 1984 utilized a bolt runner. This was removed and led without by A Pollitt on May 8 1984.

1981 March 14	**The Stirrer**	D Towse, C Jones
1981 March 18	**Pil**	M Roberts, I Alderson
1981 March 29	**Go For Gold**	D Towse
	Pre-dates an ascent by T Freeman.	
1981 March 29	**High Plains Drifter**	A Pollitt, C Lyon
1981 April	**The Really Exciting Climb**	T Freeman, G Roberts, N Radcliffe
1981 April 2	**The Norman Conquest**	A Pollitt, N Clacher, P Bailey
1981 April 9	**Moonwind**	A Pollitt, P Bailey
	Moonwind Direct climbed (as described) by A Pollitt, P Bailey on October 14 1981.	
1981 April 19	**The Electric Butterfly**	N Clacher, M Worthy, N Harris
1981 May 9	**Sunny City**	A Pollitt, P Bailey, H Clover, N Clacher
1981 May 9	**Excursion**	I Alderson, M Roberts
1981 May 13	**Dyslexic's Delite**	P Leavers, T Hooper
1981 May 30	**Jackdaw Chimney**	A Smith, I Birchall
1981 May 30	**Romeo**	P Leavers
1981 May	**Carrigan's Groove**	K Carrigan, D Hall
	Originally broke out of Mayfair. Climbed as described by A Pollitt, P Williams June 27 1983.	
1981 June 3	**Making Movies**	C Lyon, M Coles, P Leavers
1981 June 6	**Eastbound Train**	P Leavers, A Rubin
1981 June 11	**Kanly**	D Towse
	Claimed as The Master Physician but the 'new' name seems to have stuck.	
1981 June 12	**Skateaway**	A Pollitt, P Bailey
1981 June	**Axle Attack**	M Griffiths, L McGinley
	Both led the route.	
1981 June 13	**Old Sam**	C Lyon, D Lyon
1981 June 20	**Ichneumon**	G Roberts, C Brear, A Parsons
1981 July 2	**Dumbell Flyer**	S Haston, I Johnson
1981 July 5	**Juliet**	A Pollitt, H Clover
1981 Aug	**Get on the Beam**	I Alderson, G Alderson
1981 Aug	**Passionate Friend**	T Freeman, D Summerfield
1981 Aug	**Nailed up and Bleeding**	G Roberts, D Summerfield
1981 Sept 15	**Crazy Horses**	A Pollitt, N Clacher
1981 Sept 24	**Tunnel of Love**	C Lyon, A Moore
1981 Oct 27	**Jungle Love**	A Pollitt, N Clacher
1981	**The Exploding Rabbit Thing**	I Alderson, D Towse
1982 Jan 2	**Eight-Footed Exercise**	A Pollitt, N Clacher, H Clover, P Bailey
	So named due to the variety of footwear worn. Seems similar to 'Punx Funk' a route climbed previously by P Leavers (1977).	
1982 Jan 16	**The Three Musketeers**	T Freeman, N Radcliffe, D Summerfield
1982 Jan 17	**The Texas Shuffle**	A Pollitt, N Clacher, D Hall
	Direct Start by A Pollitt sometime later.	
1982 Jan 27	**Street Stroller** and **L'Indienne**	A Pollitt, N Clacher
1982 Jan 28	**The Maiden**	A Pollitt, N Clacher
	Pitch 1 had been done by J Moffatt, A Pollitt in 1981.	
1982 Feb 21	**Plas Newydd Groove**	N Clacher, D Prendergast

1982 March 4	**The Burning Sphincter** J M Redhead, A Newton

Direct Start by J M Redhead sometime later.
Soloed by T Freeman later.

1982 March 13	**The Cringe** T Hodgson, N Clacher
1982 April 9	**Whitewash** J Edwardson, J Dobie, N Clacher
1982 April 9	**Gear Freak** J Dobie, J Edwardson, N Clacher
1982 April 9	**Paul's Wall** J Dobie, J Edwardson, P Whitmoore
1982 April 10	**Larks a Bumbly** J Edwardson, N Clacher, J Dobie, P Whitmoore
1982 April 10	**Bananarama** N Radcliffe, D Summerfield, T Freeman
1982 April 16	**The Last Grasp** J Dobie, J Edwardson, N Clacher, P Whitmoore
1982 May 5	**Imminent Crisis** R Fawcett, W Wayman

Had been climbed previously using some aid by T Hodgson.

1982 May 12	**Kiwi Direct Start** A Pollitt (solo)
1982 May 22	**Autobahn** D Lyon, A Moore
1982 June 1	**Limestone Cowboy** T Hallard (solo)
1982 June 2	**Doenitz** K Howitt, D Towse

*Top roped prior to the lead. Pitch split and the original finish was up
Hydro. Climbed as described by A Pollitt, K Howitt, D Towse on June
6 1982.*
The Direct Start was added by T Jones on February 24 1986.

1982 June 6	**Rock On** and **Face Value** T Hallard, J Hallard
1982 June 10	**Puerto Rican Harlem** A Pollitt, P Bailey

Probably the same line taken by A Kick in the Head (aided).

1982 June 16	**Burgess Wall Right-Hand** A Pollitt, A Boorman
1982 June17	**Physical Diagnostic** T Hodgson, N Clacher
1982 June 18	**23 Skidoo** H Watkins, B Jones

Possibly a free version of Brer Rabbit.

1982 June 21	**Coiled Spine** C Brear, G Roberts
1982 June 27	**Fool's Paradise** T Hodgson, N Clacher
1982 June 30	**Scum Bag** H Watkins, B Jones
1982 July 2	**The Graduate** T Freeman (solo)
1982 July 13	**Big Licks** T Freeman, G Roberts
1982 July	**Hugh's Groove** (2) H Watkins, B Jones

FFA by A Pollitt, P Bailey on July 15 1982.

1982 July 16	**Think Void** T Hodgson, I Jones
1982 July 22	**The Water Margin** N Clacher, K Simpson

*A fine discovery. Alt pitch 7 by N Clacher, T Hodgson on August 29
1982.*

1982 July 26	**Space Mountain** G Gibson, P Gibson
1982 July 27	**The Disillusioned Screw Machine** (1) J M Redhead, A Pollitt

*Pitch 1 by J M Redhead, K Robertson some days earlier. Aid point
eliminated by T Jones but the pitch was not completed.*
FFA by A Pollitt, P Williams on June 14 1983 – a major plum.

1982 Summer	**Tales of Future Past** M Leach (unseconded)
1982 Aug 3	**Panorama** G Gibson, M Lynden

Variation by G Gibson 10 August 1985.

1982 Aug 3	**Corner Start** to Purple Haze G Gibson (solo)
1982 Aug 5	**Astro Blaster** A Pollitt, T Freeman

Climbed on sight.

1982 Aug 7	**The Bloods** J M Redhead, K Robertson, A Pollitt
	Pitch 2 added by A Pollitt, A Grondowski, P Williams on July 5 1983.
1982 Aug 13	**Manhattan** J Codling, S Allen
	Variation by G Gibson (unseconded) on August 3 1985.
1982 Aug 23	**Rest and be Thankful** D Lyon, C Lyon
1982 Aug 30	**The Breck Road** T Jones
1982 Aug 31	**Route 3 Direct, The Cake Walk, Vienna** and **Driving the Dumper** A Pollitt, T Hodgson
	Cake Walk Direct by G Gibson (solo) on May 20 1984.
1982 Sept 2	**Pumped in Pumps** A Pollitt
	Soloed in trainers.
1982 Sept 9	**Apostle** R Fawcett
	Cleaned by Andy Pollitt and peg placed with Tim Freeman. Freeman climbed the route a month later thinking the chalk was Pollitt's – it was Fawcett's.
1982 Oct 3	**Solid Reality** N Clacher, P Custy
1982 Oct 28	**Gold Rush** W Wayman, P Roberts, F Crook
1982 Oct 28	**Insidious Practices** M Roberts, I Alderson
	Top-roped prior to being led.
1982 Oct 21	**It** M Roberts, A Francis
1982 Nov 21	**Separate Elephant** J M Redhead, M Crook
	Sieged.
1982 Nov 24	**The Chain Gang** A Pollitt, T Freeman
1982 Dec 1	**Clear White Light** K Howitt, D Towse, S Jenkins
	Top-roped prior to the lead.
	Direct version by G Gibson on May 20 1984.
1982 Dec 3	**Precious Time** A Pollitt, K Robertson, J M Redhead
1982	**Green Flash** L McGinley (solo)
	Pre-dates an ascent by N Radcliffe, T Freeman (Beans on Toast).
1982	**Hom Rescue** S Haston (solo)
	Pre-dates an ascent by T Freeman (solo), (The Dropout).
1983 Jan	**Solid 6** T Hodgson
1983 Jan 2	**Homs Punk** J M Redhead, M Crook
1983 Jan 2	**Fading Colours** G Gibson, P Gibson
1983 Jan 9	**Dave's Wall** T Hodgson, B Connelly
1983 Jan 9	**A Touch too Much** A Pollitt, T Freeman
	Some wag commented in the Lyon's Sports new route book. "First ascent logged by A Pollitt, T Freeman" as a tree stump was used to by-pass the initial roof before the pair bouldered it out later that afternoon.
	Soloed by T Hodgson, 1986.
1983 March	**The Visitor** M Griffiths, E Jones
1983 March	**Flakeaway** D Towse
1983 March	**Firefly** M Crook, D Towse
1983 April	**Scary Canary** M Crook, D Towse, K Howitt
	Sieged. Nevertheless an excellent find.
1983 April	**After the Goldrush** W Wayman, N Shepherd
	The first of many 1983 new routes by Bill Wayman.
1983 April 9	**Legal Separation** T Hodgson, M Wilson

1983 May 11	**Klondike** and **Solid Gold** W Wayman, F Crook
1983 May 11	**Yellow Belly** D Lyon, C Lyon
1983 May 12	**Price of Gold** W Wayman, F Crook
	Variation by A Pollitt (unseconded) on August 22 1984.
1983 May	**Werry's Woof Woot** J Moffatt
1983 May 12	**The Jehad** D Towse, K Howitt, S Jenkins
1983 May 13	**Vagal Inhibition** K Howitt, D Towse, S Jenkins
1983 May 13	**Pershing II** D Lyon, C Bundock, P Ward
1983 May	**Masada** K Howitt, D Towse, M Roberts
1983 May	**Primrose Walk** D Towse, M Roberts
1983 May	**Melkor** D Towse, M Roberts (AL)
	The first route on Yellow Wall.
1983 June 2	**Space Case** A Pollitt, N Clacher
	A major line which renders Tears of a Clown defunct.
1983 June 5	**Precious Metal** and **Gold Star** F Crook, W Wayman
1983 June 5	**Krugerrand** and **Lucky Strike** W Wayman, F Crook
1983 June 6	**The Hurting** C Lyon, D Lyon
1983 June 8	**Pure Gold** W Wayman, F Crook
1983 June 10	**Quicksilver** A Pollitt, P Williams
	The first addition by this team.
1983 June10	**The Alchemist's Dream** and **Pale Shelter** D Lyon, N Clacher
1983 June 11	**En Gedi** and **Midas Touch** W Wayman, F Crook
1983 June 11	**Sheik Yer Money** R Fawcett, P Williams
	The first of many of Ron's new routes of this period.
1983 June 12	**The Violator** G Gibson, P Gibson
	The first of Gary's many routes of this period.
1983 June 12	**Love over Gold** W Wayman, F Crook
1983 June 14	**Gorgo** A Pollitt, P Williams
	The first route to be climbed on Monster Buttress.
1983 June 16	**The Bearded Clam** A Pollitt, P Williams
	Another excellent discovery.
1983 June 17	**Anchovy Madonna** A Pollitt, P Williams
	An instant classic.
1983 June 17	**Rapture** J Moffatt, E Jones
	Jerry's first major new route of the year here.
1983 June 19	**String of Pearls** D Towse, M Raine
	Opened up the blanker section of Yellow Wall.
1983 June 21	**Adequate Compensation** M Raine, D Towse, N Foster, T Freeman
1983 June 24	**The Pirates of Pen Trwyn** A Pollitt, P Williams, R Fawcett, G Fawcett
1983 June	**Wings of Perception** J Moffatt, P Williams
	The area's hardest route to date.
1983 June 25	**King Krank** M Griffiths
	A fine companion route to his own Axle Attack.
1983 June 25	**Too Low For Zero** D Lyon, C Bundock
1983 June 25	**Charlton Chestwig (The World's Finest Climber)** R Fawcett, P Williams, A Pollitt
	Ron was tackling the crux while Paul and Andy were sitting on the wall below. A dizzy old Lancashire gent enquired if Ron was "as good as Mallory". Completely ad-lib Paul told him that "him up there,

that's Charlton Chestwig the world's finest climber". Our friend was so impressed he "couldn't wait to tell the wife". Ron fell off crippled with laughter. The route now had a name.

1983 June 25	**Pen Trwyn Patrol** R Fawcett, G Fawcett, P Williams, A Pollitt
1983 June 26	**Flash in the Pan** F Crook, K Crook
1983 June 27	**The Continuing Adventures of Charlton Chestwig** A Pollitt, P Williams
1983 June 27	**Private Investigation** D Lyon, C Lyon

Originally started up Too Low For Zero.
Climbed as described by R Fawcett some time later.

1983 June 27	**Power Failure** D Lyon, C Lyon
1983 June 28	**Gold Digger** P Williams, A Pollitt, D Lyon

Paul's first new route here.

1983 June 30	**Pocket City** A Pollitt, P Williams
1983 June 30	**Captain Fingers** A Pollitt, P Williams, M Crook

Climbed 'direct' by R Fawcett sometime later.

1983 June 30	**Magical Ring** D Lyon, C Bundock, C Lyon
1983 June 30	**The Golden Goose** P Williams, M Crook, A Pollitt
1983 June/July	**Body Torque, Needle in the Groove, The Electric Cool-Aid Acid Test, Ward 10, Fall Back** and **Sourdough** R Fawcett

An impressive list of additions.
Sourdough climbed 'direct' by A Pollitt on August 22 1984.

1983 June/July	**Mr. Olympia** R Fawcett, W Wayman, P Williams

Another fine addition.

1983 July 1	**Mr. Chips** A Pollitt, P Williams, J Moffatt
1983 July 2	**Menincursion** G Gibson, A Hudson

Another area of rock is opened up.

1983 July 2	**The Peppermint Pig** A Hudson, G Gibson
1983 July 2	**Paradise** and **The Bounty Hunters** G Gibson, A Hudson, A Popp

The latter included B Higgs.

1983 July 3	**The Wall of Blutes** P Williams, R Fawcett, P Clark, A Grondowski, J Moffatt
1983 July 3	**Birdbrain** A Pollitt, N Clacher
1983 July 3	**Twisting by the Pool** D Lyon, C Lyon

A fine creation opening up yet another superb crag.

1983 July 5	**The Visionary** A Grondowski, P Williams, A Pollitt
1983 July 6	**The Arc of Eternity** P Williams, A Grondowski
1983 July 8	**Willowbrook's** G Gibson, A Hudson
1983 July 10	**Pen Trwyn Pilots** and **Liquid Lust** D Towse
1983 July 10	**Let's Lynch the Landlord** A Hudson, G Gibson
1983 July 10	**Drip, Drip, Drip** G Gibson, A Hudson, D Towse
1983 July 10	**Salty Dog** G Gibson
1983 July 10	**Pure Mania** G Gibson, A Hudson
1983 July 10	**New Gold Dream** A Hudson, I Johnson, G Gibson
1983 July 10	**Hot Space** D Lyon, C Lyon

Little Orme's first new route of this summer.

1983 July 17	**Spine Chill** and **Second Sense** G Gibson, A Hudson
1983 July 17	**Storm Warning** G Gibson

1983 July 19	**The Hole of Creation** P Williams, J Taylor
	Probably the most bizarre rock formation on North Wales limestone.
1983 July 21	**Le Bingomaniaque** F Crook, C Bundock
1983 July 21	**The Jacuzzi Jive** D Lyon, C Lyon
	Climbed 'direct' as described by D Lyon roped solo on September 30 1984.
1983 July 22	**The Psychofant Roof** A Pollitt, D Towse
1983 July 23	**Slouching Towards Bethlehem** R Foster, P Williams, A Pollitt, T Freeman
	Hanging Rock's first proper route.
	Perthy Thrower *had been climbed a few days earlier by P Williams and J Moffatt.*
1983 July 23	**Gina** S Williams, G Regnault
1983 July 23	**White Linen** J Carpenter, C Dyke
1983 July	**Patience** C Dyke, E Regnault, C Darlington, J Carpenter
1983 July 24	**De Torquemada** P Williams, A Pollitt, R Foster
	Re-climbed after losing a crucial hold by A Pollitt on August 18 1984.
1983 July 24	**Jerusalem is Lost** A Pollitt, R Foster
1983 July 25	**The Wall of Goutes** P Williams, A Pollitt
1983 July 25	**The Picnic** A Pollitt
1983 July 26	**Gripper Clipper** A Pollitt
1983 July 26	**Babylon by Bus** A Pollitt, P Clark
1983 July 27	**Spanish Train** A Pollitt, P Clark
1983 July 30	**Thunder Road** A Pollitt
	Another big line falls.
	Pitch 1 led by N Foster.
1983 Summer	**Noggin the Nog** N Shepherd, M Barnicott
1983 Summer	**Gorilla's Delight** M Crook, P Williams
1983 Aug 3	**The Thin Red Line** (1 rest) G Gibson
	Rest point eliminated by A Pollitt, W Wayman, N Clacher on September 30 1983.
1983 Aug 3	**Amateur Dramatics** C Bundock, N Clacher
1983 Aug 7	**No Red Tape** G Gibson, P Gibson
1983 Aug	**Masterclass** J Moffatt
	After numerous attempts spread over several days Jerry finally pieced together this audacious route – the hardest on the coast so far.
1983 Aug 18	**Di's Delight** I Jones, B Connelly
1983 Sept 21	**Prospectors** W Wayman, F Crook, P Clark
1983 Sept 21	**Silver Surfer** M Crook, A Newton
	New Wave Finish by J Dawes, P Clark on February 7 1984.
1983 Sept 25	**Once in a Blue Moon** G Gibson, A Popp, P Gibson
1983 Sept	**Back to the Egg** D Towse, K Howitt
1983 Sept 28	**Karma** D Towse, M Crook
1983 Oct 2	**Silent Voices** M Crook, A Newton
1983 Oct 3	**Tips** M Crook, A Newton
1983 Oct 4	**Gandalf's Groove** M Crook, A Newton
1983 Oct 8	**Big Kazoo** M Crook, A Newton
1983 Oct 8	**Beaverbrook** W Wayman, F Crook
1983 Oct 11	**The Cynical Pinnacle** P Williams, I Sayers

1983 Oct 13	**Too Pooped to Whoop** W Wayman, F Crook	
1983 Oct 15	**White Seam** W Wayman, F Crook	
1983 Oct 22	**Tokoloshe Man** P Williams, I Sayers	
1983 Oct 23	**The Gold Coast** I Carr, C Hardy	
1983 Oct 24	**Flying Lizard** M Crook, A Newton	
1983 Oct 27	**Uaeba** and **Pen Trwyn Pillar** W Wayman, F Crook	
1983 Oct 30	**Goodbye Mickey Mouse** D Lyon, C Lyon	
1983 Nov 4	**Gold 'n Delicious** W Wayman, F Crook	
1983 Nov 5	**Meanstreak** and **Gold Wall Girdle Part 11** W Wayman, F Crook	

1983 Oct 13   **Too Pooped to Whoop** W Wayman, F Crook
1983 Oct 15   **White Seam** W Wayman, F Crook
1983 Oct 22   **Tokoloshe Man** P Williams, I Sayers
1983 Oct 23   **The Gold Coast** I Carr, C Hardy
1983 Oct 24   **Flying Lizard** M Crook, A Newton
1983 Oct 27   **Uaeba** and **Pen Trwyn Pillar** W Wayman, F Crook
1983 Oct 30   **Goodbye Mickey Mouse** D Lyon, C Lyon
1983 Nov 4   **Gold 'n Delicious** W Wayman, F Crook
1983 Nov 5   **Meanstreak** and **Gold Wall Girdle Part 11** W Wayman, F Crook
　　　　　　　G.W.G. with T Jepson.
1983 Nov 12   **Vic 20** W Wayman, E Stroud
1983 Dec 3   **The Space Hunter** M Crook, S Haston, A Newton
1983   **Polit Bureau** S Haston

1983 Bouldering

Summer   **Parisella's Overhang** and **Clever Beaver** J Moffatt
　　　　　　Originally called Beaver Cleaver by M Crook. Holds fell off leaving a
　　　　　　far harder problem.
　　　　　　Steve Haston was heard to say "There exists no route which is more
　　　　　　IN there" ribbing Moffatt for his saying that Stoney Middleton's Little
　　　　　　Plum was . . . out there!
Summer   **Muscular Obscurity** T Freeman
　　　　　　The shorter, original roof had been done previously by several
　　　　　　climbers.
1984 Jan 17   **Greenham Girls** D Towse, M Roberts
1984 March 4   **Washington Waltz** K Sharples, I Riddington, G Hoey
1984 March 6   **Span Ban** C Smith, P Clark, M Kemball
1984 March 31   **Clap Trap** G Gibson (unseconded)
1984 March 31   **The People Mover** G Gibson, A Ingham
　　　　　　Pitch 2 added later the same day by G Gibson (unseconded).
　　　　　　"I thought I'd take a look at the wall Andy Pollitt had proclaimed
　　　　　　unclimbable". A true statement – though from a youngster back in
　　　　　　1979 – with Tim Freeman.
1984 April 7   **The Black Hole** G Gibson, S Melia, S Chesslett, T Hodgson
1984 April 7   **Livingstone, I Presume** G Gibson (unseconded)
1984 April 7   **Bush Doctor** G Gibson, H Gibson, A Ingham
1984 April 7   **Electric Avenue** A Ingham, S Melia, T Hodgson, S Chesslett
1984 April 14   **Napalm Sunday** G Gibson, H Gibson
1984 April 15   **Bush Rush** G Gibson
　　　　　　Soloed in trainers.
1984 April 17   **And All Hell Broke Loose** D Lyon (roped solo)
1984 April 20   **Notta Bleck, Good Friday Groove** and **Into the Gap** C Lyon, D Lyon
　　　　　　(AL)
1984 April 25   **Mad World** D Lyon, C Lyon, H Watkins
1984 April 27   **The Space Race** A Ingham, S Melia
1984 May 15   **Sweet Dreams, The Reflex, Clowns of God, Time Gentlemen Please,**
　　　　　　A Fine Time to Die, Touch the Dead, Golden Goosed Creature and
　　　　　　Seaside Rendezvous D Lyon, N Clacher
　　　　　　A good day!

1984 May 19	**The Turquoise Tortoise** and **Homo Sapien** G Gibson (unseconded)
	The latter became an instant classic. Despite Editorial sapience Homo
	sapiens claimed to be more sapient.
	The upper part of The Turquoise Tortoise had been climbed in 1982
	by T Freeman, A Pollitt but left unrecorded.
1984 May 20	**School Mam** and **Call it Black** G Gibson (unseconded)
1984 May	**Owain's Chimney** N Clacher
1984 May	**Jonathan Livingstone Seagull**, **Gibbering Wreck** and **Rainbow**
	Warrior N Clacher, D Lyon
1984 May	**XPD** and **Royal Sovereign** C Lyon, N Clacher, D Lyon
1984 May	**Barracuda** and **Whispering Death** D Lyon, N Clacher, C Lyon
1984 May	**A Cry of Angels** D Lyon (roped solo)
1984 May	**Man O' War** C Lyon (unseconded)
1984 May	**Masochist's Chimney** N Clacher, C Lyon (both solo)
1984 May	**Ramp Romp** C Lyon (solo)
1984 June 9	**New Moon on Monday** D Lyon, N Clacher
1984 June 12	**Krankenstein** S Lewis, B Masterson
1984 June 15	**Ape's Hit** A Pollitt, T Jones
1984 June 15	**Libertango** A Pollitt, M Atkinson
	The first of the 'Super routes' on L.P.T..
1984 June 16	**Face Race** S Lewis, M Pretty
1984 June 21	**Mean Mother** S Lewis, M Pretty
1984 June 25	**Statement of Youth** B Moon (unseconded)
	The result of an eight day workout producing one of the country's
	most stunning rock climbs. The first route also to have eight bolts
	placed for protection.
1984 June 27	**Readers' Wives** A Pollitt (unseconded)
	"(Laughter) . . . I've just found out what Readers' Wives are."
	Johnny Dawes sometime the following year.
1984 June 27	**Pearl from the Shell** T Hodgson, S Chesslett
1984 June 27	**Searching** T Hodgson, S Chesslett, P Custy
1984 June 27	**P.C. Wimpout** T Hodgson, P Custy, S Chesslett
1984 June 27	**Afterglow** S Chesslett, T Hodgson, P Custy
1984 June 28	**La Bohème** A Pollitt (unseconded)
	Another major addition.
1984 June 29	**Guano on Sight** T Hodgson, S Chesslett, I Jones
1984 June	**Damn the Jam, Midnight at the Oasis, Strangers in a Strange Land,**
	Amphibious Wreck and **Molasses Wall** D Lyon, N Clacher
1984 June	**The Flim Flam Man** C Lyon (unseconded)
1984 June	**Lazy Sunday** and **Learning to Crawl** D Lyon (solo)
1984 June	**Helter Skelter** and **Spirit in the Sky** N Clacher (solo)
1984 July 1	**Early Bird** D Lyon, D Summerfield
1984 July 1	**Fraggle Rock** N Clacher, C Lyon
1984 July 1	**Winebar Wall, 'Tel Shady** and **No Comebacks** C Lyon, N Clacher
1984 July 1	**Chasing the Dragon** N Clacher, C Lyon
1984 July 4	**The Dude's Rap** D Lyon, C Lyon
1984 July 6	**Sister of Mercy** D Lyon, D Summerfield
1984 July 7	**If I Die in a Combat Zone** C Lyon, N Clacher
1984 July 12	**Only Fools and Horses** D Lyon, C Bundock

1984 July 16	**The Eleventh Hour** P Clark (unseconded)
1984 July 20	**Ivan Skavinski Skavar** and **Abdul the Bull Khamir** D Lyon, D Summerfield
1984 July 20	**Grog on the Ground** C Lyon, R Griffith
1984 Aug 16	**White Hopes** A Pollitt, M Atkinson
	So named due to a previous caption in High Magazine of the first ascensionists.
1984 Aug 17	**Dive, Dive, Dive** A Pollitt (unseconded)
1984 Aug 24	**Crunchy Toad IX** S Lewis (unseconded)
1984 Aug 24	**Blast Peru** A Pollitt (unseconded)
	The beginning of new interest shown in this crag.
1984 Aug 25	**Any Which Way but Loose, Captain Pugwash, Storm Keeper** and **Boltzmann's Constant** D Lyon, D Summerfield
1984 Aug 25	**The Pink Pinkie Snuffs It** D Staniforth, R Curley
1984 Aug 26	**Gone with the Gonads** T Hodgson, A Ingham
1984 Aug 26	**Sidekick** M Atkinson (unseconded)
	Another major addition.
1984 Aug 28	**Teenage Kicks** and **Good Taste!** A Pollitt (unseconded)
	Two more stupendous lines fall.
1984 Aug 28	**Under the Boardwalk** M Atkinson, A Pollitt
	"Under the boardwalk, down by the sea, on a blanket with my baby that's where I'll be . . . ".
	An example of Atkinson's taste in music?
1984 Aug 28	**Black Money** and **Storm on the Sea** D Lyon, D Summerfield
1984 Sept 2	**Mr. Nobody** D Lyon, D Summerfield
1984 Sept9	**Stolen Corpse** M Crook (unseconded)
1984 Sept 15	**The Thin Turquoise Line** G Gibson, S Whalley
1984 Sept 19	**Rompsville** S Lewis (unseconded)
	Named with his tongue firmly bulging in his cheek. First cleaned and attempted in May. Lewis finally completed the pitch four months after his first attempt. It saw two one-day repeats that week!
1984 Sept 21	**Night Glue** A Pollitt (unseconded)
	"No the name has nothing to do with the bolt heads being glued at night."
1984 Sept 22	**Contusion** G Gibson (unseconded)
1984 Sept 23	**Skin Deep** G Gibson, S Whalley
1984 Sept 29	**T.S.P. Extension** A Pollitt (unseconded)
	An obvious gap.
	So named because it's a "short hard finish to an old route".
1984 Sept	**Alien Forces** M Crook, A Newton
1984 Oct 2	**Voodoo Child** A Pollitt, P Williams, M Atkinson
1984 Oct 4	**Wall of Voodoo** A Pollitt (unseconded)
1984 Oct 13	**2211** P Clark (unseconded)
1984 Oct 21	**Methylated Laughter** D Lyon, G Smith
1984 Oct 29	**SS20** D Lyon, D Summerfield
1984 Oct 29	**Nuclear Winter** D Lyon, A Pollitt
1984 Oct 30	**Eliminator** D Lyon, D Summerfield
1984 Nov 2	**Welcome to the Pleasure Dome** D Lyon, D Summerfield
1984 Nov 5	**Solo on Sight** N Clacher (solo)

1984 Dec 25	**The Fun House**	G Gibson (unseconded)
1984	**The Space Race**	A Ingham, S Melia

Top pitch originally climbed with a peg and huge sling for protection. This was removed and then led without by G Gibson sometime later.

1984	**No Boring Holds**	J Dawes (on sight solo)

He has since soloed many other arêtes and grooves on these concrete ramparts.

1985 Jan 1	**Hom Day Wall**	D Towse, M Crook, J M Redhead
1985 Jan 1	**The Complicated Muse**	G Gibson (unseconded)
1985 Jan 1	**The Star Spangled Banner**	G Gibson, H Gibson, M Jones
1985 Jan 6	**Precious Little**	G Gibson, S Whalley, M Jones
1985 Jan 12	**Pyrites of Pen Trwyn**	G Gibson, M Jones, H Gibson
1985 Jan 12	**Miner Forty-Niner**	G Gibson (unseconded)
1985 Jan 12	**The Cold War**	G Gibson, M Jones
1985 Jan 19	**Hagar the Horrible**	N Clacher, H Watkins
1985 Jan 19	**Norman's Wisdom**	G Gibson, N Clacher
1985 Jan 19	**No Arc No Bark**	G Gibson (unseconded)
1985 Jan 20	**Night Time Rendezvous**	G Gibson, M Jones, D Lyon
1985 Jan	**Touchstone**	C Lyon, D Lyon (AL)
1985 Jan	**Talisman**	D Lyon (unseconded)
1985 Jan 27	**Nightwatch**	G Gibson (unseconded)
1985 Feb 1	**Chock a Block**	N Clacher, D Summerfield
1985 Feb 2	**Barking up the Wrong Tree**	G Gibson (unseconded)
1985 Feb 2	**Another Dead Christmas Tree**	G Gibson (unseconded)

Direct Start by T Kay (solo) some time later.

1985 Feb 16	**Captain Percival**	M Jones, G Gibson
1985 Feb 16	**Winterreise**	G Gibson, M Jones, N Clacher, T Hodgson
1985 Feb 16	**Secondhand Daylight**	G Gibson (unseconded)
1985 Feb 16	**Small Bore**	G Gibson, T Hodgson
1985 Feb 17	**Platinum Blonde**	G Gibson (unseconded)
1985 Feb 17	**Afterthought**	G Gibson, M Jones
1985 Feb 21	**Hot Club**	G Gibson, J Adams
1985 Feb 21	**Beauty is Only**	G Gibson, M Jones
1985 Feb 23	**The Bloxwich Blockhead**	G Gibson (unseconded)
1985 Feb 24	**Testament**	C Lyon, C Bundock
1985 Feb 24	**Burslem Boys**	G Gibson (unseconded)
1985 Feb 26	**Making Memories**	N Clacher, H Watkins
1985 Feb 26	**Slapstick**	G Gibson (unseconded)
1985 Feb 26	**Gobachops**	G Gibson, D Summerfield
1985 Mar 6	**Identity Crisis**	N Yardley, S Hollinshead
1985 March 6	**Morse** and **Ask Politely**	P Leavers, J O'Donoghue, R Roberts
1985 March 6	**Luke Skywalker**	P Leavers, J O'Donoghue
1985 March 8	**Foolish Ghoulish**	G Gibson (unseconded)

A sustained effort to produce a magnificent piece of climbing. The wall above the last bolt had been climbed previously by D Towse on July 10 1983 as part of Liquid Lust – a route traversing in from the left.

1985 March 16	**Sussudio**	D Lyon, D Summerfield
1985 March 17	**Skin Game**	G Gibson (solo)

1985 April 16	**Jungle Jive** P Williams, T Taylor	

Involved one of Trwyn's most extensive gardening operations.

1985 April 17   **Human Erosion** R Wood, T Walker

1985 April 17   **Savage the Cabbage** F Crook, G Gibson, S Melia

1985 April 20   **Crab Slab** and **Just Along for the Ride** G Gibson, N Clacher

Another new crag developed.

1985 April 20   **The Get Along Gang** N Clacher, G Gibson

1985 April 20   **Capturing the Coelacanth** G Gibson (unseconded)

1985 April   **Slime Crime** D Towse, A Moug

1985 May 2   **Wu-Shu Boys** P Williams, M Barnicott

1985 May 19   **Game for a Laugh** N Clacher, D Summerfield

1985 May 24   **Amnesia Seizure** and **Funky Dung** D Lyon, D Summerfield

1985 June 20   **Glory Days** D Summerfield, N Clacher, P Freeman

1985 June 26   **Hydraulic Transmission** M Hammill, M Raven

Showed a renewed interest in Craig y Don's Upper Tier.

1985 June 27   **New Wave** M Hammill, C Lyon

1985 June 28   **The Cruel Sea** C Lyon, M Hammill

1985 June 28   **Bodyworks** D Lyon, D Summerfield, C Lyon

1985 June   **Self Abuse** and **Mystic East** D Summerfield, D Lyon (AL)

1985 June/July   **Road to Nowhere** M Hammill

Climbed in parts. Not linked but claimed anyway!

1985 July 3   **Nimitz** M Hammill, C Lyon

1985 July 7   **Frozen Moment** M Hammill, C Lyon, C Bundock

1985 July 7   **Fly by Night** N Clacher (solo)

1985 July 7   **Exocet** M Hammill, C Bundock (AL) C Lyon

Pitch split in cave.

1985 July 10   **E.C.M.** C Lyon, M Raven, M Hammill

1985 July 16   **Dough Nutz** D Towse, G Smith

1985 July   **Follow You Follow Me** and **The Fall Guy** D Summerfield, D Lyon

1985 Aug 17   **Ankle Attack** K Simpsom (unseconded)

1985 Aug 30   **Opus Pistorum** M Ryan, D Staniforth

1985 Aug   **Big Mac** and **French Fries** D Summerfield, D Lyon (AL)

1985 Aug   **Squall** and **The Brotherhood** D Lyon (unseconded)

1985 Aug   **Vaquero** D Lyon, D Summerfield

1985 Sept 1   **Watcher in the Woods** and **When the Lion Feeds** D Lyon, D Summerfield

1985 Sept 4   **Reading Henry by the Road** M Ryan, D Staniforth, D Leadbeater

1985 Sept 6   **Gary** T Hodgson, K Simpson

1985 Sept 6   **Wind and Worrying** D Lyon, D Summerfield

1985 Sept 7   **Treat Me like a Rag Doll** M Ryan, R Owens

1985 Sept 11   **Life's a Joke** D Lyon, D Summerfield

1985 Sept 18   **Cockleshell Bay** N Clacher, J Dobie

Yet another new area discovered.

1985 Sept 22   **Future Days (. . . Here's To)** D Lyon (unseconded)

1985 Sept 23   **The Green Sponge, The Oyster Catcher** and **Variation** N Clacher (solo)

1985 Sept 23   **Adam's Roof** N Clacher, J Dobie

1985 Sept 26   **The Benji Bee** N Clacher (unseconded)

1985 Oct 9	**Beanstalk** Miss K Goodey, C Goodey
	Colin Goodey's return to new-routing on Great Orme, this time with his daughter Katherine, after thirty five years.
1985 Oct 10	**The Lizard of Oz** P Littlejohn, M Wooldridge
1985 Oct 12	**Bigwig & Boldstreet** C Goodey, Miss K Goodey (AL)
1985 Oct 13	**Julie's Jump** K Simpson, S Trott
1985 Oct 20	**Michelle's Pillar** N Clacher, K Simpson
1985 Oct 27	**Swordfish Trombone** M Hammill, M Lovatt, D Kenyon
1985 Nov 1	**The Cresta Run** N Clacher, D Summerfield
	Almost definitely done before as an old peg was found en-route.
1985 Nov 4	**Cool Water** N Clacher, D Summerfield, D Lyon
1985 Nov 13	**The Fourth Protocol** D Summerfield, D Lyon (AL)
1985 Nov 24	**Moulfess** Miss K Goodey, C Goodey
1985 Nov	**Sheik Yer Money Direct** D Lyon, D Summerfield
1985 Dec	**Edge of Darkness** D Lyon, N Clacher
1985 Dec 15	**Footloose** Miss K Goodey, C Goodey
1985	**Too Much, Too Young, Too Soon** G Rimmer, R Owens
1985	**Too Little, Too Old, Too Late** D Kenyon, R Owens
1986 Jan 11	**Alexandra Sagnenko** N Clacher, D Summerfield, P Freeman
1986 March 8	**Little Buttress** C Goodey, S J Goodey, S Goodey
1986 March 26	**Turn The Turtles, Turn** M Raine
1986 March 26	**Turtle on Sight** M Raine, S Quinton, G Smith
1986 March 26	**Heightmare** G Smith
1986 March 26	**Turtle Ring Your Mother** G Smith, M Raine, S Quinton
1986 March	**Field of Blood** C Lyon
1986 March	**Anno Domini** D Lyon
1986 March	**It's a Kind of Magic** and **Black Dog** D Lyon, C Lyon (AL)
1986 April 6	**Xexu** D Lyon, C Lyon
1986 April 12	**Mumbo Jumbo** N Clacher, R Kaye, D Summerfield
1986 April 27	**Thank You Johnny** K Simpson, S Chesslett, S Winstanley, N Clacher, P Bailey
1986 April 27	**Brothers in Arms** D Lyon, C Lyon
1986 April	**Shimdahir, Walk of Life, Take It or Leave It** and **Fun in the Sun** D Lyon, D Summerfield (AL)
1986 April	**The Bear's Tears, Sorrowing Wind** and **Pale Rider** D Lyon, C Lyon (AL)
1986 April	**Lost Lens Corner** R Griffith, C Lyon
1986 April	**Condition Red** and **Trilogy** D Lyon
1986 April	**The Fat Man** D Lyon, D Summerfield, C Lyon
1986 May 4	**Fears for Tears** and **Tears as Souvenirs** D Lyon, D Summerfield
1986 May 7	**Absolute Beginners** N Clacher, D Summerfield, A Pollitt
1986 May 8	**Pink and Black** D Lyon, D Summerfield
1986 May 9	**The Turtle Run** D Lyon, D Summerfield
1986 May 11	**Purple Tight Fright** D Lyon, D Summerfield
1986 May 16	**Helgar's Fury** N Clacher, R Kaye
1986 May 22	**The Triad** D Lyon, D Summerfield
1986 May 27	**The Irishman Must Go** S Haston, R Kaye
1986 May 29	**Parting Shot** D Lyon, D Summerfield
1986 May	**Thanks** D Lyon, D Summerfield

1986 June 5	**The Silmarillion** K Simpson, N Clacher	
1986 June 12	**Dave's Rent a Drill Co.** N Clacher, K Simpson, D Lyon, T Raggett	
1986 June 19	**Lucky Eddie** N Clacher, K Simpson	
1986 June 21	**Up to the Hilt** T Freeman	
	A major problem solved.	
1986 June 30	**Trivial Pursuits** A Ingham, P Bailey	
1986 July 2	**Primeval** G Smith, P Hawkins	
1986 July 13	**Speed Livin'** and **Red October** D Lyon, D Summerfield	
1986 July 15	**The Mile High Club** N Clacher, A Ingham	
1986 July	**Zawn Creature** and **Riders in the Chariot** G Smith, D Summerfield	
1986 July	**Orca** G Smith, P Hawkins	
1986 Aug 3	**Man on the Run, Invisible Touch** and **Opal Moon** D Lyon, D Summerfield	
1986 Aug 8	**Spitting Image** N Clacher, D Summerfield	
1986 Aug 10	**Telegraph Road** D Lyon, D Summerfield	
1986 Aug 17	**Ride Across the River** D Lyon (solo)	
1986 Aug 19	**Madness and Mayhem** D Lyon, N Clacher	
1986 Sept 5	**Against All Odds** D Lyon, N Clacher	
1986 Sept 7	**The Paranoid Schizoid** D Lyon, N Clacher	
1986 Sept 12	**Bonking the Donkey** D Lyon, N Clacher (AL)	
1986 Sept 17	**Bored Daughter Meets the Powerbulge Boys** G Smith, P Hawkins, C Parkin	
1986 Sept 20	**Physical Abuse** M Lovatt, J Dunne, G Rimmer	
1986 Oct 12	**Moonshine** D Lyon, C Lyon	
1986 Oct 24	**Aerial Multigym** T Hodgson	
1986 Oct 26	**Confuse the Aardvark For 3-5 Year Olds** P Pritchard	
1986 Nov 4	**Space Delivery** P Pritchard, T Hodgson	
1986 Nov 8	**Rupture** P Pritchard, N Harms	
	On sight.	
1986 Nov 30	**Moon Madness** D Lyon (rope solo)	
1986 Nov	**The Wirral Whip** M Collins	
1986 Dec 4	**All Fall Down** N Clacher, D Lyon	
1986 Dec 7	**Top Gun** D Lyon, D Summerfield	
1986 Dec 14	**Planned Obsolescence** D Lyon, M Hammill	
1986	**Crinkle Crack** G Smith	
	Previously done with 1pt by D Lyon in 1984.	
1986	**Crinkle Crank** G Smith, P Hawkins	
1986	**Sèverine** C Smith	
1987 Jan 7	**Lost Empires** D Lyon, D Summerfield, N Clacher	
	(A Major addition!)	
1987 Jan	**Snakes and Ladders** J Dawes	
1987 Jan 8	**The Crigyll Outlaws** N Clacher, D Summerfield, J S Dobie	
1987 Feb 6	**Red Herring** D Lyon (rope solo)	

INDEX

Mountain Rescue

In the event of a serious accident where assistance is required, a message giving all the factual information about the patient(s) location (crag, climb, pitch etc.) should be passed on to the North Wales Police at the nearest Police Station, or at the Headquarters (Telephone – Colwyn Bay 57171), or by dialling 999.

The Police will contact the respective Rescue Team, and as co-ordinators, will obtain further assistance (e.g. helicopter) as directed by those affecting the rescue.

After an accident, please report in writing directly to the Hon. Secretary, Mountain Rescue Committee, 9 Milldale Avenue, Temple Meads, Buxton, Derbyshire, giving particulars of the date of the accident, extent of injuries, name, age and address of the casualty, details of the MRC equipment used and the amount of morphia used (so that it can be replaced). Normally this will be done by the local Police and/or the Rescue Team involved, who will also require the names and addresses of the persons climbing with the injured party.

Avoid making rash or unconsidered statements to the press; refer any journalists to the mountaineer who has overall charge of the rescue.

HELICOPTER NOTES
In the event of a helicopter evacuation ALL climbers ON or OFF the cliff should take heed. A helicopter flying close to a cliff will make verbal communications between climbers difficult and small stones etc. will be dislodged by the rotor downdraft. All loose equipment must be secured and climbers in precarious positions should try to make themselves safe. A smoke grenade may be dropped from the helicopter to give wind direction.

The persons with the injured party should try to identify their location. NO attempt should be made to throw a rope to the helicopter, but assistance should be given to the helicopter crew/personnel if required.

A helicopter will always be flown into the wind to effect a rescue and on landing there are three danger points; the main rotor, the tail rotor, and the engine exhaust. The helicopter should not be approached until directed to do so by the air crew.

090 160 140 300 60

Frank Corner leading the second (aided) ascent of Great Wall.   *Colin Goodey*

George Smith making the first free ascent of Crinkle Crack.

Dave Summerfield